Revolution!

The Explosion of World Cinema in the 60s

PETER COWIE

faber and faber

First published in 2004
by Faber and Faber Limited
3 Queen Square London WC1N 3AU
This paperback edition published in 2006

Typeset by Faber and Faber Ltd
Printed in England by Mackays of Chatham, plc

A CIP record for this book
is available from the British Library

ISBN 0–571–22716–3

10 9 8 7 6 5 4 3 2 1

For Françoise and Robin

Contents

Acknowledgements

My thanks go first and foremost to the directors and technicians who kindly gave their time to reminisce about their experiences of the late fifties and the sixties: Bernardo Bertolucci, John Boorman, Jörn Donner, Miloš Forman, Philip Kaufman, Jerzy Kawalerowicz, John Korty, Walter Lassally, Richard Lester, Dušan Makavejev, Walter Murch, Gillo Pontecorvo, Fons Rademakers, Karel Reisz, Alain Resnais, Francesco Rosi, Volker Schlöndorff, Vilgot Sjöman, Bertrand Tavernier, Agnès Varda, Andrzej Wajda and Krzysztof Zanussi.

I chose these individuals because their passionate commitment to complex and thoughtful film-making seems so manifestly characteristic of the sixties and its spirit. They are also without exception sympathetic to cinema as an international art form, dissolving barriers of language and politics.

Others I knew during those years, and to whom I would have talked for this book, have unfortunately passed away, among them Lindsay Anderson, André Delvaux, Satyajit Ray, Louis Malle and François Truffaut.

I am also most grateful to those friends who gave useful advice and essential phone numbers and addresses: Michel Ciment and Pierre Rissient, both experts themselves on the period, Tom Luddy in San Francisco, Hercules Bellville in London, Bengt Forslund in Stockholm, Lorenzo Codelli in Italy and Jacek Bromski, who welcomed me so warmly to Warsaw.

I also want to record my continued appreciation to my editor at Faber and Faber, Walter Donohue, and especially to Richard Kelly, whose editing of the manuscript proved both rigorous and learned. Dave Kent of the Kobal Collection has been an invaluable source of advice and photographs for this title. Finally, a nod to Rachel Alexander, who always promotes my books so well but rarely receives an acknowledgement after the fact, and to Laura Morris, my friend and literary agent.

NOTE

Throughout the text, direct quotations from the interviews made for this book are printed in italic, to distinguish them from other sources.

Introduction

'Oh, how I was young once!'
    'Elle' (Emmanuelle Riva) in *Hiroshima mon amour*

Cannes, 18 May 2002. Exactly thirty-four years to the day since it was scheduled to screen in the festival competition, and rarely glimpsed in the intervening years, Alain Resnais' *Je t'aime je t'aime* unspools in the Salle Buñuel. Afterwards, the prolonged standing ovation seems to honour not so much *Je t'aime je t'aime* itself as the man behind it. For an audience considerably younger than the snow-haired Resnais, this resurrected treasure from 1968 evokes a decade that began with the election of John F. Kennedy and the nascent hopes of a generation born during the throes of World War II. Resnais' masterpiece, *Hiroshima mon amour*, had appeared at Cannes in 1959, nimbly experimenting with time and emotion, and setting a benchmark to which younger directors in Europe would aspire.

Now, on the cusp of his ninth decade, Resnais addresses a few modest words to us, buffs and admirers, as courteous and as precise as he had proved when I first met him in the lobby of the old Cameo-Poly art-house in London in 1962. Perhaps surprised that *Je t'aime je t'aime* still works in an age of special effects and pulsating action cinema, he merely thanks everyone for having 'stayed to the end'.

The evening wears a wistful tinge, too. To many of us, this particular film was 'the one that got away' when the Cannes Festival collapsed during the chaotic events of May 1968. Resnais has made features at regular intervals since the sixties, but few have appealed to large audiences beyond his native France. So he stands tonight as a symbol of everything that made the sixties such a charismatic era. *Je t'aime je t'aime* recalls the risk-taking that characterized the period, the overriding sense that film was a medium that knew no artistic limitations.

Where lie the roots of this manifest burgeoning of talent? The French *Nouvelle Vague* or 'New Wave' seized so much attention that it almost obscured the flowering of film in many other countries. Wajda, Kawalerowicz and Polanski in Poland; Fellini, Antonioni, Rosi, Bertolucci and Bellocchio in Italy; Bardem and Saura in Spain; Reisz, Anderson and Richardson in Britain; Ray in India; Imamura and Oshima in Japan; Carlsen, Sjöman and Widerberg in Scandinavia. These directors together unleashed a movement as revolutionary and enlightening as the Impressionist upheaval in the pictorial art of the nineteenth century.

How did the cinema reflect a period of abundant change – in fashion, in music, in sexual mores and political sentiment? As social historian Arthur Marwick has noted, 'Economic expansion began in the fifties, but the social benefits came in the sixties.' He cites 'the growing power of young people, the particular behaviour and activities associated with them, the changes in family relationships, the new standards of sexual behaviour'. In *Saturday Night and Sunday Morning*, the emblematic character of Arthur Seaton declares: 'What I want is a good time. All the rest is propaganda.' As the director of that film, Karel Reisz, told me in 2002, the newly materialist element was clear: 'Here was a generation in full employment, who had money and were able to control their own lives. The outsiders became the insiders, and I rather liked studying that . . .' Reisz's analysis is true not only of Britain: the standard of living in France, for instance, leaped upwards with each passing year, and by 1960 had increased by 50 per cent in a decade.

Tempting though it remains to label the sixties as an Age of Cinematic Enlightenment, a more justifiable epithet might be the Age of Anxiety. All over Europe, directors gazed, Narcissus-like, into the navel or the mirror, questioning their role in society, and even – like Guido in Fellini's *8½* – their profession as film-makers. Bergman posed the most profound and most metaphysical questions of all: what is the nature of God? Does spiritual loyalty outweigh the artistic imperative? Bertolucci remorselessly interrogated himself and his contemporaries on the issue of political commitment – as, on a good day, did Godard. The nature of emotional commitment obsessed first the Spaniard Juan-Antonio Bardem (in his compelling 1957 study of guilt, *Death of a Cyclist*) and then Michelangelo Antonioni, who found man's moral armour buckling under the corrosive assault of hedonism and new technologies. Uncertainty replaced the doughty dedication to post-war recovery and emancipation.

Love and its ambiguous ramifications came under the microscope in films by Bo Widerberg (*Love 65* and *Elvira Madigan*), Leopoldo Torre-Nilsson (*The Hand in the Trap*, *Summer Skin*), Eric Rohmer (*Ma nuit chez Maud*) and François Truffaut (*Jules et Jim*). It was a time when conjecture seemed to outrank conviction, and to vacillate was better than to assert. And yet every so often, thankfully, a provocative talent such as Francesco Rosi or Gillo Pontecorvo in Italy, or Glauber Rocha in Brazil, would subvert this dangerous languor with a film that challenged the social *status quo* without a hint of compromise.

Certain films of the sixties offer manifest proof of the impact of the New Wave on older and more established directors. Neither Fellini's masterpiece 8½, nor Wajda's equally impressive *Everything for Sale*, nor Bergman's sublime *Persona* could have been made in quite the same audacious idiom had it not been for the swiftly changing currents in cinematography, sound and narrative form. Meanwhile, in Eastern Europe, where allegory came to hand as a means of outfoxing the apparatchiks, film-makers such as Němec, Schorm, Jancsó and Makavejev queried the tenets of a Brave New Communist World, a society in which betrayal had become a virtue.

This book thrives, if it thrives at all, on interviews with some of the period's most influential film personalities. Some were young and inexperienced. Some had served their apprenticeship and already achieved a certain reputation. Their memories dwell first and foremost on their own work, but their anecdotes and digressions also illuminate pivotal moments of the decade, such as the abrupt termination of the Cannes Festival in 1968. They attest that high seriousness in art contrived to flourish alongside satire and frivolity in a spirit of cheerful contradiction. From Barthes to the Beatles, from Marcuse to Mick Jagger, from the Sorbonne to Haight-Ashbury, everything was subject to speculation.

In Britain, Princess Margaret and her husband Tony Armstrong-Jones would go for runs on Tony's motor bike, clad in black leather, eager to mix with the likes of Jagger, Burton and Taylor. Unfamiliar affluence was catered to by a new brand of high priest: in Paris, Pierre Cardin with his first *prêt-à-porter* collection in 1959, Yves Saint Laurent and, better still, Courrèges with his flair for the mini-skirt; in London, fashion designer Mary Quant (with her Louise Brooks 'bob' created by Vidal Sassoon), models like Jean Shrimpton and Twiggy, and David Bailey, the photographer who caught their glamour. Coco Chanel, survivor of another generation, had retreated to an exile of sorts in Switzerland after having an affair with a Nazi officer during World War II, but she returned to Paris to design the costumes for Alain Resnais' *L'année dernière à Marienbad*.

The challenge to traditional standards of behaviour rose to an irresistible crescendo. Joe Orton's play, *Entertaining Mr Sloane*, pushed the sexual envelope to a new limit in 1964. Across the Atlantic, the flower-children of Santa Barbara celebrating Bacchus in the nude during John Frankenheimer's *Seconds* (1965) were absolutely characteristic of the mid-sixties, just as the audacity of James Wong Howe's cinematography on that movie proved that American cinema was receptive to change. The battle in the US courts over the 'pornographic' scenes in Vilgot Sjöman's Swedish film *I Am Curious Yellow* underlined not just the courage of maverick publisher Barney Rosset and his Grove Press but also the entrenched conservatism of 'Middle America' where sex was concerned. Then, in June 1969, *Oh! Calcutta!* opened off-Broadway to confirm the trend set by *Hair* the previous year – that 'carnal knowledge' was very much the idiom of the future.

In France, 'the shock of the new' (to borrow Robert Hughes's phrase apropos modern art) reverberated through every layer of society. In music, there was Jacques Brel and then Johnny Hallyday. In literature, the mind-stretching novels of Robbe-Grillet, Duras and Sarrault. In theatre, the plays of Genet and Beckett (then resident in Paris). In philosophy and sociology, the figures of Lévi-Strauss, Morin and Barthes emerged. And when that tide receded, numerous films sparkled amid the flotsam and jetsam. Social pundits have chastized the sixties for their puerile political polemics, but few have found it easy to dismiss the prodigious output of films in so many countries.

This was a decade in which the superlative sprang to everyone's lips. Tennessee Williams told Elaine Dundy that *Sgt Pepper's Lonely Hearts Club Band* was 'the most original, the most beautifully poetic album of songs' he had ever heard. Tony Palmer went further, claiming in the London *Observer* that 'If there is still any doubt that Lennon and McCartney are the greatest song writers since Schubert, then [this week] – with the publication of the new Beatles double LP – should surely see the last vestiges of cultural snobbery and bourgeois prejudice swept away in a deluge of joyful music-making, which only the ignorant will not hear and only the deaf will not acknowledge.'

The composer and songwriter Serge Gainsbourg, already admired for his smoke-rimmed ribaldry, recorded 'Je t'aime . . . moi non plus' with

Brigitte Bardot, but she refused to sanction the release. So Gainsbourg cut the disc with Jane Birkin, a demure English girl he had met on the set of a minor movie. Birkin, glimpsed three years earlier in Antonioni's *Blow Up*, made the song into an erotic monody for the sixties.

Looking back in 2001, Godard's iconic heroine, Anna Karina, recalled: 'All we knew was that we were having fun. We had no idea that so many years later people even in Japan would go to see our films . . .'

In 1958, a single screening changed the course of my fledgeling career as a writer. Of course, I had seen scores of films from the age of about nine onwards, but they enthralled me merely to the same degree as did sporadic visits to the annual touring circus. I grew up as an only child in the green heart of rural Gloucestershire, after the Second World War. My father – a poet by vocation and, since the late twenties, an admirer of the emerging arts of film and jazz – would take my mother and me to a tiny local cinema to see the latest Tarzan movie. I soon preferred westerns, and James Stewart in *Where the River Bends* and Alan Ladd in *Drum Beat* became heroes with whom I could identify and who distracted me from my fearful, inchoate regimen at successive schools, with their bullying boys and patronizing teachers.

The notion that film could be anything other than mere diversion was shattered quite by chance. My parents had moved to London in 1954, and my visits to 'the pictures' increased. Hollywood engendered all manner of fresh technologies – VistaVision, CinemaScope, 3-D, Cinerama, stereophonic sound. I discovered the huge, cavernous mystery of such theatres as the Odeon at Marble Arch and the Forum in the Fulham Road. Vast posters proclaimed the macho allure of Kirk Douglas in *Act of Love* and *Such Men Are Dangerous*, or Guy Madison in *The Command*. I revelled in the gimmickry of 3-D in *House of Wax* and the arrival of Cinerama in 1952 with its enveloping girth and frustrating tripartite image. Yet Hollywood was synonymous with money, with industry, with tycoons and with palm trees in search of a paradise. How, I thought so boldly and pompously, could someone at eighteen be absorbed by anything other than the meaning of life, man's place in the universe and the improvement of his lot?

My grandmother, recently widowed, sailed from New Zealand to see us in 1958. One evening, we sallied forth together to the Gala Royal in Edgware Road, a repertory theatre prized for its double bills. The main attraction was *I Am a Camera*, a worthy and still underrated adaptation of John van Druten's stage play, with Julie Harris as the definitive Sally Bowles, illuminating the grey horizons of Isherwood's pre-war Berlin. When it was over, I remember glancing with inexplicable admiration at some people who were leaving after the film, disdaining the opportunity to wring full value from their two-shilling ticket. My parents, having arrived in London from the dominions in 1936 with thirty such shillings to their name, sat fast as the ice-cream vendors drifted down the aisles.

The supporting feature was Ingmar Bergman's *The Seventh Seal*. Not only did it carry subtitles, something I had possibly never encountered before, but it dealt with issues that I had always believed to be the exclusive property of literature: the meaning of life, the fear of death, the nature of love, the struggle between good and evil. Of course, such issues were easily located in the Anthony Mann westerns I so adored. But *this* was something else . . .

About halfway through *The Seventh Seal* (perhaps after the burning of the witch), my grandmother struggled to her feet and announced in a loud and embarrassing whisper, 'I'm going home to cook the dinner. There's too much talk about death in this film.' My mother agreed and the two affronted women grumbled away into the darkness. To my surprise and pleasure, my intrepid father remained beside me. When we reached home near midnight, he and I talked avidly, not just about the brilliance of Bergman's technique and the tingling moments of suspense, but also the issues raised by the film. In retrospect, the conflict between traditional belief and a cynical materialism in Bergman's world chimed with the changing mood of the late fifties.

But what was so wrong with cinema in the fifties? Movies like Fox's *D-Day, the Sixth of June*, *Land of the Pharaohs* or *Night People*, using the fashionable format of CinemaScope, looked splendid in a large theatre. But their emotions, however worthy, oozed artifice, and they basked in a complacent vision of America as the benign leader of the old world. The Nazis had been quelled and now the Russian Communists posed an even more insidious threat to the wholesome, starched-shirt values of Middle America. It was an age circumscribed by decorum. Simone de Beauvoir visited America in surprisingly sympathetic mood in 1947 and yet found nobody debating political and social issues, not even students.

Many of these fifties productions now emit a nostalgic charge. Rugged heroes like Paul Newman, Rock Hudson or Robert Stack seemed as immutable as the graven images of Mount Rushmore. In stodgy spectacles like *The Silver Chalice*, *Giant* and *The High and the Mighty*, they stood for Integrity. In practice, their image was as false as the thickly caked make-up demanded by the emerging colour processes. *House of Wax* was not just one of the more entertaining of fifties Hollywood products; its title could apply to the entire Eisenhower decade as far as the movies were concerned. Biblical epics poured from the studios during the mid-fifties, reaching their apogee with *Ben-Hur*. For all their costumed artifice, they still seemed more honest than studio pictures dealing with big business and big 'issues' such as *Executive Suite* or *The Man in the Gray Flannel Suit*. There are critics who worship the vivid melodramas of Douglas Sirk, but even a dazzling formal exercise like *Written on the Wind* now smacks of fifties hypocrisy, with money and liquor the convenient villains to hand. An old master like John Ford could make an enduring masterpiece with *The Searchers*, although its merits lay unrecognized at the time. One year later, Stanley Kubrick's audacious *Paths of Glory* (1957) could be viewed as an isolated masterpiece amid the enveloping dross. In its controlled fury smouldered a younger generation's resistance to the studio matrix.

European cinema did not fare so poorly in the first dozen years after the war. Neo-realism in Italy influenced many a master of the subsequent New Wave across the continent. Visconti, Fellini, Antonioni, Bresson, Tati, Bergman, Bardem, Lean and Carol Reed established names for themselves long before the late fifties. In France, as Agnès Varda recalled for me, 'It's true that the French cinema at that period was very conservative, rather flat – Delannoy or Autant-Lara, for example. There were some masters none the less, like Clouzot and Clément. But classical, in the case of Clément – what has been called "the French quality" . . .' The comedian Fernandel attracted large audiences (and his films still regularly pad the schedules of French channels). And Brigitte Bardot emerged full-blown from the head not of Zeus but of the sly, disreputable Roger Vadim. If Bardot embodied the forbidden fruit, so too did Hammer horror films in Britain, with their spectral menace, their cheesy effects and their lurid X-rating.

When change became manifest around the turn of the decade, first reactions were mixed. Penelope Houston, the editor of *Sight and Sound*, brought to her writing a robust Anglo-Saxon pragmatism. Never one to fret over the entrails, she observed, come 1961, that 'The absolutely contemporary, sixties film may be nothing very marvellous in its own right: *The Connection* is boring and fascinating by turns, *À bout de souffle* runs out of gas before the end. But because the films are contemporary, talk our own language, are made with total freedom from studio disciplines and restrictions, they make a good deal of routine, competent studio film-making look solemn and constricted . . .'

This book will not discuss every director at work in the sixties: there are encyclopaedias for that. Besides, many estimable film-makers pursued their profession without caring much for radical change – James Ivory, for example, or Ronald Neame, or Pierre Etaix. The most 'successful' European films of the decade, in financial terms, were the James Bond productions: they are revived more frequently, and adored more passionately, than any of the films mentioned in this book. But they were straightforward commercial vehicles, and whether it was Terence Young, Guy Hamilton or Lewis Gilbert at the helm, the result was as sleek and impersonal as a new machine.

Some would maintain that the quality of international film-making during the late fifties and early sixties surpassed anything before or since. As Mark Le Fanu argued in a recent article, 'A measure of bleakness is part of the human condition and it used to be possible to reflect this in art. Many of the old-style art house films were indeed gloomy, but often the lucidity of their form acted to convert that pessimism into something closer to aesthetic exaltation.' Yet it's probably fair to say that just as many interesting films are being produced today, by cinéastes as varied as Almodóvar, Kiarostami, Kaurismäki and Zhang Yimou. The difference lies in the way they are greeted and supported. The committed arthouse audience has dwindled, dispersed among tens of millions of television households and clustered at several hundred festivals. The hegemony exerted by Hollywood (and, more significantly, the English language) has coincided with the triumph of US brands like McDonalds, Coca-Cola, Starbucks and The Gap. The Reagan–Thatcher revolution has seeped across national frontiers, homogenizing society and blunting any misgivings the materialist ethic might arouse. Sponsorship is the golden calf in whose name much culture has been sacrificed.

Ah, well . . . the sixties may have succumbed to many failings, but complacency was never among them.

1 Once Upon a Time in the Fifties

It's almost as if the earth had been visited by some strange force, but a positive force – in the period from somewhere in the fifties up to the late sixties, when you had this explosion of cinema.
  Phil Kaufman

The dramatic changes in world cinema during the sixties were not accomplished at a stroke; nor did the rising generation of directors want for inspiration from those who had gone before them. Throughout the previous dozen years, some mighty talents had been at work in Europe, and many of them would continue making films well into the period discussed in this book.

Although a vanquished nation in the aftermath of Mussolini, Italy recovered its passion for cinema almost immediately. In fact, Italian film production had not been interrupted to a demoralizing degree, and De Sica and Visconti had produced such masterworks as *The Children Are Watching Us* and *Ossessione* long before the Russians entered Berlin and World War II was brought to a close. Within a few months, Rossellini was shooting *Rome Open City* and, the following year, *Paisan*. Visconti trekked to Sicily in 1947 to make *La terra trema,* just after De Sica had directed *Sciuscià* in the suburbs of Rome.

Born in Pisa in 1919, Gillo Pontecorvo had joined the Italian Communist Party in 1941 and became a leader of the Italian resistance during the war. Afterwards, he became an assistant to a number of film directors and began making his own documentaries. He can well recall the profound impact of neo-realism at the time.

PONTECORVO: *My youth in Mussolini's Italy and the outbreak of war was influenced by the need to survive, and from this arose a love of social commitment. In film, the form for that commitment was of course neo-realism, which in turn reflected Italian political life. It was above all the affection for human faces that made neo-realism*

> *so special. My two favourite films of that period are* Paisan *and* Umberto D. *I was very friendly with both directors, Rossellini and De Sica. They encouraged me to make my first feature while I was still doing documentaries. I loved Eisenstein, also Nikolai Ekk, but it was the Italians who influenced me above all. And this is not just nationalism, I assure you!*

Italian audiences did not respond to the roughshod reality of the neo-realist films, and even Italian critics remained somewhat aloof. Abroad, however, neo-realism inspired directors in many countries (as the interviews in these pages will attest). The man who gave neo-realism a new surge of life in the late fifties and early sixties was **Francesco Rosi**. He had served his apprenticeship with Visconti on *La terra trema* (1948), and during the fifties, like Antonioni, he set the foundations of his career in place with *La sfida* (1958) and *I magliari* (1959).

ROSI: *The Zeitgeist of the explosion in world cinema was in large measure affected by what my generation had experienced in the postwar period. Italy was a country destroyed by war, and one that was emerging from a dictatorship; the nation had to be rebuilt, physically, materially and morally. We learned this through the visual expression provided by Rossellini, Visconti and De Sica. Through this incomparable medium that is the cinema, they gave Italians the chance to recognize themselves, and through the characters on screen the opportunity to live out their hopes, their dreams and their defeat.*

Of course, neo-realism did not immediately have an enormous success at the box-office, so it was only a certain portion of the public that was touched by the movement. But I believe that our observing of this cinema, in its depiction of the entire complexity of Italian reality and Italian society, made us aware of the need to participate in this reconstruction – and of course of the importance of the cinema as such. I think we were convinced that, through the cinema, we had the means to show something that belonged to everyone, not just as spectators but also as citizens. So to make people reflect, to share in emotions that concerned their society – that was a conscious motivation on our part.

The American cinema, too, was in some degree revolutionized by neo-realism: directors like Dassin and Kazan were influenced by its major works. Kazan used to tell me that he considered me as his younger brother!

Luchino Visconti's *La terra trema* (1948)

Of course, Rosi had the good fortune to come under the wing of some of Italian cinema's major talents of the time.

ROSI: *I made one film as an assistant with Antonioni* (I vinti), *and one film with Monicelli* (Proibito), *shot in Sardinia, and three films with Luciano Emmer. I also worked as a screenwriter, for example on Visconti's* Bellissima, *alongside Suso Cecchi d'Amico and Visconti himself. I also wrote an outline for a film called* Processo alla città, *with Ettore Giannini, who was a great stage director, and with whom I worked two years before entering the cinema.*

But what marked my 'formation' in the cinema very much was my first stint as an assistant, with Visconti on La terra trema. *It was inspired by a great realistic novel by Giovanni Verga,* The Unfortunate Ones. *But the film was not shot to a shooting script at all. The actors were non-professionals – they were all young lads and people from this small village on the seaside. Visconti worked with a very small crew, a documentary crew. They had intended to make three documentaries on Sicily, but Visconti was so impressed by Verga's novel that he made just one and forgot about the other two! He worked with the local boys on the dialogue, because he was using direct sound, which was rare in Italy at that period – and in Sicilian dialect.*

I had a wide variety of tasks, everything from writing up the descriptions of the setting and the characters to translating the dialogue from Sicilian into Italian and keeping a kind of diary of the progress of the entire film. Franco Zeffirelli was the other assistant, and he rehearsed with the actors after Visconti had discussed each scene in detail.

It was a film shot entirely in natural settings, and it took six months to shoot. This experience marked my approach to the cinema later, my method of working: realism, without falsifying reality – you understand? My interpretation of reality, the restitution of that interpretation in the images. Natural décors are not a formal necessity for me, any more than they were for Visconti at that time, but they reflect an adherence to the atmosphere of the characters, to the life of the characters. From my first films, La sfida *and* I magliari, *but above all with* Salvatore Giuliano, *I made a leap forward in terms of method, but I owe it in large part to that apprenticeship I served on Visconti's film.*

© Ponti-De Laurentiis Cinematografica

Gelsomina (Giulietta Masina) blows her trumpet in *La strada* (1954), watched by Zampanò (Anthony Quinn, centre)

While Vittorio De Sica seemed reluctant to venture stylistically beyond the faintly sentimental frontiers of his personal neo-realism, **Federico Fellini** caught the whiff of change in the air. Two films, shot in 1953 and 1954, looked forward to a period in which neither unvarnished realism nor poetic realism would be sufficient. *I vitelloni* and *La strada* seemed effectively to marry the traditions of the often sumptuous Carné–Prévert on the one hand, and of the ascetic Rossellini on the other. The music of Nino Rota alone proved enough to distinguish these films from other Italian productions of the period: Rota's scoring, tinged always with an infectious nostalgia, gave an elegance to even the most humdrum of everyday sequences. And *I vitelloni* amounted to exactly that – an assortment of everyday experiences in the lives of young men in a seaside resort during the winter months. As they drift around the streets and beaches, only one, Moraldo (Franco Interlenghi), musters the courage to escape his melancholy surroundings; the rest are left to fritter away their youth. These young men represent a condition, a state of mind, one that

Antonioni would describe in a similar way in his *Le amiche* two years later. *I vitelloni* is a memorable microcosm of Italian provincial life at that period, subtly played by Alberto Sordi and Franco Fabrizi among others, and replete with sharply etched scenes (such as a fancy-dress dance, where each character adopts a disguise approximating to his own ideal).

Fellini's other portal film of the fifties, *La strada*, made a household name in Italy for Giulietta Masina. Married to the director since 1943, she had appeared in some of his earlier work, but in the character of Gelsomina she created the definitive image of the clown-like outcast, teased and exploited by those about her and yet clinging obstinately to a wide-eyed optimism. Gelsomina lingers on the fringes of other people's happiness, like a shivering animal beside a fire. She runs like a duck, has no care for sex, but has the eye of a lynx. Learning of her death, the circus strongman Zampanò gets drunk and staggers down the beach; there he sobs and claws ineffectually at the sand. Like all Fellini's great personalities, he has just recognized not just that, as Wilde wrote, 'Each man kills the thing he loves,' but also man's craving for an image of beauty to which he can aspire. Fellini, like Bergman, knew how to mine his childhood for material. The countryside in *La strada* recalls the area round Gambettola where Fellini spent his summer holidays, just as the seaside mood of *I vitelloni* evokes the Rimini where the director was born.

From the early fifties, **Michelangelo Antonioni** drifted apart from the neo-realist movement. 'The only useful way of adhering to neo-realism', he said, 'is to take an interest more in the interior than in the exterior – to express sentiments before choosing décors.' At once both a romantic and a moralist who disapproves of material opulence and purely physical passion ('Eroticism', he said, 'is the disease of our age'), Antonioni brought a clinical eye to bear upon his characters. Specialists in Italian cinema had already applauded his slow-burning technique as evinced by *Le amiche* and *Il grido*. Jacques Doniol-Valcroze wrote (apropos of *Un condamné à mort s'est échappé*) in *Cahiers du cinéma* in 1957: 'It is perhaps only the edge of a pen-knife that [Antonioni] is thrusting into the opaque surface of the door that opens on to hope and liberty, but one knows since Bresson that a spoon-handle is sometimes enough; and through the breach others will pass and, already with *Le amiche*, a gust of air from another world.' Made in 1955, *Le amiche* indicates Antonioni's development of a highly personal film language. His characters betray their feelings little by little as the camera follows them with an unhurried discretion. The pressures of the city become forceful and realistic as

Antonioni dwells for a long moment on some bystanders or an architectural outcrop, before panning round to discover his men and women, like aliens in the pallid environment.

'Some film-makers decide to tell a story and then choose a décor that suits it best,' said Antonioni in one of the numerous interviews that followed his breakthrough in the early sixties. 'With me it works the other way around: there's some landscape, some place where I want to shoot, and out of that develops the theme of my films.' Thus the Po Valley of *Il grido*, made in 1957. The intensity of the anti-hero Aldo's anguish in this lament of a film is heightened by the vistas of forlorn countryside that confront him as he wanders in search of an inner peace. The women he encounters, despite their devotion and unselfishness, cannot attune themselves to his ill-expressed need for companionship. Aldo (Steve Cochran) stumbles pathetically along his inexorable path towards suicide, but more intriguing than this denouement is Antonioni's treatment of the mysterious, fog-shrouded countryside. This, one felt at the time, marked a step beyond neo-realism.

Born in the final year of the Great War, **Ingmar Bergman** was a clear generation older than such soon-to-emerge talents as François Truffaut, Miloš Forman or Dušan Makavejev. Yet his influence on such younger directors would be immense, more because of what he dared to say rather than the manner in which he said it. Bergman excited the imagination of critics, audiences and film-makers alike, more than any director of the fifties – just as Jean-Luc Godard was destined to become the avatar of the sixties. For many, Bergman loomed as the Shakespeare of the cinema; for others, like the late Dilys Powell, his films exerted the impact of a 'mailed fist'. But none could deny his versatility – blighted romance, historical fresco, comedy *à la* Marivaux, the study of old age.

Smiles of a Summer Night won a major award at Cannes in 1956, giving Bergman the freedom in Sweden to shoot *The Seventh Seal*, which fast became his emblematic work. Retrospectives were organized in a frenzy, revealing earlier gems such as *Summer with Monika* and *Sawdust and Tinsel*. Bergman's genius was extolled in the pages of *Cahiers du cinéma*. Godard wrote: '*Summer with Monika* is the most original film of the most original of directors. It is to the cinema today what *Birth of a Nation* is to the classical cinema.' When *Wild Strawberries* won the Golden Bear at Berlin in February 1958, Godard sent a tongue-in-cheek telegram to

Ingmar Bergman confers with Bengt Ekerot (Death) on location for
The Seventh Seal (1957)

Cahiers: '*Wild Strawberries* proves Ingmar greatest stop script fantastic about flash conscience Victor Sjöström dazzled beauty Bibi Andersson stop multiply Heidegger by Giraudoux get Bergman stop.'

French critics such as Jean Béranger and Jacques Siclier wrote about Bergman tapping into the fifties *Zeitgeist,* and how the dread of nuclear Armageddon explained the fervour with which *The Seventh Seal* was embraced. Looking back, I don't agree. What set the pulse racing about Bergman was above all his technique – his audacious close-ups, his use of flashbacks, his sophisticated treatment of female characters, his utterly persuasive grasp of historical mood and the brilliance of his team – Gunnar Fischer behind the camera, production designer P. A. Lundgren and editor Oscar Rosander. Then there were the actors, all accustomed to working with Bergman on stage during the autumn and winter months: Max von Sydow, only twenty-six when he started filming *The Seventh Seal* and yet convincing us all that he was at least fifty; Maj-Britt Nilsson, Eva Dahlbeck, Bibi Andersson, Harriet Andersson, embodiments of feminine allure; and good old Gunnar Björnstrand, striking the sceptical note.

Bergman broached his metaphysical themes with disarming skill, daring to ask fundamental questions – both of himself and of his audience – that one associated more readily with poets and novelists, or painters such as Rembrandt and Goya. His geographical 'isolation', far to the north in Stockholm, added to the mystique of his appeal. It was tempting to assume that all Swedes were like those described in Bergman's films, and therefore quite a shock to meet Scandinavians who denigrated Bergman for an ignorance of social reality in his own country. Fellini, liking Bergman as a man and admiring him as a polar opposite, called him 'a mixture of magician and prestidigitator, of prophet and clown, tie salesman and priest who preaches. That's what an entertainer must be.'

For a variety of reasons, the film landscape of Poland seemed more exciting in the mid-fifties than that of other Communist countries such as Hungary or Czechoslovakia. As the late Boleslaw Michalek wrote: 'Polish film-makers [between 1955 and 1958] had managed to establish contact with the psychological realities of their own time. It was this sense of contact, this repeated stabbing at the most sensitive areas of the national consciousness, which enabled the film-makers so immediately to win the support of the Polish public, which had previously shown itself as somewhat sceptical about the national product.'

Andrzej Wajda would become the Ingmar Bergman of Eastern Europe, a prodigious talent in film, television and theatre. Crucial to his formation as a director was the Polish national film school in the provincial town of Łódź, an academy where he, Roman Polanski, Krzysztof Zanussi, Jerzy Skolimowski and many others would study.

WAJDA: *The only period in Polish cultural history that is truly unique occurred at the beginning of the nineteenth century. Poland did not yet exist, and artists, poets mostly, took upon themselves the duty to speak for a society, for a nation. In a way, the Polish cinema of the fifties inherited this solution, and the circumstances were quite similar because Poland was under the Communist regime and artists thought of themselves in the same terms as their forebears of the Romantic era. And they – we – wanted to create a bit more than just a regular film director would.*

But to truly understand Polish cinema at that period, one must look beyond Łódź. We have to go back to 1945. Before the war, a group of neophyte directors created a kind of left-wing discussion club called START – in effect, a film society. Everything – studios, facilities – was destroyed in Warsaw during the war. Many resident film-makers emigrated to the United States. Others came back to Poland with the Red Army – Aleksander Ford, for example, and Stanislaw Wohl. They assumed the leadership of Polish cinema, and they decided to launch a film school. They hated the Polish films of the pre-war period. They wanted to tackle war themes on screen. For us, and them, the closest thing to our hearts was Italian neo-realism, because the Italians were describing the world of poor people, and we were also poor, and during the Nazi Occupation we had been working like manual labourers. So we recognized a similar set of circumstances. The work of De Sica, Rossellini and others came very early to Poland.

We also saw films from Britain like Odd Man Out *and* The Cruel Sea *– not* The Third Man, *however, as it showed the Russians as spies! The French historian Georges Sadoul, on behalf of IDHEC, had come to Warsaw with a selection of films from the French and German avant-garde of the 1920s and 1930s – René Clair, Fernand Léger,* The Cabinet of Doctor Caligari *and so on. The season was an eye-opener, and demonstrated to us that a history of film really did exist. So we entered not just into the world of cinema but also into the wider intellectual world.*

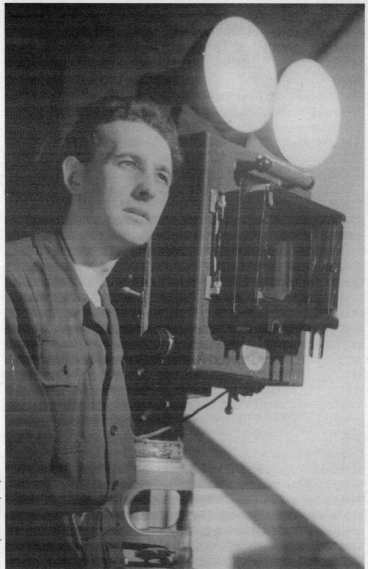

Courtesy of Andrzej Wajda

Andrzej Wajda in the mid-fifties

Wajda's near-contemporary **Jerzy Kawalerowicz** graduated from the Kraków Film Institute, and made his directorial début with *The Village Mill* in 1952. He, too, felt the impact of the Italian directors, and appreciated the effect that could be achieved with 'non-professional' performers.

> KAWALEROWICZ: *I was more influenced by neo-realism than by the French New Wave. That was after all the first contact that we had with foreign films after the war. The neo-realists were themselves much influenced by the Soviet film-makers of earlier decades.*
>
> *There were no studios here in Poland, because they had been destroyed during the war. There were no actors, so we had to use amateurs. The amateurs created a certain climate in the film, a climate of realism, and only gradually were they replaced by professional actors – who then followed their example, and even copied their style, thus retaining a certain realism in the films.*

> WAJDA: *The atmosphere at Łódź was not very good when I joined in 1950, because the school had been created when social realism was at its height. The school exercised a stronger political censorship control over the work of the students than I would have over my own feature films in subsequent years. For example, Andrzej Munk was preparing a love story involving two people suffering from tuberculosis – not an uncommon situation during the post-war years. And Munk wanted me to play the young man. But the school authorities told him he could not make the film, because the subject was too pessimistic. Instead, Munk had to make a portrait of a woman who spent her life as a weaver. But this kind of censorship ceased in 1956, when Gomulka came to power.*

15,000 Polish workers had revolted on 15 June 1956 and rioting ensued, in response to which the Polish Communist Party reinstated as Party Secretary Wladislaw Gomulka, head of the Polish United Workers' Party, who had once been imprisoned by Stalin. Gomulka began a fourteen-year spell in charge of Poland, during which time the totalitarian aspects of the regime were somewhat relaxed. **Krzysztof Zanussi**, who is now head of Studio TOR in Warsaw and, alongside his friend and colleague Krzysztof Kieślowski, the most talented film-maker of the post-Wajda generation, sets the mood of Polish cinema in the fifties in its historical perspective.

ZANUSSI: *In the general world, something happened that was unique and not often noticed, especially in the West. In 1956, Khruschev ousted Beria in Russia; there was the uprising in Hungary; and there was a dramatic twist in Poland, which was sympathetic to the events in Budapest. China, in the person of Chou En-Lai, discouraged the Russians from intervening in Poland. So we got some concessions in October 1956, including the comeback of Gomulka. And comebacks were almost unknown at that time . . .*

There followed a period of relative liberalization – quite remarkable. Later on, they tried to recoup the situation, but they never did. In this context, the Łódź School, even in the Stalinist night, was a kind of island, heavily infiltrated but always retaining some sort of civil pride. This was the time of Wajda, the time of Polanski, when the political pressure was enormous. But there was a kind of aristocratic resistance at the school. They were Communists, OK, but they were not vulgar Communists. They supported Communist artists like Brecht, but privately leaned more towards Western Communists like Picasso, who was forbidden. At Łódź it was whispered of Picasso, 'Now there's a great Communist artist for you . . .'

WAJDA: *Around the time Gomulka came to power – which is also when Polanski arrived at Łódź as a student – the film school itself changed. They now wanted students to have an all-round knowledge of different subjects, not just film-making – drawing, history of art, literature and foreign languages. The most important thing about the school was that the students could make 'studies', rather than just absorbing what their teachers told them. I made three such films, one documentary, two fictional stories.*

Krzysztof Zanussi found his career nurtured in the embrace of the 'Unit' system, a mode of production that stood at the very heart of the revolution in fifties Polish film.

ZANUSSI: *The Unit system goes back to the thirties. A group of socialist, leftist film-makers wanted to make a co-operative for artists, and they started it, and then they later all became Communists. After World War II, they came back and wanted to have the same system. But of course then the 'Hollywood' mode was imported from Moscow – after all, Mosfilm Studios was modelled entirely on Hollywood. So suddenly these film-makers were trapped.*

But after 1956, when a degree of liberalization entered into things, they immediately came back to their co-operative ideals, and set up more independent groups.

Usually the Unit was created when there was a leader, someone to whom they wanted to give the opportunity to make their own films – Kawalerowicz, Wajda and so on. My Unit, TOR, was founded in the mid-sixties for Stanislaw Różewicz, who was regarded as a classical film-maker at that time, and who had missed out when the studios were originally created ten years earlier.

The Unit was essentially an ambassador for one's projects to the Ministry. So I would see someone in an office who said, 'I like your script, and I will submit it on behalf of my Unit.' He would then get approval, draw up a budget, and supervise the production. The only country in which there were no censors involved in film production was Poland. Very interesting, from a cultural point of view, because on the one hand we had the institution of censorship – unlike East Germany, unlike Hungary, unlike the Czech Republic, unlike Russia. Poland was the only country where you could find in the phone directory an Office of Censorship – which was a blessing. Indeed, we were always fighting to preserve it, it was a great achievement, and it was not integrated. When our film was finished, we had to submit it to a censor, but there was no censorship beforehand.

The Russians, and East Germans, in fact most others in the Communist bloc, had one dedicated individual who checked if the script was correctly realized – a bit like a producer, except that this person was not interested in money, only in the ideological aspects of the film. Under the Unit system in Poland, the head of the Unit did not need to report if we were changing the script. It was entirely his responsibility. Then, when the film was completed, it was submitted to the committee, and the Minister of Culture could argue with the censor if he wanted. It was a very good system – relatively speaking . . .

Jerzy Kawalerowicz was appointed head of the KADR studio unit, and presided over a tightly knit team that boasted skilled craftsmen such as production designer Roman Mann, screenwriter Jerzy Stefan Stawiński, cinematographer Jerzy Lipman and composers Tadeusz Baird, Krzysztof Komeda and Wojciech Kilar. Stable directors included Tadeusz Konwicki, Kazimierz Kutz and Janusz Morgenstern.

KAWALEROWICZ: *There were eight Units at the outset. The studio system was created in 1955 not by the administration but by the film-makers themselves, and it fostered a trend towards more artistic films. Previously, the state was the agent for the film. One presented the screenplay to the state authorities, then the budget, and then the appropriate committee made a decision to approve it or not. Whereas the most important thing about the Unit system was that the one who created the film decided everything, unlike today. It was the first time in history that a director had the power to decide everything concerning his film – and that system survived a long time. A majority of Polish directors made their films via KADR – Has, Kutz, Scibor-Rylski . . .*

Wajda had attracted the attention of Aleksander Ford, who appointed him assistant director on *Five Boys from Barska Street*, which went into production in late 1953:

WAJDA: Five Boys from Barska Street *was a subject that I myself had wanted to do initially. My training as assistant on the Ford film was different from what I had experienced at school, because for the first time I saw how the film-making process really worked. My teachers in the directing faculty at Łódź had not been really directors themselves. The weakest faculty at Łódź was the actors' workshop – how to work with actors. I think that it's a weak point of every film school, if there is an acting faculty, as at Łódź, for example. But of course hiring professional actors takes money, so . . .*

Back in July 1953, the novelist Bohdan Czeszko had argued fiercely with the 'Film and Screenplay Qualification Committee' about the adaptation of his book, *A Generation*, which concerns the activities of a group of youngsters during the Nazi Occupation. When eventually the screenplay was approved, Aleksander Ford was asked to direct it. He demurred, urging the authorities to allow Wajda to take the helm under his supervision.

WAJDA: *I was like a producer on this film, because it was such a team effort. The entire group that created the film, they were all beginners – from Polanski the actor to Lipman the cinematographer. It was fantastic, because we were the 'Generation' fascinated by cinema.*
I did not want to make an official Communist subject. The central committee of the Party had been assuming that A Generation *would*

emerge as a lumpenproletariat film. It was scheduled to celebrate the tenth anniversary of the Polish People's Republic. But we had shot the film the way we wanted, and in only a few months, on location mostly in Warsaw and Łódź. We had to do the interiors in the studios, because the lighting was too complicated.

When A Generation *was first screened for the Politburo in 1954, in a heavily guarded resort house surrounded by barbed wire in Konstancin, I found that the criticism of the 'comrades from the leadership' was devastating. As a result, the film was delayed for many months and I was forced to reshoot certain scenes. The Party imagined that it would turn out to be a propaganda movie in the idiom of Sergei Gerasimov, and when they saw the result they raised a lot of obstacles and prevented the release for more than a year.*

In *A Generation*, a young apprentice named Stach (Tadeusz Łomnicki) is attracted to Dora (Urszula Modrzynska), who runs an underground Communist group. They try to help the Jews, but Dora is eventually arrested and Stach finds himself compelled to lead the group. The film reeks of sadness, showing how war appears a beguiling game to Stach and his companions, and how gradually it converts them into bitter fighting machines: love and devotion to a cause are linked indissolubly in Stach's mind. When *A Generation* reached France, Ado Kyrou wrote in *Positif*: 'As far as I know, Wajda is, apart from Lizzani, the only director since the days of [Dieterle's] *Blockade*, some of the Borzage films and the pre-war Soviet cinema, who has integrated love into a revolutionary story or, more accurately, has not divorced these two primordial forces in man: love and revolt.'

Wajda's next film, *Kanal* – like both *A Generation* and *Ashes and Diamonds*, the other two parts of his 'trilogy' – ends inexorably in death for its heroes. Set at the very nadir of Polish fortunes in 1944, it focuses on the final hours of the Warsaw Uprising. The remains of a company of resistance fighters are forced to take refuge in the city's sewers. Struggling for survival in groups of three or four, they are slowly trapped and eliminated. *Kanal* is based on a true incident, and in certain parts recalls the very first Polish films made after the war. Yet at heart it is a romantic work, the two love stories that run through it serving once again to throw into relief the patriotic fervour of Wajda's nation. If there is a flaw, it is that the film's narration sounds diffuse, and an excess of characters makes it difficult for any one of them to emerge as unforgettable.

WAJDA: *It was difficult to persuade the authorities to give the green light to make* Kanal, *because the Warsaw Uprising was not a good topic at that time. After all, in essence it had been a revolt against Communist power. As the Red Army approached, people rose up to take the capital, and to establish the government in defiance of Stalin.*

Every film made and screened in Poland had to be authorized by the appropriate committee. But they would not approve my critical point of view, so the Party would not touch the idea. Fortunately, in the three years since the screenplay of A Generation *had been evaluated, the composition of the committee had changed. Now it was filled with writers and directors, not just bureaucrats – people like Kawalerowicz, Stawiński and, especially, Tadeusz Konwicki, who was then literary director of the KADR team.*

During the final year of the war, when I helped with the resistance, I had been in Kraków, not Warsaw. I had fled there following the arrest of prominent members of the underground in Warsaw. Thanks to the fact that I had not seen the Uprising with my own eyes, I think that made Kanal *much better, because I kept a distance from the events themselves. The screenwriter, Jerzy Stefan Stawiński, described his own story, and had indeed written the film originally for Andrzej Munk as a pure documentary. At a certain point, I abandoned the project. But when the approval came through, I didn't hesitate for a moment, because, not having a background in documentary, I knew I would do* Kanal *in the studio. Besides, hardly any ruins still existed in Warsaw, apart from the bit in the Old Town that we show in the closing sequence of the film.*

It was with his next film, *Ashes and Diamonds*, that Wajda was finally able, after a couple of stalled attempts, to cast a charismatic young actor who would attain iconic status: Zbigniew Cybulski.

WAJDA: *I first encountered Cybulski in Kraków, when we were just members of a group of young people who didn't really know each other really well. We all used to meet in a summer camp for artistic students. But we did know who was who, and when we were casting* A Generation *we remembered him. Unfortunately, his part in the film was almost entirely cut out at the editing stage, because the censors did not like the scene where he goes to a Jewish cemetery. He didn't yet wear his famous sunglasses . . .*

Then he was all set to play the leading role of Cadet Korab in Kanal, *but the schedule clashed with his commitment to another film, and he hadn't told us about the conflict of dates. When it came to* Ashes and Diamonds, *I wasn't one hundred per cent sure about Cybulski taking the role of Maciek, because in general he did not resemble this 'voice' from the Resistance: he belonged to one generation later. But that's why the film and his character in particular were so largely accepted by the new generation. Both Cybulski and I had seen James Dean in* Rebel without a Cause . . .

Cybulski had an almost zoological way of acting, and for hours we watched gorillas in a zoo during a trip to Paris. What we particularly liked about this was connecting very small movements with big, very unexpected outbursts of movement.

Ashes and Diamonds, still the richest and most enduring partner in the trilogy, was also taken from a novel, by Jerzy Andrzejwski. Maciek is a young and handsome intellectual whose university aspirations have been frustrated by the war. The film hinges on his procrastination, and his infatuation with young barmaid Krystyna, coupled with the gathering disillusionment that accompanies the final stages of the war and almost dissuades him from assassinating the Communist Party Secretary, Szczuka.

Wajda's style had grown more baroque since *A Generation*: *Ashes and Diamonds* brimmed with magniloquent symbols such as burning glasses of vodka and an inverted crucifix (touches the director concedes were 'invented on the spot' rather than scripted). Yet Wajda's capacity for laying bare the truth behind the façade of war remains remarkable: as when the blanket slips from a young woman on a stretcher to reveal the bloodied, crushed leg beneath.

Ashes and Diamonds ranks with *The Seventh Seal* as the most exhilarating film of its period, defiant in the face of death and destruction, refusing to let the flame of romance be extinguished, just as the two love stories in *Kanal* had defied the fate of Warsaw's resistance fighters. Wajda's courage as a director reaches its height in the film's exquisite finale, as Cybulski runs, dying, through a terrain covered as far as the horizon with refuse of every kind. Inexorably, he slows to a lurch, and then a crawl, bringing his legs up to his midriff in a foetal crouch of agony. He himself has become a mere item of garbage, rejected by society, and yet defiantly wearing the sunglasses that would become his iconic trademark as an actor.

© Film Polski / ZRF Kadr, courtesy of BFI Stills, Posters & Designs

Zbigniew Cybulski in *Ashes and Diamonds* (1958)

Throughout his trilogy, Wajda obliges his audience to conspire with the characters, so that one enters the grim, grey reality of a country savaged by war and sandwiched between a brutal Fascism on one side and a rigid, monolithic Communism on the other. Somehow, one was more moved by the fate of Maciek and his pals than by the soldiers in US war movies of the decade. As Wajda himself cheerfully admits, 'It was a coincidence that the three films made up a trilogy.' And indeed most of us were swept away by the force of *Ashes and Diamonds* before catching up with *A Generation* and *Kanal* at art-houses during the late fifties. With only a handful of festivals flourishing at that juncture, one relied on the foresight of distributors to bring such films to London or New York. Thus, one would see *L'avventura* before *Il grido*, and *The Seventh Seal* before *Sawdust and Tinsel*.

Wajda's own tastes in film-going had evolved partly in tandem with what was made available to Polish cinéphiles.

WAJDA: *Because of the way that foreign films were distributed here at that time, a special commission would review the prints that had been sent to Poland by the producers or major distributors, before clearing them for local release. But before the films were sent back, there were a couple of unofficial screenings in an upstairs room in the film buildings on Pulawska Avenue, and we were able to get in to see them.*

We had stopped liking neo-realism, and started to prefer American directors like Huston (The Asphalt Jungle). *When Cybulski sniffs the blood on his hands in* Ashes and Diamonds, *for example, he does so with a strange reflexive movement. This gesture transports us from the world of symbols into reality, where biology, with its unpredictable reactions, rules. It was this that excited us during work on* Ashes and Diamonds, *and brought us closer to the behaviourism of the American cinema.*

We didn't like Russian cinema because it was too slow. The American cinema struck us as being much faster in tempo. When we had a first screening of Ashes and Diamonds *for the crew, Adam Pawlikowski – who was old enough to have fought in the Uprising himself – said, 'I don't know if it's a good film or a bad film, but it's the first time I've seen Polish actors playing so energetically!' And that was the best compliment I could have had.*

Roman Polanski also attended the film school at Łódź, and at first seemed likely to make a career as an actor. He featured in Wajda's *A Generation* as young Mundek, and later recalled the experience with huge enthusiasm. 'For us, it was a film of tremendous importance,' said Polanski. 'The whole Polish cinema began with it. It was a marvellous experience . . . The whole crew was very young. Wajda was very young, very sincere. We worked day and night . . . he believed in what he was doing – this was something utterly new in Poland (these were still the Stalinist years). The film was different, young.'

After this early break, Polanski started branching off on his own zigzag path. By 1958 he had made various shorts, and the best of these, the enigmatic *Two Men and a Wardrobe*, cropped up at art-houses and then in film-society programmes at the end of the fifties. A sly fable, it follows the wanderings of two men who stumble out of the sea carrying a large wardrobe and enter a town in an attempt to discharge their load. 'I wanted to show a society that rejects the non-conformist,' said Polanski, 'or anyone who is in its eyes afflicted with a moral or physical burden.' At last the men must leave the land – leave life – and vanish into the waves. Polanski catches in this film the grotesque and the cruel, the perverse and the defective aspects of humanity and of the architecture enveloping it. *When Angels Fall* (1959), another short, is the only film prior to *The Pianist* (2002) in which Polanski refers to the war that so obsessed his contemporary directors in Poland, and the brief, hectic battle scenes have much to say about the arbitrary barriers that war can create between men.

If Poland was playing host to a particularly brilliant flowering of new talent, there were other harbingers of the radical changes to come, some of these in countries less known for their cinema traditions. The finest Greek director of the post-war period, **Michael Cacoyannis**, had already shot scenes on location in city streets for his first film, *Windfall in Athens* (1953), while the French and British, for example, were still very much confined to the studio environment.

Throughout the fifties, Cacoyannis chronicled the tragicomic lives of Athenians, bringing the best out of actresses such as Elli Lambetti, Melina Mercouri and Irene Pappas. The distinctive rough-edged texture of his imagery owed much to the work of Walter Lassally, the British cinematographer who contributed to *Momma Don't Allow*, a short documentary about a north London jazz club made by Karel Reisz and Tony Richardson in 1955. Three years earlier, Lassally had also shot one of the earliest documentaries by Lindsay Anderson, *Wakefield Express*. Anderson was an Oxford graduate who had helped establish the influential film magazine, *Sequence*, after the war. He campaigned for personal commitment on the part of the film-maker and an unstinting adherence to the truth when showing social conditions. Lassally thus would serve as a link between one of the fifties' great European directors (Cacoyannis) and three of the most fervent advocates of change during the same period (Anderson, Reisz and Richardson).

The first Greek feature Lassally shot for Cacoyannis was an all-location film, *A Girl in Black*:

LASSALLY: *He had hired me sight unseen through a recommendation of Lindsay Anderson's at Cannes. I arrived in Athens on a very hot, sultry August evening in 1955, to be met by Cacoyannis and his leading man and his leading lady, in evening dress. I think they must have expected some kind of English gentleman. Off the aeroplane stepped this schoolboy, because I looked ten years younger than I actually was! I was twenty-eight, looking eighteen.*

Having experimented with lightweight cameras on *Momma Don't Allow*, Lassally was shocked by the equipment awaiting him.

LASSALLY: *At the time in Greece, they were using very old-fashioned Debrie cameras, and we imported an Arriflex from Germany for* A Girl in Black, *because that's what I'd asked for. To my horror, when it arrived it turned out to be the first blimped Arriflex they had ever made. I said, 'I can't operate that!' I was very wary of operating the camera. When I was confronted with this monster, much larger than the cameras I had been used to, there was nothing for it but to strip the thing down and restore it to its 'mute' form in order to shoot the film! So* A Girl in Black *was filmed without any kind of sound – guide track or anything – and was entirely post-synced from beginning to end.*

In 1956, the Spanish director **Juan-Antonio Bardem** made an alarmingly brilliant study of guilt and betrayal, *Death of a Cyclist*. Two lovers run down a cyclist by accident on a sombre stretch of road and, in panic, leave him to die. She (played by Lucia Bosé, former beauty queen, and muse to Antonioni in two early films) is the wife of a successful industrialist, he a university lecturer. As a blackmailer enters the story, and as the lovers begin to lose their self-control, Bardem not only reveals how a crime of chance leads inexorably to a crime of premeditation, but also hints at the unrest and corruption running like venom through Spanish society. Bardem's visual approach to his material kept an audience on its toes, cutting away from conversations at unexpected moments and subjecting the characters to unusual close-ups. The technique mirrored the restless state of mind of the guilty couple.

One had the notion that if such senior directors as Cacoyannis and Bardem (both of them born in 1922) could take risks in departing from the often contrived artifice of their national film industries, and if Wajda and his colleagues in Poland could sustain their momentum, then a generation ten years younger might propel the cinema into a new era. Their parents had been shattered by the war, and their early years marked by austerity. Now, as the sixties beckoned, many were ready to escape from the past and to hope for a better future.

2 Cinéphiles to Cinéastes: France in Transition

All of us at Cahiers *thought of ourselves as future directors. Frequenting ciné-clubs and the Cinémathèque was already a way of thinking cinema and thinking about cinema.*
  Jean-Luc Godard

In the summer of 1954, in a small coastal village in the south of France, **Agnès Varda** was shooting *La Pointe Courte*. An extraordinary début, the film escapes the kind of classification that every critic loves to ascribe. Instead, this reportage of two lovers visiting a small village near Marseille evokes on the one hand *La terra trema* and on the other the rhetorical theatre of Racine – and all constructed in the deconstructed style of William Faulkner's novel, *The Wild Palms*. Certain compositions – one character's face in profile, the other staring into the camera – anticipated the work of Bergman in *The Silence* and *Persona*. At twenty-six years of age, Varda manifested a talent as exciting as anyone in Europe at the time, and appears in retrospect as the clearest harbinger of the 'new wave' to come.

VARDA: *I'm always amused when people say that I'm the grand-mother of the New Wave, because I made my first feature film in 1954. And I had wonderful luck, in that I knew absolutely nothing at all about film-making . . .*

I studied at the École du Louvres, but I knew I did not want to end up in the provinces sorting out files. You can be broad-minded about everything, but not about really dusty archives! I quickly real-ized that I loved painting. But when I started learning about art at that college I was extremely young, just eighteen, and the teacher spent three months on Cézanne alone. At eighteen, that was just too difficult. I learned things when I was young, but it was too early on, and it meant nothing.

But I did read numerous books by the surrealists and on surrealism. I was a fan of Picasso, who was not yet really fashionable during the

. Agnès Varda (looking through viewfinder) directs *La Pointe Courte* (1954)

early fifties. I loved everything one could lay one's hands on during the late forties and early fifties – the American authors like John Dos Passos; I read James Joyce but didn't understand it very well – perhaps only a little of what he wanted one to understand. And I felt that the cinema was just in the process of illustrating the theatre and the novel. I'd seen maybe five or six films. I'd seen the Carné–Prévert collaborations, because I loved Prévert. They were classic films, classic in style, but very fine. So I began to recognize that the cinema had not exploded in the way that Impressionism, Cubism or Fauvism had done.

I found a post as a photographer at the TNP (Théâtre National Populaire) and ran into a lot of painters. Where photography was concerned, I knew how to 'look' – or at least I tried to know how to 'look'. I had a certain eye, I knew about lenses, wide angle, et cetera, which were the equivalent of what one called 'the rendering', just as in painting one learns about texture and the palette.

Silvia Monfort and Philippe Noiret in *La Pointe Courte* (1954)

One book impressed me greatly, Faulkner's The Wild Palms. *In it there are two completely different stories – two youths, conscript prisoners, who escape during the flooding of the Mississippi. What intrigued me was the subtle, authentic effect of an image, of a sound. What I learned in reading the book was something more subtle. So I read chapters one, three and five just like that – the story of the two prisoners, and then chapters two, four and six – about the Mississippi. Then I started all over again, reading in sequence, chapters one, two, three, four and so on, and I discovered the dialectic, the opposition, the osmosis, the mysterious undercurrents of understanding.*

The director of the TNP, Jean Vilar, was the first to introduce Bertolt Brecht to France, so I read a lot about the Brechtian distancing effect, and it was very interesting because it stated that one should move people not by pathos but by something concrete. One proof of that was the admirable film by Resnais, Night and Fog, *which certainly used distanciation in an extraordinarily effective way, and with the intelligence and a detachment that purifies the emotion. So, it's the notion of recovering emotion by means of a structure that does not seek pathos. So once I grasped that in my little mind – and here in this very studio where I have lived for such a long time and where I worked as a photographer – I wrote my film in the courtyard on Saturdays and Sundays.*

During the war, Varda had been sent to shelter in Sète, where she would eventually shoot *La Pointe Courte*. She talked to the fisherfolk there, listened to their stories and their everyday conversations, went home and wrote down what she had heard, with the expressions and the phrases somewhat exaggerated.

VARDA: *I remember a woman who told me that she was no longer very young, and she said, 'We've already shat half our shit' – phrases like that, not really embarrassing, but strong, impressive images that always struck me. And, for example, they talked about a woman who'd lost her memory, and said 'She's a forgetter' – I thought that was nice.*

I knew Sète very well, this fishing village on the Mediterranean that had to struggle against the big shots who sold cultivated oysters. So there was a social conscience, which is how people gather strength. The scenario was of a couple, Philippe Noiret and Silvia Monfort, and their problems, and a group of fisherfolk and their problems, with no link between the two except a unity of place. In this place there are the fisherfolk, and in this village which is the birthplace of the young man played by Noiret. There is one 'chapter' about the couple talking together and one 'chapter' about the fishermen who are trying to organize themselves into a kind of union to combat the rich folk who want to prevent them from fishing.

The Noiret character brings his woman there, who does not know this place where he grew up. He is going to try to show her, through the place where he comes from, who he is, and perhaps that their love can work out. So this film is very theoretical. I was already very interested in time, and what time does to a couple. It was funny because I was only twenty-five years old and this was what I was writing about.

At that period, feature films cost about seventy to eighty million old francs. I had some luck when my father died and I had around two million francs (about 200,000 francs today), and then my mother was sweet and sold some investments that she had, in order to loan me some more.

And I told the whole crew that the capital of money was such and such, sixty million I think it was. I created a co-operative – I was a real pioneer, because now everyone does that. And I said, we can't pay anybody, neither Philippe Noiret, who was making his film début, nor Silvia Monfort, who was somewhat known. We created shares – fifty for an actor, thirty for the editor, etc. We said that if ten francs come in, then five will go to the budget and five to the crew. It was a good idea, a nice little Utopia – except that the film didn't make any money! Anyway, I shared out what there was with everybody, and after ten years I bought out the shares, just about tripling their value.

When Alain Resnais, who I liked very much, agreed to do the editing on the same terms, I gave him just enough to buy lunch. So as not to have to pay for hiring an editing room, I borrowed a machine and did it all off my own bat. Resnais lived in the neighbourhood, so he rode to work on his bike and did the editing here.

Alain Resnais' career had taken root in the unglamorous terrain of the documentary. His twenty-minute study of Van Gogh had earned an Oscar in 1949; ahead of him, of course, lay masterpieces like *Night and Fog* and *Hiroshima mon amour*. For now, two major figures in film history had found each other early in their careers.

RESNAIS: *Agnès Varda and Jean-Pierre Melville were the first ones to say, in effect, 'No, one does not need formal training to make a film.' Of course, the rules have their occasional exceptions in that not every assistant would indeed become a film director and vice versa. All right, Becker was assistant to Renoir and others, but they are different crafts.*

So I met Varda after she contacted me to edit her film. I was an editor, but I had only cut short films. I went to the IDHEC (Institut des Hautes Etudes Cinématographiques), in the editing section. I had no intention of becoming a director.

In those days, there were amateur film societies that would meet once or twice a month and show films on 16mm, 9.5mm or 8mm.

I would just play around at weekends and shoot on 16mm, but not professionally. So when Varda called me, I jumped on my bicycle to her place, not far from where I lived. She showed me her rushes. I first said I couldn't do it, but she insisted. And she had a workshop (which is still the same today), so I said, as a joke, 'You have a big room here. Just call the lab and they'll send you the editing table.' I didn't mean it but she took it seriously and as she was very dynamic she called the CPM lab and they were so taken aback by her request that they said, 'Well, yes, we do have an old one, and, fine, we can lend it to you.'

Luckily I was friends with Henri Colpi, the editor (who was involved with the sound mixing of Varda's film), and I could ask his advice as I was not feeling too sure.

VARDA: *Resnais was a very good editor. He said, 'Editing is not like ironing a badly cut dress. It must honour the decisions initially made by the director.' In other words, this was a quite slow and very special film, and he said, 'The montage should respect your project,' which is so unusual. It's interesting because he made a decent editing job of a project that seemed strange to him, and he said that it inter-ested him in connection with his own research. He has often said that the structure of* Hiroshima mon amour *owed something to the structure of* La Pointe Courte *because there were these two worlds. He helped me generously, he applied his intelligence to the film and he made a self-effacing, discreet montage where my project was concerned. We had to post-synchronize everything, though, because I had no sound, and all that was difficult.*

I don't quite know where I got the idea of making La Pointe Courte *in that way I did. It wasn't a photographer's film, it had a very special narrative structure, with specific ideas such as, for instance, there being no sound perspective. So people would go down there in that direction and yet continue talking as if they were still here. We decided to retain the dialogue in close-up (the conversation involving the couple was distant) but it was very literary, theatrical with little emotion. Obviously people in the movie business said that it was a UFO, extraordinary but unreleasable.*

The film was finished in 1955 and André Bazin got it screened at Cannes. Finally, it was released in 1956 in a very small cinema, Le Studio Montparnasse, run by Jean-Louis Cheray, who was the only one who had the courage to show it for three weeks. In the reviews there were some very amusing expressions – 'one swallow who heralds springtime', and a critic called it 'the first ring of a great pealing of bells', silly things like that.

The film was well received everywhere among film societies, cinémathèques, museums, and film historians – but not by the public. In fifty years there have been only 10,000 admissions. But it attracted an instant following among cinéphiles. As a result, I remained a photographer, but luckily for me I made documentaries as well.

I've said that the roots of the New Wave could be found almost everywhere, but the explosion really occurred in France. Perhaps there was Wajda, and then Jean-Pierre Melville, whose methods were classical but did not exactly involve something new. I simply came 'out of the blue' as they say in America, but still La Pointe Courte was the first film by a young woman. Don't forget that, apart from the genius of Welles, everyone – even Antonioni, who was assistant to Renoir – had been an assistant, first or second assistant. I'd never been a cinéphile, never been to film school, had no film-maker friends and had never been a part of the Cahiers du cinéma group. I had no film education whatsoever, so I was completely raw. But that had proved my strength – my stupidity and my strength I should say, or rather my ignorance. And to think that one had made a film without premeditation, and that it was, in a way, the germ cell of the New Wave . . .

So prolific would the output of French film-making become during the late fifties that the New Wave seemed to appropriate every vestige of innovation that was changing the character of European cinema. The truth is that the French could not have had a more advantageous situation. General de Gaulle's regime presided over a shake-up in politics, social behaviour and the arts. The minister of culture, André Malraux, established a network of *Maisons de Culture* throughout the country, starting in Le Havre. The arts were thus brought into close-up for a wide public, who could see stage productions, ballet, art exhibitions and films all under one generous roof. Government subsidies for film-making encouraged private producers to take more risks than hitherto. Meanwhile, a teeming generation of cinéphiles, nourished at film-society level and above all in Paris by La Cinémathèque Française, was eager to convert its theorizing into practical movie-making.

Passionate debate has long been the seedbed of French culture. Already in 1949, many of the personalities associated subsequently with the New Wave had founded a film society called 'Objectif 49'. André Bazin, the *éminence grise* of the modern French cinema, along with Alexandre Astruc, Jacques Doniol-Valcroze, Pierre Kast and others, resolved to give an airing to films that had failed to gain release or recognition. In the early fifties, young cinéphiles (none more eloquent than Jacques Rivette) began to foregather at Henri Langlois' Cinémathèque in the rue d'Ulm. Their critical reaction to American B-movies as well as to European mavericks like Roberto Rossellini coloured the pages of *Les Cahiers du cinéma*, the yellow-covered monthly that nourished the writing skills of François Truffaut, Claude Chabrol and Eric Rohmer among others. In the words of Rohmer, 'Nobody can enter the Olympus of *Cahiers du cinéma* if he is not a *metteur en scène*.' Truffaut rammed home the *politique des auteurs* in his weekly column in *Arts* magazine, while dealing unmercifully with the beached whales of an earlier generation such as Autant-Lara or even Carné. He damned with faint praise the glittering work of Roger Vadim, who 'only speaks of what he knows well: today's girls, fast cars, love in 1957'.

Vadim, though, worked intelligently within the commercial framework of the cinema, while deploying its new-found technical delights such as colour and CinemaScope. *Et Dieu . . . créa la femme* (1956), which made Brigitte Bardot an international star, was a Gallic equivalent of Douglas Sirk's *Written on the Wind*, made in the same year: both films revelled in the 'Scope format, brightly spangled colours and an 'overheated' narrative structure.

Less garish and flamboyant, the work of **Jean-Pierre Melville** (born back in 1917) encouraged the younger generation. With their crepuscular melancholy, their Paris streets agleam after the rain, and their implicit fatalism, Melville's films inspired everyone from Godard (*À bout de souffle*) to Chabrol (*Les Bonnes Femmes*). His adaptation of *Le Silence de la mer*, from the atmospheric novelette by Vercors, was already a straw in the wind in 1949. *Bob le flambeur*, released in 1956, paid homage to both the French *série noire* and the Hollywood B-movie. Here, Melville used the latest, fast film stock to catch the light of Place Clichy and Place Pigalle at dawn.

Melville may be regarded as the godfather of the New Wave by many, but his films still observed the schematic structure of the American gangster film. When all's said and done, nothing that Melville does well in

Bob le flambeur was not being done just as impressively by the young Stanley Kubrick in *The Killing* during the very same year. Like Kubrick, Melville took his criminals seriously. He could not have countenanced the frivolity of Godard in *Bande à part*, for example, or Truffaut in *Tirez sur le pianiste*. Ultimately, Melville never quite fulfilled the promise of his early years. During the sixties, his work became more sluggish and less audacious, although *Léon Morin, prêtre* was an austere, controlled exercise in the Bresson idiom. His premature death in 1973 robbed him of a place in the forefront of the New Wave.

Roberto Rossellini exerted the most authoritative influence over the young French film-makers. His lean, almost ascetic style appeared like a wondrous antidote to the stifling artifice of French cinema in the early fifties. Already confirmed as a great documentarist with films such as *Rome Open City* and *Paisan*, Rossellini now applied a similar aesthetic to fictional subjects. 'With *Voyage en Italie*,' wrote Antoine de Baecque and Serge Toubiana in their biography of Truffaut, 'Rossellini showed them that it was possible to make the simplest films in the world, in telling a love story with two characters in natural surroundings.' In 1955, Rossellini decided to produce a series of films on different aspects of French society at the time. He approached various neophyte directors, among them Rivette, Godard, Rohmer, Truffaut, Rouch and Chabrol. The project did not mature, but Chabrol did at least write an original screenplay, which would develop into his first feature, *Le beau Serge*.

A survey in the magazine *L'Express* in 1957 had already referred to a 'Nouvelle Vague de la jeunesse', and in June 1958 Françoise Giroud published a successful book entitled *La Nouvelle Vague, portrait de la jeunesse*. It propounded the need for fundamental change in French society, but the title was seized upon as a nickname for the insolent, insouciant young directors arriving on the scene. Godard and Truffaut were by no means first out of the gate.

Indeed, in December 1957 **Claude Chabrol** began shooting *Le beau Serge*. It took him nine weeks, on a budget of thirty-eight million francs (around £40,000), and was filmed entirely in real interiors and in the streets of a bleak provincial town, according to the precepts laid down by Melville regarding the use of natural light and locations. Financed with money from within his family, this maiden feature was followed almost immediately by *Les Cousins*. Jean-Claude Brialy and Gérard Blain starred in these films, and in both the characters' close friendship

© AYJM, courtesy of The Kobal Collection

Serge (Gérard Blain) and François (Jean-Claude Brialy) in Chabrol's
Le beau Serge (1958)

succumbs to the pressure of envy and mutual disgust. Chabrol would
build on these opening salvos and proceed to create a bourgeois world
disfigured by furtive lust and reckless crime. Truffaut may have written
the definitive book about Hitchcock, but Chabrol's career runs alarmingly close to the Master's. A stream of near masterpieces featured the
director's wife, Stéphane Audran – *Les Biches*, *La Femme infidèle*, *Juste
avant la nuit*, *Le Boucher*, *La Rupture*. Chabrol knew how to use the
best technicians (Henri Decaë and Jean Rabier behind the camera; composer Pierre Jansen; his perennial editor, Jacques Gaillard) to give a sinister sheen to his Manichaean explorations of human frailty and guilt.
They were not New Wave films in the received sense of the term, but they
were as sophisticated as any European cinema of the period.

Louis Malle, scion of a prosperous industrial family in northern
France, had jumped straight from the Paris film school, IDHEC, into acting as director, cameraman and editor on Captain Jacques Cousteau's
underwater documentary, *Le Monde du silence*. Shooting and post-
production dragged on for more than two years. But at Cannes in 1956

the film appeared as a triumph, snatching the Palme d'Or from under the nose of Bergman's *Smiles of a Summer Night* and pitching Malle's name forward as a competent all-round young film-maker. By the spring of 1957, Malle was ready to embark on his own first feature – some months earlier than even Chabrol. *Ascenseur pour l'échafaud* was based on a thriller by Noël Calef. 'I was trying to portray a new generation through the characters of the children,' he later told Philip French. 'A description of the new Paris. Traditionally, it was always the René Clair Paris that French films presented, and I took care to show one of the first modern buildings in Paris . . . I showed a Paris, not of the future, but at least a modern city, a world already somewhat dehumanized.'

One of France's toughest critics, Georges Sadoul, wrote in 1957: 'This autumn, in the studio where *Ascenseur pour l'échafaud* was made, its director Louis Malle celebrated his twenty-fifth birthday. This event should bring luck to the French cinema. His film, which is excellent, has received the Prix Louis Delluc immediately on completion.' *Ascenseur pour l'échafaud* still looks fresh for several reasons: the casting of Jeanne Moreau in a hard, unsympathetic role as the unfaithful, scheming wife intent on murdering her husband; the jazz score composed by Miles Davis; and the brooding cinematography of Henri Decaë (who, alongside Raoul Coutard, would become the key technician of the French New Wave). 'When I made *Ascenseur pour l'échafaud*,' said Malle, 'I didn't know what *mise-en-scène* was. I had that wonderful strength that comes from naïveté, in other words a tremendous will to make movies.'

Les Amants, directed by Malle in 1958 from the cultivated pen of Louise de Vilmorin, drew inspiration from an eighteenth-century story. Decaë's languorous tracking shots precisely counterpoint the brittle, patchy comedy style that Malle uses to describe the social milieu inhabited by Jeanne Tournier (Moreau), a woman bored by both husband and lover and yet tempted still by another man. The maddening vacuity of the *haute bourgeoisie* that Malle pins down so well frames one of the most lyrical love sequences in film history. To the accompaniment of the vibrant, sensual chords of Brahms's first Sextet for Strings, Jeanne Moreau and Jean-Marc Bory stroll across wide, moonlit fields, the passion between them rising silently to its climax in the bedroom scene. Jeanne's departure with her lover at dawn throws out a challenge. Malle cocked a snook at the cowardice implicit in scores of 'women's movies', with their marital reconciliation in the final, tearful reel.

At this juncture, **Volker Schlöndorff** was a German student in Paris who would soon stun the French intelligentsia by passing out second in Philosophy for the whole of France. Determined to make his career as a film-maker, he went on to study at IDHEC, and plunged into the mood of the time.

SCHLÖNDORFF: *In 1958 I was eighteen going on nineteen, and just starting to become a film-maker. I know that if I try today to explain to film students how we got started, the fact is that I thought every new generation would do that. I didn't know it was exceptional for just that generation between 1958 and 1965. I thought that old people grow older, and then came a new generation and there was a revolution, and then we would get old ourselves, and the next one would come.*

In 1959 I started to go to La Cinémathèque Française in the rue d'Ulm in Paris. I had just graduated, with Bertrand Tavernier sitting next to me in the same class, and already we had decided that we would become film-makers. But since I was an intern in the school, we could only have Thursday afternoon and Sunday to go into town, and so that's when we caught up with movies. Once I was free, I took a room in a small hotel in Paris, in the rue Descartes, next to rue Mouffetard – where Agnès Varda made her documentary L'Opéra Mouffe – and the rue d'Ulm, where the Cinémathèque was located. We went there every evening for three movies, at 6.30, 8.30 and 10.30. Half were silent movies, but there were also newer films like Les Mistons *or* La Pointe Courte.

It wasn't the films on the screen that influenced me so much as the people around me, because in the third row you had all the guys from Positif. *Truffaut was already more established because he wrote for* Arts *. . . Some were just about to become film-makers, or had just made their first feature, like Chabrol, who had done* Le beau Serge, *which had been first screened at the Ciné-Club de La Sorbonne, in the vast auditorium.*

So when these people became film-makers, we in turn became their assistants because we were around ten years younger than they were, and they were already established as film critics, if not yet as film directors.

An aesthetic revolution happened literally during the screenings. If there was a certain type of movie, it would be booed throughout the projection, not only when the curtain came down – that happened to Claude Autant-Lara, or Clouzot's Le Corbeau. There was always an incredible debate going on. Old Fritz Lang came to show The Tiger of Eschnapur, *which he had just completed in Germany, and they all raved about how good it was, but I thought it was totally appalling and ridiculous – just because I knew these German actors, and the way they performed struck me as totally impossible.*

So I'd say that the revolution took place in those screenings as well as anywhere else. There were two ciné-clubs – the Cine Qua Non, and then the Studio Parnasse, on Tuesday nights, where Monsieur Cheray conducted quizzes, and usually Bertrand Tavernier knew the answers and got a free ticket for the next weekend. It was such a seedbed of bacteria, and everything was interacting with everything and everybody else. It was also very sectarian, because as soon as there were three guys who liked one movie, there were three others who thought it impossible, with an almost religious fundamentalism about film-making. Debates raged in the streets outside where everybody was queuing, because not everyone got into the most popular screenings, and even if you did get in, there were often terrible fights on the staircase to get a seat.

Bertrand Tavernier, son of a Lyonnais poet, had first studied law but soon fell under the spell of film and its history. He would become one of the most zealous of film buffs in the late fifties.

TAVERNIER: *Sometimes I was lacking in perspective, I was too busy discovering the history of the cinema – the masterpieces, <u>and</u> the films which had been underrated, neglected. So we were busy fighting for some directors who were not at that time accepted, and we were really in advance – Samuel Fuller, Joseph Losey . . . Later on, we discovered that Fuller had been praised by Manny Farber, but it took many years . . . We loved Delmer Daves, but that did not prevent us from admiring John Ford or Murnau. We adored the films of Renoir, John Ford, Becker, Max Ophüls. At the same time we were trying to re-evaluate directors like Cottafavi and Freda, who had been despised because they did not belong to the neo-realist movement.*

We were curious about many different kinds of cinema. With my friends from the Nickel-Odéon film society, we created a club to show the films we could not otherwise see. Italian and American films mostly – Don Siegel, Andre de Toth, Sam Fuller – a lot of them are still my heroes. But we were not only obsessed by the Hollywood cinema, our interests were wider.

I didn't miss a single film by Bergman, and we liked the early films by Fellini, Wajda, Kawalerowicz – but at the same time we were finding some Hollywood directors who were just as 'personal' – John Ford, Anthony Mann, Robert Parrish. And some films presented to us as classics – Jacques Feyder's La Kermesse héroïque, for example, or the documentaries of Joris Ivens – we found to be stiff, boring and dated.

It is true that at the end of the fifties, when the New Wave appeared, a lot of European cinema, and maybe Hollywood cinema, was becoming stiffer. There was less air, a lot of directors were less in shape – Duvivier, Autant-Lara, Clouzot. The cinema that had worked so well until the beginning of the fifties was running out of breath. Also in England, where the cinema had been superb, it was becoming so lifeless, and suffered from a lack of imagination and a lack of contact with what was happening in the world – certainly by comparison with the films of Jennings, Powell and Pressburger, Launder and Gilliatt, Cavalcanti, Mackendrick. The same thing was happening in Italy.

So suddenly a window was opened and there was a new attitude. But we have to put it in perspective – our attack was on the films of the previous five or six years, not on all the cinema that had gone before. Some of the attacks were rather unfair, and some of those directors attacked now need to be rehabilitated. But it's true that we also needed what happened.

Agnès Varda also appreciated the galvanic role of the film society:

VARDA: *In fact, there would not have been a New Wave without the audience. The audience nourishes the film society: the post-war film society, militant or Catholic, or committed ones like 'Travail et Culture' where they watched Renoir's La Marseillaise . . .*

There was an enormous number of film societies, and the audience that had learned to love the work of the older auteurs was ready also to discover new talents. Thus the New Wave was marked by the auteur theory, and not by studio factory production. On one side you had the cinéphiles, and the pack of critics, and on the other the originals, and I was among the originals.

Schlöndorff remembers the Paris film community as extremely intimate – after all, the French film academy had only a dozen students, compared to the hundreds enrolled in numerous schools throughout Europe today.

SCHLÖNDORFF: *It was a world in which everyone knew everybody else. And all roads led back to La Cinémathèque Française, where these people had grown up seeing tons of films. My political involvement began because the area round the rue d'Ulm – Montagne Ste Geneviève – was very run-down, almost a slum district with very old houses, small hotels and apartments, where the Algerians lived. The Algerian War was on, and every night there would be riots, and swoops with the police and their machine-guns. The first reports about torture had come out while we were studying at Henri IV, so we circulated Henri Alleg's book,* La Question, *which homed in on the topic and had been banned.*

French film-makers shied away from tackling the Algerian issue, which, ever since the first bomb attacks by the FLN (Front de Libération Nationale) in late 1954, had perplexed and enraged the French intelligentsia. During 1957, the left-wing French weekly magazine, *France-Observateur*, was seized no fewer than thirty-four times. Not until 1962 would Algeria receive its independence following a referendum; and, as we shall see, not until 1966 would an Italian, Gillo Pontecorvo, make the definitive film about the conflict.

SCHLÖNDORFF: *So the political turmoil synchronized with the films we saw. Documentaries started appearing. At the same time, they invented what was called the 'Scopitone' – in the café-bars, you had these big machines like a juke-box, and you put in your franc and you had not only sound but also a short film.*

The first films of Bergman were shown, and I'll never forget the afternoon when we went to see Sawdust and Tinsel. *I was still in college, and before that they screened* Les maîtres fous (1955) *by Jean Rouch, about the African exorcists – and far more than* Citizen Kane *or the classics, this made one realize how much more could be done with film as a medium. I had the feeling that this was almost the centre of everybody's lives!*

The revolution in cinema was only slightly political at that juncture – it was far more about aesthetics. But, of course, like every generation, we had to be anti-establishment, anti-bourgeois. And when the same thing happened five or six years later, when I came to Munich in 1965, it already seemed to me like a replay, like an import . . .

As **François Truffaut** was shooting the early scenes of *Les 400 coups* in November 1958, he suffered the loss of his friend and mentor, André Bazin, who died of leukaemia at the age of forty. Truffaut dedicated his début feature to a man widely regarded as the greatest critic of the post-war era in France. But many in the French film establishment were hoping that Truffaut would come a cropper with *Les 400 coups*. He had been instrumental in defining the *politique des auteurs* in the mid-fifties, and now he alone would be held to account if the film failed. From its opening sequences, however, *Les 400 coups* showed Truffaut to be as fresh and inventive in his technique as anyone in the New Wave. Spontaneity – the property and appearance of the passing moment – was everything to Truffaut. The caustic young critic who had been the scourge of Clair, Carné and Autant-Lara now revealed himself as sensitive, emotional and romantic in equal measure.

'The moment I first touched the camera,' Truffaut said in 1968, 'I quite simply realized my life's dream. Perhaps that's what settled me down. But I never dreamed of making films and then deciding not to do them. Even as a critic, I certainly dreamed about *Les 400 coups*, I dreamed about *Tirez sur le pianiste* and I dreamed about *Jules et Jim*, which I had read six years earlier. And I dreamed of these films as though I had already shot them. I was merely afraid of not being able to make them, but I never dreamed of them as being more beautiful or more aggressive.'

Les 400 coups was strongly influenced by the work of Jean Vigo, whose *Zéro de conduite* tackled many of the same issues as Truffaut's autobiographical film – the problems of a young boy, Antoine Doinel, misunderstood and maltreated by everyone from parents to schoolteacher. Made on a budget of just thirty-six million old francs, *Les 400 coups* expressed (wrote the *Guardian* in England) 'in so far as any one film could do so, the principles of the New Wave – with its rebelliousness against order, and its brusque inattention to the niceties of film form'. Truffaut did not like films that were technically self-conscious. 'The sincerity of a film', he wrote, 'is much more important than its technical perfection, which tends to leave only an impression of coldness.' One felt an exhilarating rush when watching the film for the first time, as though a bird had been released from a cage. Truffaut's joyful use of the 'Scope format, Henri Decaë's fluent camerawork and the spontaneity of the youngsters' behaviour all seemed fresh and hopeful in the final year of a grim decade.

Alain Resnais' *Night and Fog*, screened at Cannes in 1956 against the diplomatic protests of the German government, still stands as the greatest study of the Nazi camps. Narrated by Michel Bouquet in a flat, merciless monotone, this rigorous documentary about Auschwitz says more in thirty-one minutes than Spielberg with *Schindler's List* or even Claude Lanzmann with *Shoah* could show over many hours. Resnais' grave and visually inventive tribute to the French National Library (*Toute la mémoire du monde*) won widespread praise in the same year.

RESNAIS: *I grew up with the idea that in order to learn the craft, one had to be an assistant or second assistant for a very long time. According to the rules of the game, one could understand the principles of film-making only if one had made three films in each capacity. Only then could you be a director. That was the tradition, and it could be explained by the fact that there were no books on the subject. One had to work out one's own rules. To my knowledge, nothing existed to help us find our directions.*

Cinema is a strange thing because no film requires the same level of intellectual effort as any book does for the audience. And I wondered why that was, why even in those amateur film societies, where no commercial pressure was exercised, one could not find real rebel films, anything really different – but then perhaps I missed some things. The surrealist movement with people like Breton, Aragon, Renoir and Buñuel was very interesting to me.

I used to read Sight and Sound, Positif, Les Cahiers du cinéma, Cinema Nuovo *and* Sequence. *I went to London once to get back copies of* Sequence, *reached a small studio, entered and suddenly saw Lindsay Anderson, back from his shopping. We started talking and went on for hours, both very excited. I regard his film,* This Sporting Life, *as a masterpiece.*

After the war, there was tremendous curiosity in all foreign films, because on the whole we were deprived of films during the war, apart from some Italian titles. Then they talk of the Golden Age of French Cinema and really, apart from some films, of course, by Clouzot and Becker, there was scarcely anything new. Hence the hunger for films.

The number of spectators rose enormously in those days. I was a great fan of British and American cinema and naturally Ingmar Bergman's work came as a big shock.

I was a member of the Cinémathèque, and Henri Langlois would introduce a film only once a week. He could never finish his sentences, but it was fascinating stuff. I discovered the great Russian directors, so different from what I was used to, especially coming from Brittany as I did. Having said that, no Soviet film-maker really amazed me, other than Boris Barnet and some of the Soviet films made in the fifties, like Ballad of a Soldier. *On the whole, compared to the classic works of the thirties, I found the new Russian cinema very disappointing.*

Karel Reisz was the inspiration for my work as an editor. His book, The Technique of Film Editing, *showed me how to shape formal links between shots not only in terms of content but also with the framing and camera movements. So, thanks to Karel Reisz I was able to work on my film* Le Chant du styrène. *Even today, I could still find which pages described it in his book. I also liked his films, incidentally!*

Resnais embarked on *Hiroshima mon amour* in the summer of 1958, leaving for Japan to shoot the interiors in Tokyo just as Truffaut was finalizing his preparations for *Les 400 coups*. He worked with a predominantly Japanese crew, apart from Sacha Vierny, who photographed the scenes in Nevers where the Emmanuelle Riva character endured her first, shattering love affair. Eiji Okada, who played her Japanese lover, could speak hardly a word of French and had to learn his lines phonetically in order to loop them satisfactorily in Paris in January 1959.

Hiroshima mon amour, which Louis Seguin in *Positif* hailed as 'perhaps as important a film as *Citizen Kane*', demonstrated Resnais' abiding gift for working with a novelist–screenwriter.

RESNAIS: *My French producers commissioned a film about the atomic bomb. I agreed, but only if Chris Marker would write the script. At first he said yes, and then retracted, as he thought a friend of his would do it better. Meanwhile, I viewed a lot of Japanese films. I then told the producers, 'Look, just take some of those films from Japan you showed me as I don't think I can do any better. I'm opting out of the project as it stands,' to which they then said, 'Would you agree to visit Japan with Françoise Sagan?' I said yes, why not, but* we did not get to meet for some reason. In fact, there was money to be spent in Japan, for just material, pedestrian reasons, and we talked about writers I liked – Raymond Queneau, Jean Genet and Marguerite Duras (who was not famous then, but whom I liked).

Now, Olga Wormser, the historian who had been the technical adviser – almost co-scriptwriter in fact – on Night and Fog, knew Duras and talked to her. Marguerite was rather amused at first and said, 'Resnais, yes, I've got to meet that boy.' So we agreed to have a drink and I spent the afternoon explaining to her why I was not making a film on the atomic bomb. I said, 'You see, it's strange that while we are sipping our cup of tea, planes are going round the globe loaded with these atomic bombs twenty-four hours a day and it should really affect our life, but it doesn't quite. So perhaps we should just make a film not on the subject itself but on the notion of threat, of atomic death lurking in the background.'

She called me three or four days later with a stretch of dialogue between a Japanese man and a French woman debating as to whether the fish were contaminated or not – as simple as that. So, I told the producers that if Marguerite Duras wanted to write a script, I was interested, but that the film would not be a documentary at all. They, too, were intrigued, so we all met and we drew up a contract and Marguerite began writing.

At the time, I found that French cinema was going in circles and that perhaps if we were to ask writers who had no experience with film to write screenplays, we might come up with something different. Certainly this created some fresh enthusiasm, and for Marguerite, that was an adventure. This climate lasted for about five to ten years, at least until about 1965, whereby people who had not been involved in film-making found it very exciting to be able to write for a visual dramatic story. Nowadays it is common practice.

I have never pretended to write a script. But I shrank from the idea of adapting a book. I wanted to have a script especially written for the cinema. I said to Marguerite, 'Bear in mind that it will be for the cinema, and remember that the spectator has no means of rewinding the print and watching again, as a reader would do with a book.' That was my only advice.

In my youth, one was accustomed to the presence of a scriptwriter in French films, except for René Clair, or Jean Renoir for La Règle du jeu, which was then criticized for the very fact that the director had *written his own script. Then there was Chaplin, of course, but these instances were rare. Since those days, we have found out that in Hollywood directors like Capra, Ford, George Stevens all actually worked a lot on the script.*

As these comments show, Resnais was not an *auteur* in the fashionable sense of that word in 1959. Like Hitchcock, like Welles, he relied considerably on his screenwriters, whether it be Duras for *Hiroshima mon amour*, Jean Cayrol for *Night and Fog* and *Muriel*, or, eighteen months later, Alain Robbe-Grillet for *L'année dernière à Marienbad*. *Hiroshima mon amour* adheres meticulously to the shooting script by Duras. Even when the novelist had given him some alternatives, Resnais would shoot them all and then select the one originally recommended by Duras.

The completed film struck a series of resounding chords in its youthful audience. Its cool and yet ominous references to the atomic devastation in Japan brought home – at least to British audiences – the relevance of recent anti-nuclear marches to the atomic weapons site at Aldermaston in 1958, led by Bertrand Russell, championing the cause of disarmament. Then there was the film's extraordinary structure. Memories were interwoven with the present, displaying not only a compulsive logic but also a confidence that matched even *Kane*. More than anything else, it was the casual brilliance with which Resnais flitted back and forth in time that ensured *Hiroshima mon amour* a crucial niche in the history of the cinema. Nicolas Roeg's *Don't Look Now*, Kieślowski's *The Double Life of Veronique* and Christopher Nolan's *Memento* are just three films that could rely on audience acceptance thanks to Resnais' ground-breaking achievement. Resnais and Duras obliged us to identify with Emmanuelle Riva's heroine to an anguished degree. Subjective flashbacks to the doomed affair with a German officer in Nevers gradually merge with the woman's current fling in Hiroshima, while the tragic evidence of the nuclear blast in Hiroshima 'rhymes', as it were, with the private agony of the Frenchwoman as she confronts the death of her German lover back in 1945.

RESNAIS: *When it came to the montage, we even thought of cartoon-like editing, with shots that grip on to the next ones to link them together, ways to bounce from one shot to another in almost a kind of disharmony. When I made* Toute la mémoire du monde, *for example, I knew one could not cut a shot in movement without it being stopped. But here I said yes, we __can__ if one links it with a side movement, but the*

*lateral movement should then be slightly faster than the forward move-
ment – well, you see, that sort of research. All this now sounds very
dusty as it is used in films constantly, like part of the routine.*

There was also the haunting, evocative music by Giovanni Fusco, who
had composed scores for every Antonioni film from his earliest documentary onwards, and would indeed go straight from composing his
score for Resnais back to Rome to work on Antonioni's *L'avventura*.

RESNAIS: *I hesitated a great deal before asking Giovanni Fusco to
write the music on* Hiroshima mon amour *because he belonged to
Antonioni, I thought. But I was so taken by what I had heard by him
. . . So Fusco came, saw the film and wrote the music in three weeks.
And we got on very well. Then Georges Delerue, who had often
directed the music for my shorts, very generously contributed the
waltz for* Hiroshima mon amour. *In order to keep the French mood
of the film, we needed a French musician and it was a magnificent
gesture from Delerue. He worked from the records of Japanese music
I had collected in order to introduce a Japanese sound into the
French music. Besides, I always like to have a waltz in each of my
films, and Fusco was very happy with that waltz by Delerue.*

Delerue would become for ever associated with the lyrical peaks of the
French New Wave through his scores for *Tirez sur le pianiste, Jules et
Jim, Contempt, Day for Night, The Conformist* and *The Last Metro*.
The interjection of wistful, poignant music on a jukebox in Hiroshima
has a double impact, on both the Riva character in the film and on us, as
opposed to the music of Giovanni Fusco, which is always heard off-
screen. Resnais likened *Hiroshima mon amour* to the form of a string
quartet, with its themes, its variations on the opening movement and so
on. 'His idea was to film the screenplay like a libretto,' recalled Duras
later, 'just as a composer would set a play to music – as Debussy did with
Maeterlinck's *Pelléas et Mélisande*.'

It is hard now to believe that *Hiroshima mon amour* was rejected for
the Cannes Festival competition in May 1959. The real reason was that
the festival feared that it might offend the United States – this was still
the Cold War era, and the 'nuclear option' was one that flew above our
heads every minute of every day. But *Hiroshima* did receive an out-of-
competition slot at the festival, won the FIPRESCI critics' award and
was snapped up by every territory in sight.

In fact, Cannes 1959 marked a watershed in the history of French cinema, with Truffaut winning the Best Director Award for *Les 400 coups* and Marcel Camus taking the Palme d'Or for *Orfeu Negro*, his brightly spangled fable of Brazilian city life. Jean Cocteau ecstatically endorsed the work of Truffaut in particular, telling everyone within earshot how good his film was. The local media proclaimed the festival as embodying a youthful renaissance in French cinema. Foreign distributors began snapping up rights to *Hiroshima mon amour*, *Orfeu Negro* and *Les 400 coups*, thus adding to those films by Malle and Chabrol already in circulation abroad.

'It was a good time to be alive,' wrote Godard later, 'and the fame that lay ahead had not yet begun to weave the shroud of our happiness.'

© Leo Mirkine, courtesy of The Kobal Collection

Jean-Pierre Léaud and François Truffaut at the Cannes Film Festival, May 1959

3 The Realist's Eye

When I started, I thought it would only take me a few months; it took three years. I made every mistake known to man; I can't even remember all the mistakes we made.
    John Cassavetes on *Shadows*

The effect of the European film-making frenzy was felt in the United States in quite different ways. In New York, the passion for 'foreign movies' blended to some extent with that city's yen for experiment in the visual arts, with painting and photography to the fore. Several film-makers tilled the fertile fields of the documentary – Richard Leacock, D. A. Pennebaker and the Maysles brothers – while others took up the Dziga-Vertov torch of formal experimentation: Ed Emshwiller, Jordan Belson and Stan Brakhage, for example. Trailblazers on the East Coast, such as Maya Deren, Jonas Mekas and James Broughton, had sustained a loud if ultimately impotent challenge to the Hollywood studio system. Their films were almost always short, and circulated among film societies and universities, rarely outside the metropolitan areas of America.

John Cassavetes began shooting *Shadows* in February 1957, before Chabrol or Malle had embarked on their first features but long after Varda had completed *La Pointe Courte*, while Wajda had already made two of the three films in his path-breaking trilogy. Indeed, *Shadows* was only released commercially in Europe in October 1960, and even later in the United States. Its impact, however, surpassed that of any other American independent film.

Cassavetes milked the advantage of being a successful young actor. He used his fees to subsidize his own persistent efforts to get a feature off the ground. In January 1957, he 'dreamed up some characters that were close to the people in [my actors' workshop] class, and then I kept changing the situations and ages of the characters until we all began to function as those characters at any given moment'. Cassavetes chose one basic melodramatic situation, in which a girl is seduced by a young white

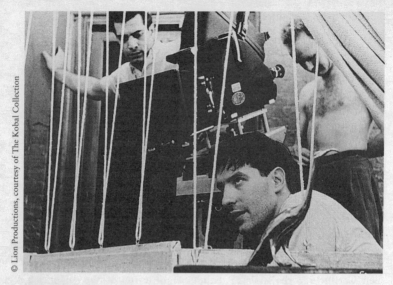

John Cassavetes directs *Shadows* (1958)

man who only finds out later that she is coloured. Accepting help wherever he could find it (and fellow director Shirley Clarke proffered the equipment), Cassavetes began shooting *Shadows* with the Italian neo-realists, early Bergman and Kurosawa as his chief sources of inspiration. 'The real difference between *Shadows* and any other picture', he said later, 'is that *Shadows* emanates from character while in other pictures the characters emanate from the story.'

He would write descriptions of his characters, and even their dialogue, and then embark on a spell of improvisation. 'First we improvise to get the feel of the characters; then as the actors become easy in the roles, we go back to the text. If it doesn't work out, then we go back and improvise some more; and again return to the text. We keep working like this till we feel complete identification between actor and role.' Once shooting began, Cassavetes would often go for broke and use an entire magazine of film – up to twelve minutes – to ensure an unbroken texture in the performances. 'Though on *Shadows* I had to scrap most of what we shot in the first of eight weeks' shooting, later on,' reflected Cassavetes, 'once they relaxed and gained confidence, many of the things they did shocked even me, they were so completely, unpredictably true.'

Shadows took eighteen months to edit, and cost eventually some $40,000. After the initial private screenings in November 1958, Cassavetes decided to reshoot whole sections of the film. More than eighteen hours of new footage was filmed, and by the late summer of 1959, only about one quarter of the original version remained in place. Cassavetes had the 16mm material blown up to 35mm, and *Shadows* received its definitive first showings in November 1959 thanks to the enthusiasm of Amos Vogel, founder of Cinema 16 and, subsequently, the New York Film Festival.

Shadows influenced many directors as far as the details of its production were concerned, but what looks vital about it still is the grimy truth of its observation. It's about a black family that, in the words of Cassavetes, 'lives just beyond the bright lights of Broadway': Ben, Hugh, Tom and the others – New Yorkers trying to get a purchase on the fringes of stable society and compromising all the time for fear of losing that precarious opportunity. The ragged strips of dialogue and the spontaneous fights are just stages in their instinctive search for pleasure and status. Ben (Ben Carruthers), the mulatto, haunts the film more than anyone; a hunched-up embodiment of melancholy, a jazz musician without a job, drifting away into the urban night as the film dwindles to a close.

If there is sympathy in *Shadows*, there is also resignation. Happiness shines briefly for Tony (Anthony Ray) and Lelia (Lelia Goldoni) in Central Park, but soon they too are drawn back into patterns of inarticulateness and high-strung recrimination. There is a form to *Shadows*, there is even a central crisis when Tony discovers that Lelia is a half-caste; but it's the film's coarse, consistent weave that counts, its unabashed glare at the seamier side of metropolitan existence and its rejection of the platitudes of Hollywood cinema.

Not that Hollywood was immune to the fostering of challenging directorial talent. **Arthur Penn** was already thirty-six years old when he caught the attention of critics in 1958 with *The Left Handed Gun*, released by Warner Bros. Penn offered a revisionist portrayal of Billy the Kid, played by Paul Newman as a confused and complex-ridden adolescent betrayed by his friend Pat Garrett. Billy (like Bonnie Parker and Clyde Barrow, real-life outlaws whom Penn would later bring to the screen) resorts to violence as a means of shocking what seems to be a drab and regimented world.

But shaking up the traditional movie genres – western, musical, thriller – has rarely made for popular success. Audiences in the late fifties were ready for a closer glimpse of the daily world in which they moved and, increasingly, of the financial goals that beckoned as the austerity of the post-war years dispersed.

Meanwhile, separated from France by that oh-so-significant Channel, Britain was enduring a crisis in self-confidence. The Suez adventure of 1956, when the government crossed swords with the combative Egyptian president Colonel Nasser, had left a lot of blushes – even some blood – on the countenance of the British government. President Eisenhower's rebuke to Prime Minister Anthony Eden seemed the ultimate affront. Meanwhile, a new generation was quickening, a generation that had grown up during the war years but had gone to secondary school and university in the aftermath of the conflict. They refused to accept the dogma and traditions of their elders.

In what would prove to be a profound cultural revolution, the first shots were fired by a playwright, John Osborne. His play *Look Back in Anger* opened at the Royal Court Theatre in London's Sloane Square in May 1956. Its leading character, Jimmy Porter, flung insults and invective at just about every institution cherished by middle England. Osborne followed up this caustic drama with a brilliant portrayal of a disillusioned artist – *The Entertainer,* in which Laurence Olivier gave one of his greatest stage performances in the leading role.

Other playwrights joined the fray – Arnold Wesker with *The Kitchen*; Shelagh Delaney with *A Taste of Honey*; Willis Hall with *The Long and the Short and the Tall*; Harold Pinter with *The Caretaker*. Simultaneously, some fresh faces were emerging on the literary scene, led by Alan Sillitoe, whose *Saturday Night and Sunday Morning* depicted a raw cross-section of working-class life in England, a country much troubled by industrial disputes, class envy and a sense of isolationism *vis-à-vis* the European continent. (In 1959, General de Gaulle had pronounced Britain not fit to be a member of the 'Common Market', as the fledgeling EC was then called.)

John Braine wrote an incisive study of financial greed set in the north of England, entitled *Room at the Top*, and when it was filmed by Jack Clayton in 1958, it signalled the launch of a whole new wave in British cinema. In terms of form – editing, camerawork, music – *Room at the Top* was not revolutionary in the manner of Cassavetes' *Shadows* or Resnais' *Hiroshima mon amour*. But in terms of content, the film was socially committed in a way that many other 'new wave' films in other

Joe Lampton (Laurence Harvey) and Alice (Simone Signoret) in
Room at the Top (1959)

countries were not – or at least, not at that juncture. It tracked the
progress of Joe Lampton (Laurence Harvey), a ruthless cad who wor-
ships the golden calf and who will use anything, including love, to get his
way. What also seemed so new about *Room at the Top* was its raunchi-
ness, embodied in the physical allure of Simone Signoret as the principal
woman in Lampton's unsavoury life. Signoret, who had already starred
in films by Max Ophüls, Jacques Becker and Henri-Georges Clouzot,
brought an exotic, cross-Channel flavour to the proceedings.

The realist tendency among British film-makers around the turn of the
decade owes its origins not just to stage plays like *Look Back in Anger*,
with its ferocious denunciation of the lack of stimulus in British life (and
especially the overweening role played by southern England). The realism came also from a little-trumpeted movement called 'Free Cinema'.
The directors involved in Free Cinema adopted a documentary
approach, and focused on working-class life. Their budgets were slim
and their films were usually short or medium in length. This was before

the mass-market era of television, and so such films were screened by film societies and in specialized cinemas around the nation. **Lindsay Anderson** and **Karel Reisz** were the foremost names in the Free Cinema movement. The third member of the squad, **Tony Richardson**, had collaborated with Reisz on the path-breaking documentary *Momma Don't Allow* and would go on to make some of the most memorable British feature films of the renaissance between 1959 and 1964.

A manifesto was issued by the founders of Free Cinema, in which they defined their aim as 'making films which share an attitude: a belief in freedom, in the importance of the individual, and the significance of the everyday'. While this manifesto clearly bespoke a collective voice, Karel Reisz remembers there being no question as to who was the driving force of the movement.

REISZ: *As far as Free Cinema was concerned, Lindsay Anderson was our publicist and our priest, and tried to pull it all together. We were keen not to be labelled polemical, political – and we weren't actually.*

Cinematographer Walter Lassally, who shot Anderson's first shorts and Richardson's first features before winning an Academy Award for his work on *Zorba the Greek*, is of the same mind as to Free Cinema's prime mover.

LASSALLY: *It was Lindsay who coined the phrase 'Free Cinema'. It wasn't really a movement, and not comparable in the least to the French New Wave – it was much too small and the influence it had was nil! But Free Cinema was very much a one-man band on the part of Lindsay Anderson. He was the energy behind it, assisted by Tony Richardson and Karel Reisz. But they had lesser parts to play, because Tony was involved in theatre and Karel had other things to do as well.*

Anderson, a discriminating critic with an unexpected fondness for John Ford, would become the mouthpiece of the cinema revolution that advanced little by little during the late fifties. In an article in *Sight and Sound* which appeared only a few months after *Look Back in Anger* had opened in 1956, he launched an attack on 'the kind of philistinism which shrinks from art because art presents a challenge'. In the piece, entitled 'Stand Up! Stand Up!', Anderson went on: 'By celebrating the merits of the trivial, we lower the prestige of the cinema and, indirectly, make it more difficult for anyone to make a good film.'

Like Oscar Wilde long before him, and like François Truffaut across the Channel, Anderson expected critics to adhere to a personal vision of the world – not to endorse the escapist, usually sentimental films that Hollywood was serving up in the fifties, but to single out those voices who were condemning the fault-lines in society. Anderson's name would become irreversibly associated with an outsider's energy and frustration, forever battering at the wall of the English Establishment, an Establishment, he would say later, that 'has a remarkable flair for assimilating its critics'. Typical of his early work was *Every Day Except Christmas*, made in 1957 and photographed by Lassally, which described the toil of porters and others in the Covent Garden fruit and vegetable market.

Apart from Lindsay Anderson's eloquent call to arms, the British cinema of the sixties was not shored up by theory or debate. Without much help from government subsidies, but to a fair degree backed by a younger generation of critics, the new wave in Britain simply pushed ahead and made films. In some cases, they were based on plays or novels; but as the decade wore on, original screenplays – and screenwriters – came to the fore.

Karel Reisz was a Czech *émigré* and made the most successful of the Free Cinema documentaries, *We Are the Lambeth Boys* (1958). Sponsored, surprisingly, by the Ford Motor Company in 1958, this film charted the daily life of young people in one of London's least prosperous neighbourhoods. '*I'd taught at secondary modern schools and also at Marylebone Grammar School,*' Reisz told me shortly before his death in 2002. '*Momma Don't Allow and certainly* We Are the Lambeth Boys *were a response to that experience.*' Thanks to Lassally's hand-held camerawork, *Momma Don't Allow* captured the energy of an evening at a London jazz club.

This new-found push for realism – grittier than its Italian forebear had been – also began to exert an impact on acting and actors. Take the example of Delphine Seyrig, shortly to become a screen icon of the period. Born in Beirut to French-Alsatian parents, Seyrig first studied acting at the Comédie de Saint-Etienne and Centre Dramatique de l'Est in France, but was drawn in the late fifties to Lee Strasberg's Actors' Studio in New York, with its Stanislavsky-influenced precepts. 'It was an essential training for me,' Seyrig would recall. 'I lived in a milieu of painters and poets that led me to act in Robert Frank's film, *Pull My*

Momma Don't Allow (1955), an early collaboration by Karel Reisz and Tony Richardson, photographed by Walter Lassally

Daisy, in 1959 and which was screened in the same programme as *Shadows*.'

Screen acting began to undergo a transformation, becoming less stilted and self-conscious. As Bergman's great collaborator Max von Sydow recalled to me, 'If I watch my old films, for example *The Seventh Seal*, I realize I do a lot of stage acting there. I have always been disturbed by the declamatory fashion in which I speak in a film like that. But then television suddenly swept through Sweden, and we were all soon accustomed to *realism* – from newsreels, talk shows . . . And then of course there was the Method school of acting, which exerted an influence in Europe also.'

Zbigniew Cybulski's informal approach to his characters – refusing to change his 'look', as a traditional actor such as Olivier would do – set the tone for the young screen idols of the late fifties. Wajda would speak of Cybulski's 'assertiveness, his impetuosity. Everyone who worked with him could feel that here was a remarkably stimulating personality who had an astonishing flair for thinking up any number of riveting bits of business . . . Though sometimes,' Wajda conceded, 'we found that on the screen they fell flat, that the exhilaration failed to get across.'

Gérard Blain, in *Le beau serge* and *Les cousins*, also adopted the dishevelled, leather-jacketed guise. Within two years, Jean-Paul Belmondo and Albert Finney had joined this group of off-beat heart-throbs. Belmondo in *À bout de souffle* adopted the Bogart approach – tough, hard-boiled, with an edge of insolence that added to his allure. Finney, despite his classical stage training, slipped easily into the proletarian role of Arthur Seaton, the pugnacious factory worker bursting his bonds in Karel Reisz's *Saturday Night and Sunday Morning*. In time, though, Belmondo would prove his ability to play more restrained roles – in Melville's *Léon Morin, prêtre*, for example – while Finney was considered by Antonioni for the male lead in *L'eclisse*, and came closer yet to securing the coveted role of *Lawrence of Arabia* in David Lean's epic.

Advances in film technology during the fifties also opened the door to directors in search of independence – not just in subject matter but also in visual and aural style.

Sound recording for motion pictures was revolutionized by the work of Stefan Kudelski, a Polish engineer working in Lausanne. In 1958, the Nagra III, a transistorized tape recorder with electronic speed control, was launched by Kudelski's company. For the first time, a unit weighing only 5 kilograms could be relied upon to produce recordings of the same quality as those achieved by the best non-portable studio recorders. Certainly, Cassavetes would have welcomed a Nagra on location while making *Shadows* in 1957 and 1958. 'We didn't even have enough money to *print* [the sound], to hear how bad it was,' he recalled. 'So when we came out, we had Sinatra singing [in a dance studio] upstairs, and all kinds of *boom*, dancing feet above us. And that was the *sound* of the picture. So we spent hours, days, weeks, months, *years*, trying to straighten out this sound. Finally, it was impossible, and we just went with it.'

For **Volker Schlöndorff**, the benefits of these improvements in the sound domain were immediately clear:

SCHLÖNDORFF: *Of course the new, lighter cameras were important – the Cameflex they used in France, and also the Arriflex. But above all it was the Nagra recording system developed by Kudelski in Switzerland. His sound recording equipment would run in sync with the film, first via cable and later with an incorporated quartz system that synchronized the two machines. Up to that point, film sound meant a whole truckload of equipment in itself, and now all of a sudden you could hang it round your neck as you were shooting. But still you could not record sound with the portable camera. So on the one hand there was the aim to go for direct sound, live sound, and on the other the impossibility because the camera was so noisy. So a lot of looping still had to be done for those kinds of scenes.*

In turn, the role of the lighting cameraman was transformed by the introduction of the Cameflex and the Arriflex. Although the Arriflex 35IIC, with its remarkable reflex viewfinder, had been introduced as early as 1935, it was only the later, lighter models that excited the New Wave directors and that fostered the growth of *cinéma-vérité* techniques. Festival-goers at Cannes in 1958 were amazed by the hand-held camerawork of Sergei Urusevsky in *The Cranes Are Flying*, which won the Palme d'Or. Urusevsky had been an army cameraman during World War II and relished the challenge of shooting on location. In one extraordinary fluid shot, Urusevsky's camera observes the heroine in close-up inside a bus, and then follows her out the door of the bus into a crowded street, swerves through milling bystanders and finally cranes up to view her moving off down the street.

Faster film stock, exemplified by the Kodak Tri-X Panchromatic Camera Negative (introduced in 1954), also enabled directors to escape the stifling embrace of the studios and to shoot in real streets and in real houses and apartments. They could rely on available light, as their cameramen could stop down much further than before. (Cassavetes used Tri-X stock to shoot the night-time sequences in *Shadows*.)

As the recollections of **Karel Reisz** and **Walter Lassally** confirm, these changes were in train before the French New Wave became fashionable. The younger generation felt confident in rejecting what was referred to in Germany and France as 'papa's cinema' – the conventional, studio-bound productions that dominated European cinema after the war.

LASSALLY: *The thing that Britain and France had in common was that the Free Cinema, or the films that followed Free Cinema, and the films of Chabrol and Truffaut in France represented an escape from 'papa's cinema'. If you look at earlier films from the fifties, they contain all the clichés of the working-class characters – they only appeared as comic relief, if at all. Studio people in Britain, the professionals, frowned on location-shooting and natural lighting.*

That barrier was broken in several countries pretty much at once, particularly in Britain and France.

I remember a conversation I had once with Raoul Coutard where we agreed that these things occur more or less simultaneously, without one necessarily being influenced by the other: whether it was Lionel Rogosin in America, or us in Britain, or cinematographers like Coutard in France or – someone I admired very much – Gianni Di Venanzo in Italy.

On Momma Don't Allow *in 1955, we used only a spring-wound Bolex 16mm camera, so the maximum length of run was twenty-two seconds, so no shot could last longer than twenty-two seconds. It was done with a sort of primitive playback system, one might say, for the dance numbers. But all the actual syncing had to be done in the cutting-room.*

The big breakthrough came with crystal-controlled motors, which Pennebaker and Leacock used in America on a converted CPR [car plate recognition] camera, which was a camera not really at all suitable for hand-holding – it was the size of a large biscuit-tin, and completely square. Very shortly afterwards, this system was incorporated in the Eclair NPR.

The Arriflex camera was considered by so-called professionals as an amateur camera, or rather a newsreel camera, and its use on feature films was very much frowned upon. For one thing, it only had 400 foot of load, and that wasn't considered enough. But the fact that it could be converted within a few minutes from a very small hand-held camera into a perfectly usable studio camera for sync sound was very important to me.

Interestingly enough, development in America and in France was more or less simultaneous. The Eclair NPR was the first self-blimped 16mm camera, so one no longer had to choose between hand-holding and sync sound, which was the case before. That's why in films like We Are the Lambeth Boys, *I had to use an improvised blimp made out of an old sleeping-bag, in order to get a few hand-held sync-sound scenes!*

REISZ: *On* We Are the Lambeth Boys, *the gear allowed you to shoot synchronous rushes. For example, you could have long sequences of debates, with boys seated round a table. Walter Lassally with his hand-held Arriflex, and John Fletcher with his Nagra enabled us to shoot unrehearsed material. It was a sacrifice of technical perfection in favour of spontaneity.*

LASSALLY: *I remember distinctly the first time I encountered a Nagra really close-up was in Greece, on one of my Greek films called* Maddalena. *The sound-man appeared on the pier of this little island where we were shooting, on Antiparos, carrying a Nagra over his shoulder and a small folding-stool – and he sat down and said, 'I'm ready!' And I was absolutely amazed, because it was unheard of for the sound to be ready before me!*

But you know, even more so than directors, I think that camera-men are a very conservative lot. And every time the film stock increased its speed, instead of using fewer lamps or smaller lamps, they just stopped down another stop!

Alain Resnais also felt the significance of the lighter cameras reaching the market during the fifties.

RESNAIS: *On my first three films, we post-synchronized everything. In-between, I would do little things like shooting commercials, so I got to know the equipment. When the Éclair Cameflex arrived, that was a revelation for me. It was a fragile piece of equipment, but the first one to take into account the cameraman's need. One could choose the angles much more rapidly and with a much better view compared to old-fashioned ones I worked with sometimes, where you would only get a wiry frame and you had to view through the film itself. It's amazing that one was able to make films under these conditions.*

The good thing about this system is that one could see instantly the result on the image itself. The Cameflex was a bit like using a 16mm camera and therefore film-making became a less solemn affair – but it enabled people like Truffaut, Rohmer and others to get a closer and faster grip on things. I really would have chosen to be a camera-man but for that you need to be strong and sturdy to carry the camera on the shoulder and I could not do that because my health had been fragile since early youth. That is why I chose editing, because it was less physical. But then everyone could carry a Cameflex!

Cinéma-vérité as a movement could not have flourished without the lighter, portable equipment that became available during the late fifties. The expansion of television throughout Europe stimulated the documentary form, and the French in particular warmed to the idea of capturing everyday reality on film, whether it be in an African village, the steppes of Siberia or on the streets of Paris itself.

Jean Rouch coined the term *cinéma-vérité* ('camera truth') in 1960 to describe the documentary he made with Edgar Morin entitled *Chronique d'un été*. Dziga-Vertov had already practised a similar technique in Russia during the twenties – *Kino-pravda*. Rouch and his disciples set themselves apart from other observers of the social scene (such as Leacock and Pennebaker in the US) by interviewing people in the streets and at their work. *Cinéma-vérité* was active rather than passive in approach, provocative rather than receptive, and its ideals were in sync with the unvarnished interpretation of reality that Jean-Luc Godard was about to launch upon the world.

Rouch, celebrated initially for being the first man to negotiate the Niger river in a dugout canoe, had begun shooting documentaries in the late forties, almost contemporaneously with Richard Leacock's *Louisiana Story*. Like Flaherty, Rouch had the instincts of an ethnographer, but he turned his back on the innate aestheticism of Flaherty's cinema. For some years, he pursued his experimental work in Africa, recording tribal customs on 16mm film. In 1955, he made *Les maîtres fous*, with the support of the enterprising producer Pierre Braunberger at Les Films de la Pleiade. Using a hand-held camera and colour stock, he recorded the bizarre rites of possession practised by the Haouka sect in west Africa. By refusing to 'stage' the ritual, and allowing – even encouraging – the members of the cult to improvise before the camera as they sacrifice a dog and devour the bloodied flesh, Rouch achieved a naked realism. The French authorities of the time were enraged and promptly sought to ban the film entirely – as did many African states, who felt that it presented the 'noble savage' in derogatory terms. After all, the men involved were clearly shown to be government officials, clerks, or shopkeepers, who had cast aside their 'Western' dress for the purposes of the ritual.

Nevertheless, the seeds of many a great documentary of the sixties lay in Rouch's pioneering film. Alongside the aesthetic revolution, an investigative urge would develop among film-makers such as Marker, Rosi, Pontecorvo, Loach and eventually Marcel Ophüls, with *The Sorrow and the Pity*. But here, as elsewhere, there was an evident desire to expose on screens that which had not been seen before.

4 The Big New Wave

> Everyone thought the New Wave was so natural . . . but it just looked natural. In *A Woman Is a Woman*, all the scenes in the apartment were filmed in a studio . . .
> Anna Karina

I PARIS BELONGS TO US

On 16 March 1960, there occurred an event as momentous as the first performance of Stravinsky's *Rite of Spring* in 1913, or the publication of Joyce's *Ulysses* in 1922. *À bout de souffle*, **Jean-Luc Godard**'s first feature film, opened in Paris. Godard had been a passionate advocate of change in French cinema, and had already attracted attention with such shorts as *Tous les garçons s'appellent Patrick* and *Charlotte et son Jules*. These had been written, financed and generally fostered by a wide circle of friends that included Truffaut, Rohmer and the actors Jean-Paul Belmondo and Jean-Claude Brialy. When *À bout de souffle* first appeared, observers assumed that Truffaut's credit as screenwriter and Chabrol's as 'artistic supervisor' meant that Godard's role was less dominant. In fact, such credits were created to pacify the technicians' union in France – although it was Truffaut who had spotted the news item that gave Godard the idea for his film. And nothing could have been more lucid than the scenario of Jean-Paul Belmondo as a relaxed, spoiled young Parisian layabout who steals fast cars to impress his American girlfriend (Jean Seberg) and refuses to commit to anything or anyone.

It soon became obvious that Godard was his own man, utterly different from anyone of his generation. Much later, he would accept creative advice and collaboration (from, for example, Jean-Pierre Gorin and Anne-Marie Miéville), but at the turn of the sixties he rewrote the grammar of film as surely as Griffith, Eisenstein and Welles had done before him. A tiny budget of 400,000 francs only encouraged his audacity when it came to editing his first feature. Sequences seem to end in mid-section, close-ups are followed abruptly by long shots, actors glance at the camera in sly collusion.

À bout de souffle may owe its sense of petty crime to Melville and its relentless pace to B-movies like Kiss Me Deadly, but the accent is unmistakably Godard's. He frankly couldn't care less about classical filmmaking, although he would (famously) concede that movies should have a beginning, middle and end – but not necessarily in that order. The world was a playground, and the distinction between highbrow and lowbrow deliberately blurred. Godard, like Harold Pinter, loved to turn concepts inside out and upside-down. 'Was I happy because I felt free, or free because I felt happy?' asks Bruno in Le petit soldat; a notice on a wall in La Chinoise declares that 'Vague ideas must be confronted by clear images'.

Between the autumn of 1959 and the late summer of 1965, Godard shot no fewer than nine features, along with sundry episodes and sketches for the 'portmanteau' films that so beguiled producers during the sixties. Fassbinder managed to exceed this prolific output a generation later, but he was a more acutely personal director than Godard, dealing first and foremost with his own troubled psyche. Godard, like Picasso in his early phase, plunged with glib abandon into any genre to hand, eager to prove that he could use it as a vehicle for his abundant reflections on life and love: 'I've always wanted, basically, to do research in the form of a spectacle. The documentary side is: a man in a particular situation. The spectacle comes when one makes this man a gangster or secret agent.'

All of his work was stuffed with cultural references, and manifested a Weltanschauung that veered from the frivolous to the misanthropic. Most of the time, his characters had a lot of fun, like the impertinent Angela in Une Femme est une femme, playing two men off against each other in a whirligig of emotions; or like Frantz, Arthur and Odile in Bande à part, a spoof on the gangster movie. But Godard's graver side emerged in Vivre sa vie, in which the lead character of Nana evokes not only Émile Zola's heroine but also other literary prostitutes such as Wedekind's Lulu. The actress who brought Nana, Odile and Angela to life was Anna Karina, a virtual muse for Godard during this period: they married in 1961 and divorced six years later.

Le Mépris (Contempt) has survived the years better than many a Godard riff of the era. Allusive, and awash with vivid colours, this adaptation of a novel by Alberto Moravia becomes a speculation on film both as an art and as an industry, with Michel Piccoli, cigarette always dan-

© Laetitia/Rome Paris, courtesy of The Kobal Collection

Raoul Coutard (with camera) and Jean-Luc Godard (with cigar)
on location for *Les Carabiniers* (1963)

gling from hand or lips, playing Godard's *alter ego*. Betrayal still seeps
through the sumptuous colour photography of Raoul Coutard and the
remarkable use of the FranScope format. (Godard made all his black-
and-white features in the standard ratio of 1:33, and his colour films in
'Scope.) The clash between Piccoli's European movie director and Jack
Palance's brash American producer was mirrored off set when Joseph E.
Levine (*Hercules Unchained*), who had invested heavily in the picture,
demanded three nude scenes with Brigitte Bardot. Godard demurred, but
offered to include just one, near the start of the film. Raoul Coutard had
already departed to work on another film by the time this crisis arose
and Alain Legrand had the pleasure of shooting Bardot in the buff, so
that the Americans would cough up the final instalment of cash.

I remember being shocked at Godard's cavalier disregard for the sub-
tleties of the original novel (*A Ghost at Noon*), and felt that Moravia's
work would have been much better served by Antonioni. With hindsight,
however, Godard's disparagement of Moravia was neither here nor
there, as he was using the book as a trigger to release his own conjectures
on the film-making process. In *Le mépris*, Godard retains the novel's

references to Homer and *The Odyssey*, but, as he said in an interview in August 1963, 'Whereas the Odyssey of Ulysses was a physical phenomenon, I filmed a spiritual odyssey: the eye of the camera watching these characters in search of Homer replaces that of the gods watching over Ulysses and his companions.' At other junctures, Godard's work seemed tiresome and trivial, like much of *Les Carabiniers*, with its pretentiously named characters and a staccato editing style that outstayed its welcome. But there was so much more to come from Godard, restless and prolific as he would remain throughout the decade.

What, then, of Truffaut? *Les 400 coups* had delighted French audiences throughout 1959, and Truffaut's clout in the local industry enabled him to help contemporaries like Godard and Rivette to bring their projects to the screen. His next film, however, *Tirez sur le pianiste*, explored an entirely different register. Indeed, the only characteristic that Truffaut's first four feature films have in common is their brilliant use of the 'Scope format. *Tirez sur le pianiste* depicts the emotional turmoil of failed concert pianist Charlie Koller (played by the singer Charles Aznavour) as he falls foul of some gangsters and tries to start a fresh life with his winsome mistress, Léna (Marie Dubois). Truffaut addresses this pot-boiling crime thriller with balletic skill, from the sickening burst of realization that Charlie's wife has committed suicide (in a manœuvre worthy of Max Ophüls, the camera races past him to the window and zooms down towards her body on the pavement), to the poetic vision of Léna swirling down a snowy slope after being shot by gangsters. The piano music of Georges Delerue sets its stamp on the mood of the film, suggesting the wistfulness and surreptitious force of the theme.

Jules et Jim (1962) established Truffaut's reputation beyond reasonable doubt. The love of two friends (Oskar Werner and Henri Serre) for the mischievous Catherine (Jeanne Moreau) is both amusing and melancholy. Catherine is undoubtedly a memorable character in the source novel by Henri-Pierre Roché, but there she is only one of several girls in the men's lives. In his film version, Truffaut combines them all – their foibles and their idiosyncrasies – into a single, wayward personality: 'A force of Nature, that can manifest itself only in cataclysms,' says Jules (Werner). For Jules, who unfortunately believes in marital fidelity, Catherine serves as mother, daughter and wife combined. Jim, the more subtle and diffident of the two, admires Catherine as a creature of instincts and liberal emotions. 'She is a vision for all men, not for one,' he concedes.

The chiselled sentences of Roché's novel are matched admirably in the film by Truffaut's own vigorous, shorthand style and by the infectious zest of Delerue's music. When asked about the attributes needed by a director to make worthwhile, satisfying films, Truffaut replied: 'Sensitivity, intuition, good taste and intelligence are the main ones. A little of each of these will yield very little, but a great deal of any one of them will make an appealing film, and a lot of all four will make a masterpiece.' More than any other product of the New Wave, *Jules et Jim* possesses these qualities in abundance. It remains, as Truffaut called it, 'a hymn to love, and perhaps a hymn to life itself'. American film buffs – and film-makers – justifiably embraced the film as the symbol of the New Wave, embodying everything that seemed fresh and impressionistic about French cinema in the early sixties.

Jacques Rivette had taken a central place among the friends of La Cinémathèque during the fifties. His cogent arguments and command of dialectic enabled him to shine even in the company of Truffaut and Godard. As a film-maker, however, he never achieved the world-wide recognition accorded to his comrades. *Paris nous appartient,* which went into production in late 1957 but did not appear for a further three years, struck an authentically original chord. Rivette's fascination with architecture and interiors provides a mysterious vision of Paris, and his characters are suffused with a literary tinge that colours all his work (right up to *Va savoir* in 2001). The dialogue sounds bookish, without quite becoming stilted. *Paris nous appartient* belonged unmistakably to the revolution in European cinema because it rejected the traditional tenets of narrative film-making, with neither of its principal strands (rehearsals for a play and a political conspiracy) coming to a climax. But *La Religieuse*, made five years later, adhered to more orthodox precepts, even if its content proved controversial. Based on Diderot's novel about life in an eighteenth-century nunnery, the film's overtones of sadism shocked the French censors. *L'Amour fou*, shot in 1968, ran for more than four hours and held the audience's interest with its clever interplay between footage shot on 35mm and 16mm, showing a theatre group preparing to stage Racine's *Andromaque*. Admiration for Rivette's technical audacity tends to be overshadowed by the cultivated complacency and verbosity of his characters. Rivette could – and can – make compulsively watchable films, but remains anchored in erudition.

Bertrand Tavernier can well remember the mood of excitement among

French *cinéphiles* as the outstanding productions of the New Wave began to multiply:

> TAVERNIER: À bout de souffle *was a shock, and I especially adored* Tirez sur le pianiste. *I was at the very first screening of* Le Signe du lion *in 1959.* Hiroshima mon amour *I saw seven times. The shorts of Agnès Varda I loved, also those of Jacques Demy. But I also loved Autant-Lara's* La Traversée de Paris *and* En cas de malheur, *and I could not understand why those two kinds of cinema could not co-exist. We always felt that Godard and Autant-Lara should not fight with each other.*
>
> *I was a press agent, and I was interested in the history of cinema, because I wanted to make films. I had to earn some money to live; I was not a good assistant director, so, thanks to Melville, I became a press agent, first with Georges de Beauregard. I became very friendly with people like Claude Chabrol and Pierre Schoendorffer (whose* La 317ème section *was one of the great films of the sixties). I made two shorts, which I didn't like; they lacked personality. I thought that I had to learn things about life first, in order not to become one of those directors – and there were many in France – who were imitating the American cinema. Louis Malle and François Truffaut succeeded in transforming certain books from American literature, in the way that* Kiss Me Deadly *by Mickey Spillane had become a cosmic, Shakespearian film and one of the best commentaries on the paranoia of the fifties – but many others missed completely.*

Tavernier is also sceptical today of the notion that the 'New Wave' achieved a novelty in all matters.

> TAVERNIER: *The New Wave introduced a lot of things, among them the notion of the director filming autobiographically. But certain ideas that were said to have been invented by the New Wave must be reconsidered now and put back in perspective. For example, the notion that for the first time critics became directors. Not true: there was a generation of film buffs writing about the cinema, like Edmond T. Gréville was writing about Stroheim and Borzage and Joan Crawford; Pierre Chenal, Marcel Carné were critics. Shooting on location? A lot of silent films had been shot on location, a lot of film noir, a lot of westerns.*

Indeed, not everyone embraced the New Wave. Following the release of *Les Cousins*, *À double tour* and *Les Liaisons dangereuses*, François Mauriac (the novelist, academician and pronounced Catholic) denounced it in the pages of *L'Express*: 'My very soul', he railed, 'revolts against this world of the Chabrols and the Vadims.' The notion of a 'new immorality' for some time obscured the technical and aesthetic advances of the younger French directors. In the magazine *Premier Plan*, published in Lyon during the summer of 1960, Raymond Borde delivered a reasoned, if waspish, attack on the movement. 'Since the end of World War II,' he wrote, 'little by little, the cinema has been recognized as of public value. The key parties – producers, exhibitors, the government, the audience – have changed their attitude under the many influences that added up their effects. The mushrooming of film societies after the Liberation has been the most decisive. An audience emerged, far more widespread than one would have imagined. Hundreds of thousands of ordinary French people attended, at some time or other, sessions at a film society . . . Fernandel has been defeated, the good old French vaudeville no longer makes money, and so much the better. The concern for art had paralysed directors. Now, the cinema has become terribly serious and encourages another kind of nonsense – a sly and insincere form of metaphysics.'

According to Borde, eighteen directors, aged between twenty-four and forty-eight years, made their first feature film in 1958 (Chabrol, Franju, Resnais and Truffaut) or 1959 (including Godard, Rivette, Rohmer, Drach and Hanoun). He pointed out that the movement's commercial and artistic evolution was influenced by the success of earlier débutants such as Vadim, Malle, Astruc, Hossein and Camus. Borde conveniently forgot Melville, who had made *Le Silence de la mer* in 1947, and Varda, who shot *La Pointe Courte* in 1954.

By 1961, with *Hiroshima mon amour* and *L'année dernière à Marienbad* behind him, **Alain Resnais** loomed as the Sartre of the new French cinema. Statuesque, austere and evincing a brilliant intellectual grasp of abstract issues, Resnais brought an astringent seriousness to a decade that already had begun to edge towards frivolity. The supreme, often perplexing symmetry of *Hiroshima* and *Marienbad* set Resnais apart as the mysterious elder statesman of the New Wave.

RESNAIS: *Although I was not fully part of the New Wave because of my age, there was some mutual sympathy and respect between myself*

67

and Rivette, Bazin, Demy, Truffaut. I did not know Rohmer so much, although I liked what he wrote; Chabrol, too, since I shared his passion for Hitchcock and Fritz Lang. So I felt friendly with that team.

If every film buff with a hand-held camera and a pair of scissors felt that he could imitate Godard, few felt able to emulate the austere brilliance of Resnais. Here was a talent who fulfilled Louis Delluc's dictum: 'A good film is a good theorem.' Like Antonioni's *L'avventura*, *L'année dernière à Marienbad* feeds on the enigmatic, on a vanishing never explained. Ostensibly dissimilar to *Hiroshima mon amour*, *Marienbad* seemed a logical next step for its director. 'In both these films,' commented Resnais, 'there is the rejection of a chronological story in which the happenings are presented in apparently reasonable order. There is perhaps the common anxiety to use mental images as a counterpoint to the dialogue.'

On *Marienbad*, Resnais enjoyed as remarkable a relationship with Alain Robbe-Grillet as he had with his previous screenwriter, Marguerite Duras. Robbe-Grillet relished working in the cinema: in 1962, he told me that he loved Orson Welles, loathed Bergman ('too metaphysical') and regarded Demy's *Lola* as the best film of the previous year. Robbe-Grillet found his work accepted with such alacrity and understanding by Resnais that when the film opened, the pair were interviewed almost as co-authors.

Yet *Marienbad* remains unquestionably a film by Alain Resnais. All of his work in the cinema has aimed to achieve realism on a mental level, even if, paradoxically, it must be wrung from artifice. The statuesque poses of the anonymous characters in *Marienbad* serve brilliantly to throw into relief the spurts of memory and imagination that occur in the cavernous château, where a married woman (Delphine Seyrig) is courted by a stranger (Giorgio Albertazzi) with whom she may or may not have had an affair the previous year. Amid the film's 'algebra of actions' (to quote Valéry's dictum), there exists a powerful human element as well. The frozen attitudes of the people in the castle lend the clue to the triumph of Albertazzi's character: he wins the woman because he can stir her emotionally, for neither Sacha Pitoëff's 'M' nor anyone else at Marienbad possesses emotions. It marks a victory of instinct over calculation, the Prince awakening his Sleeping Beauty. Delphine Seyrig returned from her fledgeling television career in New York to take the role of 'A'. Together with Resnais, she viewed silent films featuring

Delphine Seyrig and Alain Resnais on the enigmatic location
of *L'année dernière à Marienbad* (1961)

Greta Garbo and Louise Brooks, and step by step created this dream-like
creature, from her shoes to her make-up to her hairstyle.

After the baroque imagery and remote setting of *Marienbad*, Resnais'
next feature, *Muriel, ou le temps d'un retour* (1963), came as something
of a surprise. It was scripted by Jean Cayrol (who had written the commentary for *Night and Fog*) and took place in the modern surroundings
of Boulogne-sur-mer. 'Muriel' herself is never seen; she is a young woman

in Algeria whom Bernard (Jean-Baptiste Thierrée) recalls with great feeling. His romance epitomizes one of the themes of the film (a kind of mirror image of *Marienbad*) – that love cannot be resuscitated: it exists only in the past. But there are several other characters in *Muriel* and while Resnais never really succeeds in distinguishing one from another, there lingers a palpable sense of anxiety and emotional confusion, indicated primarily by the editing, which is as fragmented and unorthodox as any in Resnais' career. The influence of Eisenstein is there in the disciplined approach to montage: not a single shot may be wasted, not an inch of the frame left untended or unnoticed. A succession of striking shots, placed in the requisite order and rhythm, can accomplish a greater sensual and emotional effect than the leisurely pan or the dazzling zoom.

> RESNAIS: *On* Muriel, *I wanted to check whether we could make a film without any movements of the machinery – that means not to move the stand about, but the camera itself, yes. We could do panoramic shots.*
>
> *Our idea was to shoot a film solely with 'plans fixes' that would correspond to the script. So we would shoot one of the characters arriving at the railway station at the appointed time. Rain or shine, the camera would roll. The character goes to the station coffee shop, so does the actor, whatever that real coffee shop looks like. So we played the game almost like we would for a documentary.*
>
> *We shot the film in colour because I sensed, in Cayrol's style, something almost breathless, and I wanted to translate that into the editing, but I needed the contrasting shock between black-and-white and colour. The film had about 800 shots, which is more than the usual 400 but not 1,500 as some have claimed. And the introduction of colour with black-and-white really enhances the effect of contrast, which we wouldn't have had otherwise.*

Louis Malle's *Les Amants* had been banned in various American states, and lawyers fought for its freedom all the way to the US Supreme Court. But its financial success assured Malle artistic freedom for many years to come. At the age of just twenty-six, he had gained a head start on his confrères. If Malle's approach struck critics as eclectic, there ran through his work some very personal themes. The isolation of the individual in a bustling world seemed to fascinate him, and this underpins *Le Feu follet* (1963), which belongs among the very finest products of the New Wave. Alain Leroy (played by one of Malle's favourite actors,

Maurice Ronet in Louis Malle's *Le Feu follet* (1963)

Maurice Ronet) rests in a sanatorium after a nervous breakdown and decides, almost casually, to commit suicide. He travels to Paris and visits his society acquaintances. He joins in animated conversation with his former friends, he laughs and gets drunk in their company, but in none of them does he evoke the warmth or sympathy that might dissuade him from taking his own life. The words of his farewell note – 'I have killed myself because you have not loved me' – suggests the loneliness that has afflicted not only Alain, but also Jill in *Vie privée* (made by Malle in 1962), and Florence in *Ascenseur pour l'échafaud*. All of Malle's films, however frivolous, embody a conflict between indifference and danger. If, like Resnais, he remains an aloof figure in French film history, it is because he preferred to analyse human behaviour from a detached standpoint, not quite rejecting his privileged upbringing but mocking its foibles with tongue firmly in cheek.

Volker Schlöndorff had met Louis Malle through Roger Nimier, who wrote the screenplay for Malle's maiden feature, *Ascenseur pour l'échafaud*. Eager to break into the movies, the young German accepted the post of unpaid trainee on Malle's next film, the comedy *Zazie dans le Métro*.

> SCHLÖNDORFF: Les Amants *and* Ascenseur pour l'échafaud *were well-crafted films, almost in the French tradition. Only the casting was new, because Jeanne Moreau was more or less 'discovered'. But in* Zazie, *we did everything the opposite of how it was supposed to be done! So if the shot was a close-up, where you might be expected to use a long lens, well, we would select a fish-eye lens! Or if it was meant to be a nice tracking shot, well, we would do it with a hand-held camera! We changed the speed, too; instead of using twenty-four frames per second, we would experiment with six or eight or twelve. We would totally change the furniture in a room from one shot to another, to show the absurdity of matching or non-matching. Malle and his screenwriter, Jean-Paul Rappeneau, had studied the Mack Sennett comedies and the anarchy of W. C. Fields in* Hellzapoppin'.

Schlöndorff would then be hired by Resnais on *L'année dernière à Marienbad*, because a German-speaking assistant was needed for the location work in Munich and Schleissheim.

French directors rarely brandished their political commitment as ostentatiously as their Italian confrères. Their approach was at once more eclectic and less doctrinaire. I put it to Agnès Varda that suddenly filmmakers were talking about *real* people:

> VARDA: *Yes, Godard especially, and Jacques Demy in* Les Parapluies de Cherbourg, *for example. People experience the social divide, the social struggle – the difference between the classes and the impossibility of the classes ever meeting one another. In* Cherbourg, *the girl's mother does not want her to mix with a garage mechanic. Jacques' major films are about the impossibility of mixing the classes. Truffaut was sentimental by comparison.*
>
> *Resnais and I and others had our heart on the left, and we were not part of the* Cahiers du cinéma *crowd. Truffaut and Rohmer, for example, were rather centre-right, and a little 'Champs-Elysées', while Chris Marker, Resnais and I lived on the Left Bank. It's funny because it really was a geographical distinction.*
>
> *I have never belonged to a political party, but we voted for the left, we campaigned for leftist ideas. I think only about the poor, whereas*

Chabrol is a great cinéaste of the bourgeoisie – only bourgeois issues interest him. I've never made a film that takes place in a bourgeois family, with some drama involving a lawyer or a doctor. I've always been interested in fisherfolk, in decent folk, in the poor – from genuine feeling, not as a special case. That corresponds to a certain notion of the world. Except for the actress in Cléo, who is spoiled – she says, 'Everyone spoils me, nobody loves me.'

Richard Roud, writing in *Sight and Sound* in late 1962, said that the Left Bank was not so much an area as a state of mind. 'It implies a high degree of involvement in literature and the plastic arts. It implies a fondness for a kind of bohemian life, and an impatience with the conformity of the Right Bank.' He pointed out that the Left Bank had been a focal point for cosmopolitan refugees and the avant-garde since the turn of the century. 'The Dome was not only a rendezvous for Picasso, Joyce and Hemingway,' he emphasized. 'Trotsky and Lenin were also *habitués*.'

RESNAIS: *Given the fact that politics scarcely existed in French cinema, perhaps we could argue then that it was interesting to have some political element in the film, but, you see, this is a very formal way of discussing the issue. My attitude was that if a political aspect emerged during the process of film-making, then we should retain it, but that if nothing of a political nature emerged by itself then we would not introduce it voluntarily. I never woke up one morning consciously thinking that my film should be political. I would let the film grow like a plant or vegetable, almost like an independent dynamic in the scriptwriting stage.*

On the face of it, the revolutionary subject matter of Resnais' *La Guerre est finie* (1966) – in which Yves Montand plays Diego, an ageing Spanish Communist engaged in a clandestine resistance to the Franco regime – is as political as one could wish for. But Resnais sees it differently.

RESNAIS: *Even with* La Guerre est finie, *the political aspect was not deliberate. At my first meeting with the screenwriter, Jorge Semprun, we decided we would not talk about either Spain or Brittany. I said, 'I am a Breton, and you are a Spaniard, and that's that.' But then it turned out differently when Diego's character developed – there was the burial of a Spanish emigrant, and from then on, the script unfolded, but neither of us knew beforehand it would turn out that way.*

> *When people ask me why I make films, I always answer that 'I make films to see how films are made.' I am proud of that phrase. I am curious to see what will become of the script because there are always surprises, and in the end, generally speaking, the film does not resemble what one initially expects.*

Although one would hardly have expected to see Maurice Scherer (known to the film world as **Eric Rohmer**) on the barricades of the Quartier Latin come 1968, this reclusive intellectual contributed to the 'revolution' in numerous ways. His fecundity as a critic during the fifties, when he edited *Cahiers du cinéma*, enabled him to formulate many of the principles on which the New Wave would depend. In 1957 he wrote, with Claude Chabrol, a seminal study of Alfred Hitchcock. Rohmer's admiration for the *cinéma-vérité* movement translated into an informal technique that would distinguish his films throughout the next forty years. Two of his *Six Moral Tales* were shot on 16mm, and even when he shifted to 35mm, his imagery remained expressly informal and coarse-grained. Throughout his career, he has focused on the emotional and intellectual dilemmas of youth, and his knack for dialogue always marked him apart from a majority of the New Wave directors (although Godard, who acted in Rohmer's very first short in 1952, wrote screen conversation with a similar facility).

Rohmer's first feature, *Le Signe du lion*, may also be viewed as his most innovatory, given the fact that it was shot in 1959 (although not released until 1962). A failed composer finds himself without means in the midst of a Parisian summer and takes up with a *clochard* on the banks of the Seine, a milieu he finds more congenial than the shallow café society he has known hitherto. Like the best New Wave films, *Le Signe du lion* explores Paris as microcosm and delights in shooting on location. The film breathes a deliciously lazy *je m'en foutisme*. As the sixties progressed, Rohmer pursued his own winding path, far from the central thrust of his French colleagues. His cinema flourished in moral soil, his characters spending more time in discussion than they ever did in bed (indeed, no director of the period treated sexual relations with such fastidiousness as Rohmer). Locations were important – Saint-Tropez in *La Collectionneuse*, Lake Annecy in *Le Genou de Claire*, a wintry Clermont-Ferrand in *Ma nuit chez Maud*. Rohmer's women seemed more durable than the men who courted them with such trepidation. Referring to his *Six Moral Tales*, Rohmer wrote: 'There is

another factor that obliged me from the start to clothe the tales in literary garb. Here, literature – and this is my principal excuse – belongs
less to form than to content. My intent was to film not raw, unvarnished events but rather the account of them as given by one of the
characters.'

A certain wisdom coloured Robert Benayoun's iconoclastic piece in
Positif in 1962, in which he excoriated the New Wave for shying away
from important themes. 'They refuse to commit themselves, they escape
into formalism. There is, they claim, no subject that cannot be tran-
scended, enlarged, or contradicted by the director . . . The minute anything important or serious is touched upon, they take refuge in the
insipid or the banal.' His sly dig directed at Godard could as well apply
to Rohmer in *Ma nuit chez Maud*: 'The mental vacuum is camouflaged
by a monologue which makes random mention of a few book titles, or
gives a quotation from Gorki which, just for fun, is attributed to Lenin.'
Benayoun's spleen is understandable given the euphoria surrounding the
New Wave in 1962, but with hindsight there was infinitely more worth
than speciousness in a movement that gave the cinema a new soul (in
Truffaut), a new theorist (Godard) and a seer such as Rohmer – as well
as Resnais, the intellectual touchstone for a European generation. Not
forgetting the early work – *Classe tous risques* (1960) – of the young
Claude Sautet, a true heir to Melville.

Agnès Varda's work in the early sixties reflected her love of risk. *Cléo
de 5 à 7*, shot in the summer of 1961, demanded close attention and a
mature response from its audience. This chronicle of two anxious hours
in a woman's life is a synthesis of the best features of the New Wave. The
camera of Jean Rabier discovers a Paris that is exhilarating and, to the
foreigner, often unfamiliar (for example, the radiant use of the Parc
Montsouris). This is, for sure, a *real* city, with nary a studio backdrop in
sight. Corinne Marchand had impressed Varda with her appearance in
Lola and enriches her role here (as a pop singer) with inflected glances,
fussing with dark glasses, varying her way of walking and confronting
the camera in close-up without the slightest qualm. The screenplay, too,
is perfectly weighted, and carries a built-in suspense as Cléo awaits the
results of a cancer biopsy. Her recognition that she may be condemned
to an early death allows her to appreciate her beloved Paris with a clarity that, miraculously, Varda, Rabier and composer Michel Legrand are
able to communicate with sensual intensity. Facially, Marchand bears
some resemblance to Jean Seberg in *À bout de souffle*, but while Seberg

serves as a cipher in the shadow of Belmondo, Marchand emerges as her own proud and complex woman.

Jacques Demy, Varda's partner in private life, brought tones of tenderness and delicacy to the New Wave. *Lola* (1960), his first feature, had a champagne sparkle that reflected his romantic, often nostalgic, outlook on life. 'I prefer blue to black,' said Demy, 'births to funerals, red wine to Vichy water, the sun to the rain.' His eponymous heroine, played by the insouciant Anouk Aimée, is a dancer in Nantes whose past and future existence is reflected in the present by the introduction of various characters. Time is frozen and then accelerated; flashbacks as such appeared anathema to Demy. In its intricate construction, *Lola* recalls *Lola Montès*, the last great work of one of Demy's acknowledged masters, Max Ophüls (to whom the film is dedicated). There is a precision and deftness about the style, however, that is far more in touch with the buzz of life than the cloying arabesques of an Ophüls film. The camera of Raoul Coutard swoops and whirls, cranes and dollies with exhilarating skill.

All these films were screened, and screened again, by a network of *cinémas d'art et d'essai* in Paris. Each theatre had its own atmosphere, its own personality – Le Ranelagh in Passy, run by the urbane connoisseur, Henri Ginet; Le Quartier Latin and the Studio Saint-Germain, programmed by the avuncular Boris Gourevitch; or Le Studio 28, the oldest cinema in Montmartre, where Buñuel's *L'Age d'or* had been first shown (amid demonstrations) and which was still, when I visited it in 1963, in the hands of the same Roulleau family. The fact that neophyte French directors could get their work promptly screened would prove of inestimable importance to the New Wave.

II ITALIAN RISORGIMENTO

> *The term 'political film' is an improper, imprecise one. When one makes films about reality, when one makes films in order to reveal what reality hides – let's say, films of denunciation – we call them for want of a better phrase, 'political films'.*
> Francesco Rosi

Regarding himself first and foremost as a poet, **Pier Paolo Pasolini** was a ruthless scourge of materialism. His methods were harsh, his career prolific. During the sixties, Pasolini directed nine features and contributed episodes to five portmanteau productions. He turned forty in

© Cino Del Duca

Accattone (1961): Pier Paolo Pasolini with Franco Citti

1962, the year following the release of his maiden feature, *Accattone*. Set in a sordid district of Rome, where the director himself had lived during the early war period, *Accattone* portrays a young pimp (Franco Citti) who does himself to death and yet remains in our eyes a likeable character. Pasolini, who wrote his own screenplays, attacked his medium with an almost tensile relish. Hard, jutting faces fill the screen; men constantly provoke one another to violence; and there is always speculation as to where the next meal will come from. Accattone suffers a nasty, brutish life, the narrow confines of which are clearly seen to distort a man's character and squeeze it into rebellion. As Naomi Greene has written: 'If Antonioni was the anatomist of middle-class alienation, and Fellini the master of spectacle, then Pasolini was the poet of the Roman *borgata*.'

Bernardo Bertolucci recalls the impact of Pasolini and his personality:

BERTOLUCCI: *Pasolini was a very good friend of my father, and they were both poets. Pasolini was also a novelist, and my father helped him when he was very young to publish his first novel. For me, he was a kind of mythical figure who was coming to our home – my father*

77

was reading his poems and I was very impressed. He was one of the various 'father figures' I've had in my life. He was living in our building for a few years, and one day when I was twenty, I met him in the lobby and he said: 'You want to make movies, right?' So I, who had done absolutely nothing at all, replied, 'Of course. That's my life!' So he said, 'Okay, you will be my assistant director on my first film, Accattone.' *I protested that I had never done anything like that and he said simply: 'I've never been a director either, so let's just both start.'*

When I worked with Pasolini, I realized that here was something completely different – it wasn't in the style of neo-realism, but nor was it experimental or avant-garde in the way the New Wave was. He came from literature, and also he had graduated in History of Art at Bologna University, and so he was very influenced by art. In fact, when he began Accattone, *he said, 'My model in this film will not be the cinema, it will be the primitive Tuscany of the fourteenth century.' And you can see that influence in the enormous close-ups in the film. Also, he rejected psychology. Pier Paolo was someone who was naturally provocative. He could not help but shock. He thought that scandal had a real reason to exist.*

Because he did not have much knowledge of film-making, he invented cinema. It was as though I had the privilege of assisting, of witnessing the invention of cinema by Pasolini. One day, he said he was going to use a dolly, and somehow it was like seeing the first dolly movement in the history of the cinema. Also, his way of being political was very different from that of other Italian directors.

Pasolini, like Fassbinder in Germany a generation later, lived at the cutting edge of scandal. His episode in *RoGoPaG*, entitled *La ricotta* (1962), roused the fury of the Vatican. Pasolini was put on trial and given a four-month suspended prison sentence. This film-within-a-film features Orson Welles as the 'director' of a movie about the life of Christ – an enterprise that Pasolini himself would embark on just two years later, with *The Gospel According to Saint Matthew*. The character of Stracci in *La ricotta* is an impoverished extra who, bloated with an excess of his favourite cottage cheese, dies nailed to the Cross. At once comic and profane, this episode is dipped in brimstone, its savage irony levelled at the clerics so loathed by Pasolini.

By 1962, **Francesco Rosi** was approaching the peak of his powers as an imaginative film-maker. *Salvatore Giuliano* would become one of the defining works of the period, a film of such Sicilian authenticity that even *The Godfather* needs to pay homage to it. The benchmark for all subsequent Mafia films, this rigorous, complex film lays bare the roots of organized banditry and accentuates the latent antagonism between the north and the south of Italy. Rosi has often been drawn to the documentary approach. He does not endorse Giuliano's violence. Instead, he leaves him lurking in the shadows, hard to pin down as a personality – a concept more than a man. He captures the uncertain atmosphere of Sicily by taking his cameras into the mountains and looking down at the *carabinieri* and peasants in the villages, through, as it were, the eyes of Giuliano and his outlawed band.

The audacious interweaving of past and present still seems ahead of its time, and *Salvatore Giuliano* needs to be seen again and again before the precisely calibrated patterns of movement and subversion assume their disturbing logic. Sequences such as the frenetic trial in Viterbo emphasize Rosi's stern moral attitude towards the entire affair.

ROSI: Salvatore Giuliano *was not a neo-realist film – it was a realist film that expresses in its material a certain critical realism. Neo-realism sought to transfer reality directly on to the screen, not just a reproduction of reality but – in the best films of the movement (De Sica, Visconti, Rossellini) – with some kind of critique of society.*

Salvatore Giuliano was the first film to strip away the mystique that enveloped the Mafia, and around the compromise that the state's relationship with the Mafia involved. That was the 'mystery' behind the story. My first preoccupation was to describe the man, Salvatore Giuliano, and also the nature of Sicily and the Italy of the period – to denounce the hidden links between the power of the state, the power of the institutions and the Mafia. So the whole film is a kind of quest for the truth – an approximate search, too, because even today we do not know the whole truth about Salvatore Giuliano. We still do not know for sure who ordered the massacre at Portella della Ginestra. So this search constituted the very structure of the film's narrative.

Being a Neapolitan, I know the south, and the rules of the Mafia and the Camorra. So I decided from the outset to turn up in the small village, Montelepre, where Giuliano was born and where he had all his adventures, the village in which he could see his mother on the terrace of her house even from his hideout in the surrounding mountains. I went there and I said, 'Listen, I want to make a film about

The bandits of *Salvatore Giuliano* (1962)

Salvatore Giuliano, but I'm going to shoot it right here, in your sight, in the same houses and if possible with the same people who lived out this story.'

There were only two professional actors in the film, Frank Wolff and Salvo Randone. The majority of the cast were individuals from Montelepre or the district round Portella della Ginestra, or Castelvetrano, the three places where the story happened in reality. So it was not an attempt to do something clandestine, but rather an attempt to gain their confidence. If you show a sort of loyalty on your side then one establishes a kind of rule of mutual respect. They questioned me closely at the municipal offices in Montelepre, but finally they said yes, fine.

My second aim was to be able to provoke a kind of psychodrama among the people who had lived through this story scarcely ten years earlier. It was my dream that this would give the film a stamp of reality. With each passing day, I established with the local people a kind of confidence, almost complicity, if not exactly friendship, and they started to tell us things that we had not included in the first version *of the screenplay. So I added scenes accordingly, and this relationship between real events, real houses, people who had participated in those events, gradually embraced all my work, day after day. So it was enormously important that I was shooting in exactly the right, authentic locations. It was not a formal choice, it wasn't neo-realism – for me, it was a vital necessity, in order to translate the emotions and incidents that had been unknown to the outside world.*

Rosi would make seven films under the auspices of Franco Cristaldi, an enterprising producer who had begun his career as a newsreel cameraman, filming celebrities passing through Turin airport. He had made the acquaintance of Fiat's Gianni Agnelli, who gave him some useful introductions in Rome.

ROSI: *Cristaldi was young and courageous, he had confidence in me and so he followed me on to the set. He financed my first film,* La sfida. *One would present the finished script of the film one wanted to make to the Ministry of Entertainment. If the ministry gave its approval, its imprimatur, the Banca Nazionale del Lavoro would provide the money in advance. Because the Salvatore Giuliano scandal was such that none of the authorities wanted to get involved, the ministry said, 'No, we can't support your project.' So the bank refused, also. Luckily, Franco Cristaldi was linked with Lux Film, who agreed to support the film. We commenced production, and the more the work advanced, the more convinced I became of its vivid reality and emotions, as expressed through the ordinary people I cast in the film – especially the mother, a peasant woman who had a dozen children (one of whom had died in almost the same circumstances as Salvatore Giuliano).*

I was fascinated by the method of telling a story on film without being preoccupied in detail with the chronological order of events, of going back into the past but not in the style of the traditional flashback which is based on memories or the thoughts of a particular character – or a dream. My method was to use quite liberally the ensemble of different moments to lead the narration to the content that I wanted to express in the film.

I make 'dialectical' films, and not films as theses. I have never liked political propaganda, and I don't like forcing people to conclusions. I prefer to expose matters in such a way that the public can be informed and at the same time have the chance to reflect on the issues the film has presented. But a film cannot give the audience the chance to reflect on one thing after another, because there just isn't the time. It's not like a book, where each word can be evocative, where through each word a writer can evoke a situation. If a film has a rhythm, and a suspense, then the spectator has to think at that juncture the way in which the director wants him to think! But after the film is over – and that's why film as a medium is an open one – he can and must reflect on what he has seen.

In Salvatore Giuliano, *I differ from directors like Pontecorvo or Costa-Gavras in that my films are interpretations of reality, following reality but never obscuring it with interventions of invention, imagination or fantasy. There's a scene in* Salvatore Giuliano *featuring an elderly character, a former Sicilian separatist chief at the time, a simple man. I had the intuition of placing this man against the backdrop of Sicily and having him do something that would express his love of his country. The sun was setting and Gianni Di Venanzo, who didn't want to lose the twilight on the wall where this man was standing, urged me to start filming. The separatist was so moved that almost without my prompting him, he sobbed on camera. So, this occasion, which was dictated to me from the marvellous landscape that is Sicily in twilight, and this fellow who expressed all his love for his native land, became a very lyrical moment.*

So my method is to present reality without falsifying it and giving an interpretation through the characters in the story. I am a passionate man, but with the ambition to be rational at the same time – and my passion is typically Neapolitan. There's a conflict between the passion and rationality. I live the situations with passion, but I try to deal with them in a rational manner.

Hands over the City, Rosi's next picture, proved him to be the supremely intelligent, creative journalist of the cinema during the sixties. Each of his films delved into doubtful practices – the Neapolitan fruit and vegetable market in *La sfida*, the Mafia in *Salvatore Giuliano* and the building speculators in *Hands over the City*. Just as Antonioni had turned to Steve Cochran for the lead in *Il grido*, so now Rosi bestowed on Rod Steiger the choice role of Nottola in *Hands over the City*.

ROSI: *I had seen Rod Steiger in two films,* On the Waterfront *and* The Big Knife. *I thought he was perfectly suited to this role, and I took him to night-clubs in Naples, and had him dressed by a local tailor . . .*

Francesco Rosi by the camera with Rod Steiger (seated) on the set of
Hands over the City

The Neapolitan Camorra, claimed Rosi, consisted of political gangs who used their influence in the city council to protect unscrupulous financiers of the order of Nottola. When one of his buildings collapses, Nottola becomes the centre of a blazing scandal. Rosi, while stressing his own Marxist disapproval of the situation, shows with uncanny objectivity how Nottola, far from suffering for his capitalistic sins, merely switches political colours and, by the close of the film, stands free to speculate once more.

Ermanno Olmi had to work on a tight budget to make his first fiction feature, *Il posto*, in 1961. Costing just $15,000, this gossamer-light comedy was unencumbered by the social anxieties of a Rosi or an Antonioni. Observation – sometimes satirical, sometimes sardonic, always engaging – is the prime quality of *Il posto*; not so much its story of a diffident young man in search of a job. By using non-professional actors, Olmi remains faithful to the tenets of neo-realism while also embracing the ideals of the New Wave. 'For the boy [in *Il posto*],' he recalled in 1971,

> I needed someone who had reached the precise stage in life of my hero, someone who would not need to be taught the things that worried my character. In fact, I found such a boy in the town of Treviglio, a boy who was trying to fulfil his family's aspirations by placing himself in the big city. That's why I set the film on the outskirts of Milan.

Olmi also photographed most of his early films, something that in the US would have been rejected by the unions. He had used 'Scope for his first film, the quasi-documentary *Il tempo si è fermato* in 1959, but subsequently he preferred the flexibility offered by the hand-held camera. Two years later, Olmi confirmed his talent with *I fidanzati*, a quiet, reflective film about a worker who moves to Sicily, away from his home and fiancée. The structure is more adventurous, though, with an intricate tangle of flashbacks interspersed with documentary vignettes of factory life. In writing his own screenplays, Olmi responded to the *auteur*-ist spirit of the age, with its insistence on everyday realism in alliance with the fragmentation of the traditional narrative.

Few of the legendary directors who cut their teeth in the film studios of the forties responded to the quickening *air du temps* at the end of the following decade. Rossellini, Visconti, De Sica, Tati, Buñuel and Bresson could all be held up as admirable exemplars for a younger generation. But only two directors were inspired and perhaps even goaded to renew themselves: Ingmar Bergman (as we shall see) and **Federico Fellini**.

La dolce vita, subsequently damned with faint praise by those who prefer Fellini's less 'commercial' pictures, in fact improves with every passing year. At once a lament for the past and a dream of the future, the film etched a society in decline, a modern version of imperial Rome's final phase, with the *paparazzi* baying like barbarians at the gates of the city. Beneath its banter, its orgies and its cynical picture of Italian high society, *La dolce vita* pulses with Fellini's own fretful quest for tranquillity in a world where the still small voice of beauty is drowned in a cacophony of car horns, screaming reporters and night-club exotica. 'At home, it's always dark and deserted at this hour,' comments Marcello's father, the benign, bewildered stranger to the Babylonian whirl of Roman night life. With his use of high, detached shots and a ruthlessly thrusting camera on the ground, Fellini misses no opportunity for irony. The annulment of Nadia's marriage (symbolic of a collapse rather than a liberation) is celebrated with glee at the final party. The banal, insistent rhythm of the music as Nadia performs her striptease underscores the boredom, the immurement even, of the guests.

The exhilarating fluency of *La dolce vita* came at a price. The authorities refused Fellini permission to shoot along the Via Veneto except between the hours of 2 a.m. and 6 a.m. When Mastroianni drives Anita Ekberg home after her dip in the Trevi Fountain, Fellini recalled, 'We started off in the middle of the night and managed to "capture" a really lovely dawn, with Anita's teeth chattering with cold, Marcello worried over the punches he was to get from the athletic Lex Barker, and the photo-reporters, the *paparazzi*, jumping around the set like a lot of devils.'

Yet however vivid the fresco of life captured by Fellini in *La dolce vita*, nothing could have prepared the audiences of 1963 for the shock of 8½. Here was a film that tested the outer limits of the medium, with Gianni Di Venanzo tossing aside the cinematographer's rule book, shooting into dazzling light, using light coming through windows, light bouncing off white walls, integrating and reconciling the natural light of the location with the more coruscating light of the stage. 8½ could not have existed prior to the New Wave, but all too few New Wave films aspired to the same level of intellectual surmise as Fellini's masterpiece.

Guido Anselmi, a famous film director – clearly, Fellini himself – searches after a certain kind of truth only to end up a beaten man, obliged to accept that his artistic future is entwined in his past experiences. Guido's childhood recollections surface in fits and starts, as complex in their way as the labyrinthine memories of *L'année dernière à Marienbad*. At the core of the film dwells an overwhelming self-pity: Guido will inevitably pass his prime, just as the inmates of his imaginary harem are sent upstairs when their charms begin to fade. Fellini's childhood is more carefully portrayed in *8½* than in any of his films, including *Amarcord*. Even the monstrous Saraghina had provoked his curiosity when he had been a boy of eight years of age.

Quite apart from this personal baggage, *8½* delivers a dazzling speculation on the validity of film as an art. It describes with wit the enormous effort required to launch major production – dealing with stars, screenwriters, technicians, budgetary hassles – alongside the artist's attempt to plunder his own memories and wish-dreams for material and inspiration. The figure of Purity (played by a youthful Claudia Cardinale), dressed in flawless white, tender, smiling, and tantalizingly insubstantial, becomes a familiar signature to the work as a whole.

With *8½*, Fellini escapes from the traditional movie narrative structure and flips from standing in front of the camera to move behind it in one scintillating swoop. Guido's indecision is a microcosmic metaphor for a European world that, in the early sixties, seemed to be lurching two steps forward and one step back. The improvements in technology allied to a spectacular increase in the standard of living brought with them, as Antonioni and Losey were showing so subtly, a genuine moral dilemma. As would Wajda in *Everything for Sale*, and Bergman in *Persona*, Fellini held his chosen medium up to the light and found it wanting.

In the summer of 1960, Penelope Houston wrote of the Cannes Festival:

> Michelangelo Antonioni's *L'avventura* was shown to an accompaniment of boos and jeers, yawns and laughter, such as I have never heard in a cinema. The film spectacularly exhausted the patience of this audience; and it would probably tax any audience in the world. Yet *L'avventura*, for all its apparent failure in the most basic requirement – that of communication – is still the kind of film for which one would trade six easy successes.

Working with Monica Vitti as passionately as Sternberg had with Dietrich, and Kieślowski would with Irene Jacob, **Michelangelo Antonioni** gave visual credence to the uncertainty of the late fifties and early sixties.

On location for *L'avventura* (1960): Antonioni (in sun hat) directs
Monica Vitti, Lea Massari and Gabriele Ferzetti

Opulence, his camera seems to say, is not the only answer. Vitti's look in
L'avventura, sensual yet never vulgar, reduces those around her to
objects of vanity and emotional inadequacy. 'I think it is much more cinematic', commented Antonioni, 'to try to grasp the thoughts of a character by showing their reactions such as they are, rather than conveying
all that in a reply, having to resort practically to an explanation.'
Physical objects and landscapes evince a strength lacking in the human
beings who wander distraught among them. Antonioni gives a mysterious, sinister charge to the volcanic island in *L'avventura*, to the geomet-
ric features of modern Milan as seen from the Pirelli building in *La notte*,
and in the five-minute coda of *L'eclisse*, with its trees seething in the
wind at dusk, and blocks of flats looming against the twilit sky. But
L'avventura soared beyond these social pieces, not just because of
Monica Vitti's unfamiliar beauty but also by virtue of the director's
absolute control of his material. Deploying a language more oblique
than Godard's, Antonioni's film, premièred at Cannes just two months
after *À bout de souffle*, proved almost as influential.

The film's shoot was precipitous, for the first half was taken in bad
autumn weather on an uninhabited island off the coast of Sicily. There

was no food and very little shelter to be found (except under the rocks), and the producer left after a week. Antonioni also had trouble with some of his unit, who quit the island and were not replaced. The wonder is that the precision of Antonioni's applied technique remains the most impressive feature of *L'avventura*. On the island, slow panning and crane shots serve to set and then maintain a mood, planting people firmly in their spatial environment, isolating them against grey horizons. Characters stray near to one another without allowing their gaze to meet. A boulder rumbles suddenly down one side of the island. A storm brews malevolently offshore to the tune of a rising wind. A motor-boat sounds in the distance and then vanishes. Such touches (and Antonioni had a hundred reels of magnetic tape on hand for the natural effects), allied to Giovanni Fusco's montage of real sounds and melancholy music, underscore the frustration and essential futility of the party's search for the missing girl, Anna. It is a mood, like that of the novels of Cesare Pavese or F. Scott Fitzgerald, that brims with anxiety.

While shooting *La notte* (1961), Antonioni said, 'Man deceives himself when he hasn't courage enough to allow for new dimensions in emotional matters – his loves, regrets, states of mind – just as he allows for them in the field of science and technology.' This time, Vitti played Valentina, a young woman whose appearance provokes and seals a crisis in the marriage of Giovanni and Lidia. Giovanni, acted as though to the manner born by Mastroianni, has wearied of success as an author, and boredom stifles him as it does Sandro in *L'avventura*. As he listens to Valentina – part emancipated intellectual, part bright young teenager – he senses his lack of moral fibre. Just as Rosemary in Fitzgerald's *Tender Is the Night* bewitches Dick Diver, so Valentina acquires in Giovanni's eyes 'the elusiveness that gives hidden significance to the least significant remarks'. Valentina, uncorrupted by her family background, lingers as an ideal for Giovanni, while he strives to mend his marriage.

Vittoria in *L'eclisse*, however, possesses more experience, nourishing a new relationship on the roots of a dead affair. Alain Delon's frenetic Piero at first glance marks a superficial departure from the customary pattern of Antonioni's manhood, but beneath his impetuousness is the familiar acquiescence in the inane, and the failure to gauge a woman's emotions. Lassitude has given place here to an agitation, an inner confusion reflected in the manifest chaos of the Stock Exchange where Piero works. Vittoria feels herself outstripped by what Matthew Arnold termed the 'sick hurry, its divided aims' of urban life. Her one rapturous interlude is a visit to Verona aero-club, where she lazes in the sunshine and imbibes the tranquil atmosphere of the countryside.

Even in the late fifties, **Luchino Visconti** already wore the air of an Old Master, as someone whose first film, *Ossessione*, lay far back in the mists of 1942. *Senso* could hardly be matched in its operatic splendour and colourful rendition of a sordid affair in the turbulent days preceding the Risorgimento, but its form was scarcely innovative. *Rocco and His Brothers* (1960), though, marked a return to the neo-realist vein that courses so powerfully through Visconti's work. Rocco (Delon) is one of four brothers who migrate with their mother from the south to Milan. They hope to make a new and lucrative life in the city but Simone (Renato Salvatore), crudest of the family, lusts after Nadia (Annie Girardot), a prostitute, and his rivalry with Rocco for the woman's affections leads to degradation and murder. One has to give some kind of synopsis, because *Rocco* is a long, sprawling film that expands on a gigantic canvas. Visconti analyses the gulf between north and south, as Rosi does in his best work of the period, and he boasts a flair for creating an overwhelming mood of grief and inevitability.

More than any European director of the early sixties, Visconti adored the big screen.* I saw *The Leopard* projected in 'Scope on an outdoor screen in Locarno during the festival there in the summer of 1963. I had to drive over the Gotthard Pass that night, but the sumptuous grandeur of Visconti's compositions, allied to a conversation at dinner with Lotte Eisner, somehow kept me alert enough to survive the journey. Soon afterwards, Twentieth Century Fox made a shorter version of the film for US release, and before long the title had disappeared from circulation. An entire generation of film buffs came and went without even glimpsing *The Leopard*. Where Giuseppe Tomasi Di Lampedusa's novel is taut and perceptive, Visconti's vision is more languorous. The film is seen through the eyes of the ageing Prince of Salina (a surprisingly good Burt Lancaster) at

---

* Godard also relished the potential of 'scope, especially in *Le mépris*: 'I think it is the normal ratio,' he said in an interview with *Cahiers du Cinéma*, 'and 1:33 an arbitrary one. This is why I like 1:33 – because it is arbitrary. 'Scope, on the other hand, is a ratio in which you can shoot anything. 1:33 isn't, but is extraordinary. 1:66 is worthless. I don't like the intermediate ratios. I thought of using 'Scope for *Vivre sa vie*, but didn't because it is too emotional. 1:33 is harder, more severe. I'm sorry, though, that I didn't use 'Scope for *À bout de souffle*. That's my only regret.'

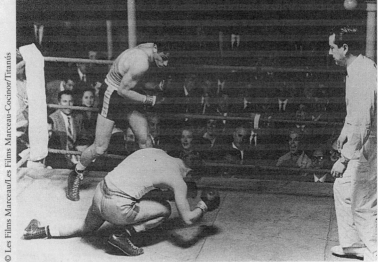

TOP *Rocco and His Brothers* (1960): Rocco (Alain Delon) in the ring

BOTTOM *The Leopard* (1963): Angelica (Claudia Cardinale) and the Prince, Don Fabrizio Salina (Burt Lancaster) together on the dance floor

his villa outside Palermo. The struggle between an old and a new order of society predominates, as it does in *Senso* (both films occur in the midst of Garibaldi's campaign). The concluding ball, held to celebrate the marriage of Tancredi (Alain Delon), the Prince's nephew, becomes symptomatic of the passage of time and of classes, as the Prince recognizes the futility of resisting the nationalist sentiments sweeping his country. The conflict within Visconti, between his Marxist philosophy and his adoration of all things opulent and decorative, gave his films a fascination even as it prevented him from being an influence on the future.

III THE BRITISH WERE COMING

> *What I want is a good time. All the rest is propaganda.*
> Arthur Seaton (Albert Finney) in *Saturday Night and Sunday Morning*

In Britain, a Tory government had come to power in 1951, and would continue to rule the country until 1964. By that time, an entire generation had grown up assuming that the Conservatives presided as of natural right. So the revolution in British cinema proved to be every bit as political as it was aesthetic in nature. Its ramifications and effects expanded rapidly. Not just film, theatre and literature underwent a seismic change; but also the popular music of the period, with the Beatles and the Rolling Stones replacing the crooners of the fifties. Although the first Beatles single, 'Love Me Do', was not released until October 1962, Britain's youth was already in the grip of music fever. In 1960, when the Beatles first became a band and performed in a Hamburg club, they had to compete with up to 300 other bands in the Merseyside area of the north-west.

Then there was the fashion of the era, with the mini-skirt symbolizing the image of 'Swinging London', celebrated so brilliantly in the shots of Julie Christie in *Billy Liar*, walking down a street in northern England, swinging her handbag as if she had not a care in the world. Designers like Mary Quant and photographers like David Bailey were emerging to give British fashion a more spontaneous, buoyant look. Although Britain was not involved in the Vietnam War, the country's young people sided with the protesters in the US, and the 'nuclear disarmament' marches of the late fifties gave way to vociferous anger directed at American imperialism. At the same time, the early impact of the Kennedy years, with the peace corps travelling the world, also chimed with a yearning for 'helping others to help themselves' among young people in Britain.

From this turbulent mood there flowed a sequence of films that did not have the glamour of the French New Wave, or the vivid imagination of the Italian cinema. But it was a 'wave' none the less, and its achievements have been either forgotten or underestimated in a turn-of-the-century mood that cherishes consumerism more than idealism. There were satires. There were fantasies. There were period pieces that drew a sly parallel with the present day. There were comedies. There were musicals. There were dramas. There were love stories. Soon there were gangster films. No genre was beyond the reach of the British cinema at the time. Television played its part in promoting an atmosphere of 'nothing sacred', poking fun at the Establishment in programmes such as *That Was the Week That Was*. Tom Lehrer reflected the mood in his derisive songs. The satirical magazine *Private Eye* was founded, and became an Anglo-Saxon equivalent to France's *Le Canard enchaîné*. 'In fact satire was as much of a force in directing the course of the sixties as were the Beats, the Beatles, hippies, cool jazz and hot protest,' Elaine Dundy wrote in her memoirs. 'The sixties, above all, was the age of disrespect for the old established hypocritical order. Right alongside the Theatre of the Absurd stood the Theatre of Disrespect.'

The British New Wave of the late fifties and early sixties proceeded from a proletarian perspective. The Nouvelle Vague in France had not shown workers actually *working*, but the British did. If in emblematic films like *À bout de souffle, À double tour*, or *Paris nous appartient*, the French were fascinated by a *jeunesse dorée*, the Brits were drawn more to the factory floor and the weekend binge. One of the least fashionable areas of England – Nottingham – received more publicity in 1960 than at any time since Robin Hood and his merry men rode through Sherwood Forest in the Middle Ages. For *Saturday Night and Sunday Morning* may be regarded as the standard-bearer of the 'new British cinema' in all its naturalistic glory, in the same way as *Les 400 coups* or *À bout de souffle* are synonymous with the French New Wave.

KAREL REISZ: *I'd read Alan Sillitoe's novel,* Saturday Night and Sunday Morning. *And I wanted to do a feature because there's never any real distribution for documentaries, so you're thirsting for a form. Albert Finney had been to RADA and had already had a season at Stratford, so everybody knew that he was the right lad for the part. He was like a puppy, he couldn't do anything wrong. He had that easy, lazy arrogance. Arthur Seaton in the novel is a kind of*

Saturday Night and Sunday Morning (1960): Karel Reisz directs Rachel Roberts and Albert Finney

wish-fulfilment figure for Alan Sillitoe, whereas we perceived the victim side of the character – he's a spiritually unsatisfied kid. Shirley Ann Field had already appeared in The Lilywhite Boys, *directed by Lindsay Anderson at the Royal Court.*

Bryanston Films, run initially by Michael Balcon, was an important factor in the British cinema of that period. As the distributor of Saturday Night and Sunday Morning, *Bryanston left us alone, partly because they felt we were dealing with material they couldn't fathom. And partly because we took virtually no money (my fee for directing was £2,000). All the interiors – six days' worth – were done at Twickenham Studios, partly because working-class interiors must by definition be small and cramped, and you have to be able to move walls.*

Saturday Night and Sunday Morning was produced by Woodfall Films, which had been set up by Tony Richardson and John Osborne to showcase their work and also to develop opportunities for other young

93

talents. They were backed by Harry Saltzman, who would use the influence and financial clout afforded him by the success of this film to produce the James Bond pictures over the next decade. Karel Reisz made the leap from short documentaries to directing a maiden feature film, and Alan Sillitoe's screenplay from his own critically lauded novel was as tight as a drum. Looking back, the film was made by a remarkably gifted team – cinematographer Freddie Francis, composer John Dankworth, editor Seth Holt, and Rachel Roberts and Shirley Anne Field alongside Finney in front of the camera.

Arthur Seaton is the quintessential anti-hero of the age, as memorable as Belmondo in *À bout de souffle* or Cybulski in *Ashes and Diamonds*. He exploits his working-class background, and exerts a revenge on British society, by seizing the cherries from the tree of life. More instinctive and less calculating than Laurence Harvey's unpleasant carpetbagger in *Room at the Top*, Arthur is a lovable, cocksure rogue, of the kind that Michael Caine would make his own some years later in films like *Alfie* and *The Ipcress File*. In Arthur Seaton's small triumphs, such as sleeping with his colleagues' wives while they are on night shift, may be discerned the movement from austerity to affluence in British post-war society. The frankness of the sex scenes, and the incandescent language, also proclaimed a new era in the hitherto staid British cinema.

For a movement that presented problems primarily concerning the proletariat, it is ironic that most of the new British directors of the sixties were well educated. Tony Richardson graduated from Oxford University, where he ran the university dramatic society. Capitalizing on his success with stage productions like *Look Back in Anger*, Richardson produced and directed *A Taste of Honey*, from Shelagh Delaney's play about working-class life in Blackpool. Murray Melvin's young homosexual is the most memorable among several good performances, and makes an intriguing contrast to Dirk Bogarde's gay barrister in *Victim*, also shot in 1961.

WALTER LASSALLY: *It was only through the great success of* Saturday Night and Sunday Morning – *which is not an all-location film, but a studio film with location scenes – that Tony was allowed to cross-collateralize its receipts against a possible failure with* A Taste of Honey. *The motivation for films like* A Taste of Honey *and* The Loneliness of the Long-Distance Runner *was entirely social and political. While Tony Richardson was no salon Communist, he was fairly committed to the social aspect, not so much to the political aspect. Tony's entry into that scene was really via the theatre. The Royal Court was the formative essence of all that movement.*

Tony still had great difficulty in setting up Taste of Honey. *It was ready to be produced in 1960, one year before it was actually made, and the distributors would not allow Tony to make it entirely on location.*

The following year, Richardson turned his attention to a more unusual film, *The Loneliness of the Long Distance Runner*. This not only introduced the melancholy, guarded face of Tom Courtenay, but also described cross-country running in very imaginative technical terms, somewhat reminiscent of Truffaut's lissom style.

LASSALLY: Loneliness *grew out of* Taste of Honey. *All the things which in* Taste of Honey *were completely new and experimental, were already tried and tested for* Loneliness, *so we could fall into a certain mode, like the hand-holding in the riot scene. It became second nature and didn't need to be discussed very much. The running sequences were discussed very, very thoroughly, and each running sequence has a slightly different character and mood to it.*

Lassally recalls that *Tom Jones* was being prepared during the actual shooting of *The Loneliness of the Long-Distance Runner*, in the same year:

LASSALLY: *Oswald Morris had been engaged as cameraman for* Tom Jones. *And Ossie, who I always admired and whose style I always felt mine resembled (reflected light, the use of not many lamps and things like that), actually tried to pull Tony Richardson away from that kind of easygoing production, back to a more studio-oriented mode of production. He said, 'You can't make a big epic period colour film in the same way as you made* A Taste of Honey *and* Loneliness.' *And Tony was saying, 'Why not?' They gradually parted company on that issue; Ossie, as it were, resigned, and I was asked by Tony to take over.*

We made a very interesting decision at the beginning of Tom Jones *following discussions about the style and way in which it was to be filmed, namely – if the costumes and art direction were impeccably in period, the camera style could be very modern. That's what gives* Tom Jones *a totally different look to the costume dramas of only a*

*year or two earlier in either Britain or America, and compared to
Tom Jones they look much less natural, and much more artificial and
studio-bound. That film contained no studio scenes, and was shot
100 per cent on location. I used a filter made of some silk hat-veiling
of the twenties, and have used the same kind of filter for all my
colour films since, in fact – because it gives a certain combination of
diffusion and softening, or 'pastelization' of the colour, which I have
always found very pleasing and very simple to achieve.*

Richardson's rollicking version of Henry Fielding's eighteenth-century
novel, *Tom Jones*, with its lascivious humour and flamboyant acting,
delighted the members of Hollywood's Academy, who gave it the Oscar
for Best Film of 1963. But Richardson's personal Oscar, for Best
Direction, led him into a creative cul-de-sac, and he limped from one
half-baked co-production to the next.

John Schlesinger, whose studies of northern England in *A Kind of
Loving* and *Billy Liar* were authentic in tone and content, was the son of
a well-to-do paediatrician. He grew up in Hampstead, and went to public school and then to Oxford. He honed his skills of observation with
documentaries for the BBC, and then with the award-winning *Terminus*,
a documentary about Waterloo Station in London, which won a Golden
Lion at the Venice Film Festival. This was noted by the Italian producer,
Joseph Janni, who asked Schlesinger to direct a feature film based on
Stan Barstow's novel, *A Kind of Loving*, in 1962. Vic Brown (played by
one of the key actors of the decade, Alan Bates) is a factory draughtsman
in the north of England. Vic is a more restrained personality than either
Frank Machin (Richard Harris) in Lindsay Anderson's later *This
Sporting Life*, or Finney's Arthur Seaton in *Saturday Night and Sunday
Morning*. But he remains subject to the same pressure of narrow, *petit-
bourgeois* vigilance and moral rectitude. Schlesinger's quiet, sensitive
direction put his film on a par with Bo Widerberg's *Raven's End*, shot in
Sweden a few months later and dealing similarly with a young man
straining against his roots in an industrial city.

If the rebellion against an ingrained class system and, by extension, the
impoverished conditions of the working population was the primary
theme of British cinema in the sixties, then the secondary theme concerned the need for more relaxed sexual relationships. In film after film,
young people (and particularly young men) face family opposition to the
romance that beckons just beyond the garden gate. Sex is something

Billy Liar (1963): director John Schlesinger confers with Tom Courtenay

clandestine, something that implies a sin not so much against an established church as against the family fortress. Vic Brown suffers from this
anguish in *A Kind of Loving*, and so too, in a more light-hearted idiom,
does the eponymous hero of Schlesinger's next film, *Billy Liar*.

Billy Liar began life as a stage play, by Willis Hall and Keith
Waterhouse. Filmed mainly on location in Bradford, it charts the fantasies and wish-dreams of Billy, an undertaker's clerk. Billy (played by
Tom Courtenay, another icon of the period), suffers from an utter lack of
understanding with his parents, and has a series of girlfriends among
whom only one (the Julie Christie character) comes near to sympathizing
with him. Schlesinger had met Christie while producing a television documentary about London's Central School of Acting, and when his first
choice, Topsy Jane, fell ill and was unable to appear in *Billy Liar*, he gave
the short but vital part to Christie. Like Schlesinger, she took the film in
her stride, with an exuberance that set off beautifully the whimsy of Billy
Liar's world.

97

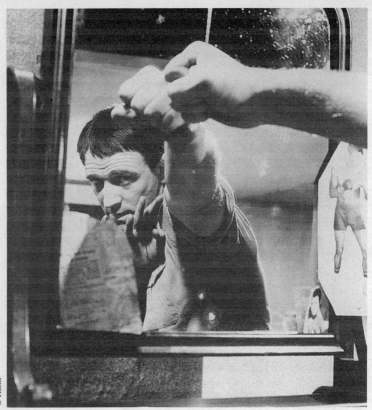

This Sporting Life (1963): Richard Harris as the pugnacious Frank

The darkest and yet most mysteriously lyrical of all the films set in the industrial grime of northern Britain was Lindsay Anderson's *This Sporting Life*, adapted in 1963 from a novel by David Storey. Anderson introduced a kind of subjective realism into British cinema. The audience is presented with a pattern of northern life in *A Kind of Loving* and *Room at the Top*; these are externalized, analytical movies, whereas *This Sporting Life* is the intensely felt vision of one man – Frank Machin (Richard Harris).

On the rugby field, Anderson breaks up the game's logical movements into a series of brutal encounters that convey Frank's own inner feelings. Surly and strong, Machin rebels against the crass attitudes of the society around him, against the *nouveau riche* arrogance of Mrs Weaver (Vanda Godsell), wife of the club chairman, and against the depraved associates of his landlady, the former Mrs Hammond (Rachel Roberts). For Frank Machin, force becomes the only effective argument to hand. Anderson shows him flexing his body, testing his strength within the narrow confines of the house, or prowling around a party like a caged animal. The film is quickened by the clash between Frank's simple, forthright ambition and the bitter, repressed nature of the widowed Mrs Hammond – a clash between innocence and experience, between the direct and the distorted.

If these New Wave studies of the north were passionate and felt, films about London and the south tended to be satirical in tone, with a distinct edge of bitterness that compared with, say, Louis Malle's scathing look at the French *haute bourgeoisie* in *Les Amants*. The moral turpitude of upper-crust London was etched in acid in Joseph Losey's *The Servant*, based on a novel by Robin Maugham that had been transformed into a brilliant screenplay by Harold Pinter. Losey approached his subject in the style of a *Kammerspiele*. James Fox's effete young aristocrat, Tony, lives in Chelsea and succumbs, inexorably, to the weasel-like wiles of Barrett, his North Country manservant played by Dirk Bogarde. The outside world – streets, shops, offices – is scarcely shown. Instead, the action unfolds in an elegant terraced house off the King's Road, creating an intense and sinister mood of claustrophobia. The conflict is not so much social as metaphorical – Faust versus Mephistopheles, a duel that each man seeks to disguise until Tony drifts into vice and Barrett's servility becomes dictatorship.

IV EASTERN EUROPE: REBELLION AND INNOVATION

As Marx's teaching dictated that History is always right, our colleagues were often shouting that History is often wrong. This was a very strong message, very close to the spirit of Greek tragedy, with no good way out.
   Krzysztof Zanussi

Can anyone be nostalgic for Eastern Europe during the fifties and sixties, when layer after layer of apparatchiks exerted their tentacular grip on the minds if not the hearts of anyone involved in cultural affairs? Well, yes – to some degree: the film buff can claim that a stream of masterpieces and near-masterpieces emerged from that oyster-rub, like (to quote one Czech title of the period) 'Pearls from the Deep'. But it seems aeons since Pula or Kraków were indispensable watering-holes for the festival pilgrim.

Miloš Forman was destined to become more successful in critical and financial terms than any other Eastern European film-maker of the post-war generation. His flair for describing young people with neither ran-cour nor captiousness made his comedies the most pleasing aspect of the Czech cinema of the sixties – that brief flowering so tragically crushed by the Soviet invasion of 1968 (cf. *The Unbearable Lightness of Being*, Milan Kundera's novel, filmed in 1987 by Phil Kaufman). Unlike most of his countrymen, Forman was not preoccupied with World War II. There was no glamour in his cinema; but nor was there squalor and depression. Instead, Forman studied individuals in their daily lives, and returned again and again to the stresses and strains of the generation gap.

FORMAN: *What was allowed to be distributed at the time in a Communist country like Czechoslovakia was the Italian neo-realist cinema. It was considered as being on the side of the proletariat, crit-icizing the capitalist society and things like that. We knew the French New Wave much less, because that was not regarded as politically correct from the Communist point of view. The only trips I could make abroad were when I accompanied a film to a festival, to see some films.*

I saw only one Polish film, Ashes and Diamonds, *at a secret screen-ing that was arranged because the projectionist who regularly screened films for the Politburo was a friend of mine. From time to time, when the ministers and the Communist apparatchiks saw films, we waited round the corner for half an hour, and then he let us go into the screening-room and showed us the film. So we were not very much in touch with what was going on around us, at least where things that were in some way progressive were concerned. From other Communist countries we got the usual stupid 'Socialist hori-zon' kind of stuff.*

Our films were, I think, less inspired by great works but more pro-voked by the stupidity of the fruits of Socialist reality. That was our reaction to seeing on the screen these wholly artificial, shallow, idi-otic kinds of pictures, not about life as it is, but about life as it ought to be in Socialist society! We wanted to see something real on the screen. Strangely enough, we did catch one or two films like Lionel

Miloš Forman, *circa Loves of a Blonde* (1965)

> *Rogosin's* On the Bowery *and Shirley Clarke's* The Connection. *But Cassavetes was not kosher enough for Communists!*
>
> *When I think today about all that period under the Communists, it was a very strange situation, because when they took over in 1948, the main revolution in the film industry was that producers were branded as capitalists. So their role diminished to something equivalent to an accountant's – which meant, paradoxically, that the filmmakers (the director, the screenwriter) became kings. So long as you conformed to the official ideology of Socialist realism, you could even live like a king. But that was virtually impossible during the first period, from 1948 to about the beginning of the sixties, because all production was under the tight control not only of the producers, of course, but of the ideologues. When, after Khruschev's speech at the Twentieth Congress of the Communist Party of the Soviet Union, suddenly the political situation loosened up a little bit, that created an absolutely ideal situation. Suddenly we were allowed to make our films the way we wanted, and we were the bosses. We were always in the lowest category to be paid, because we did not strictly conform, but we could do what we wanted.*

Jan Němec awoke spontaneously to the excitement and promise of the new decade. Of all Czech directors, he mingled memories of World War II with uncanny premonitions of the Soviet invasion of 1968. Like his compatriot Franz Kafka, he saw the sinister in every situation, and endowed even the most innocuous of landscapes with undercurrents of foreboding and anguish. He represents the revolution in sixties cinema by virtue of an unusual masterpiece. *Diamonds of the Night* (1962) unfolds in the Sudetenland, on the borders of Germany and Czechoslovakia. Two youths leap from a Nazi transport train and plunge through the forest in an attempt to shake off pursuit. Gradually they become animalistic in their gestures and frame of mind. Their minds start to wander. Memories, hallucinations and desires rise and die away like the knelling of the bell behind the credits. They imagine trees falling on top of them, ants swarming over their hands and faces, and they conjure up distorted visions of wartime Prague, with strange elongated trams and a woman who gazes impassively from a window like the subject of a Goya portrait. At length they are hunted down and arrested by a Home Guard composed of weird old men, who celebrate their capture with beer and grinding songs. Only Resnais or, much later, Tarkovsky, could match the density of expression in *Diamonds of the Night*. The memories are like a stabbing pain, injected into the audience's collective psyche. At first ambivalent and illogical, they bloom into tangible recollections and realizations. Jaroslav Kucera's hand-held camera clings obsessively to the fugitives, registering the slightest change of look on their faces.

Further south, Marshal Tito's complex congeries of republics – the Yugoslavia that produced such a harvest of gifted film-makers during the sixties – allowed politics to figure more significantly on screen. This was due in the main to Tito forever cocking a courteous snook at Moscow. Yugoslavia became the Communist nation that the West accepted with condescending sympathy. But for sheer charisma and idiosyncratic wit, the personality of **Dušan Makavejev** would prove the most engaging of all. Working in the buffer state to end all buffer states of the period, Yugoslavia, where virtually all film citizens were true Marxists ('Fifty per cent Groucho, and fifty per cent Karl,' quips Makavejev), he cheerfully wed politics with erotica, nostalgia with agitprop, and comedy with tragedy. Much marked by the influence of Godard, he did not take himself as seriously as the French director, while possessing the intelligence and knowledge of history to mock every taboo in sight.

MAKAVEJEV: *We lived in a one-party system in Yugoslavia, and there was no way out politically, as all history was viewed in Marxist terms. So belonging to a film or photography club was one way of eluding this situation, because such places were not really controlled.*

In our high school, we also made the acquaintance of some retired artisan guys, technicians who would come and give us courses in art photography. So there were a lot of niches in the system. And basically, as soon as we became freer in the early fifties, American films started arriving. So we were raised on this diet, first of Soviet films immediately after the war as kids, and then American films with Clark Gable and Gary Cooper, and then the American 'underground'. So it was not just one influence that marked our generation. Film condensed the best that was happening in politics and society.

In 1954 Henri Langlois came on behalf of his French Cinémathèque to 'bless' our film archive in Belgrade, and ended up staying a whole month. Each day, three or four more feature films would arrive by diplomatic bag, and we saw all the work of Clair, Pagnol, Feuillade, Gérard Philipe – a wonderful grounding in French cinema – and all uncensored. I was First Secretary of the Cinéma-thèque Club.

I think the riots in Budapest and in Poznan in 1956 exemplified the Old Order. Before that, the Soviet films had dominated our screens, and for a while there were no Western films at all to be seen in Yugoslavia. But then films began to emerge from Poland. I remember the series of 'black' documentaries made by Jerzy Bossak and others – so-called because of their unvarnished view of life in post-war Poland. Each documentary was an incredible statement. I remember one was about the people who had to live in houses destroyed by the bombardment of the war – full of sombre contradictions and a dark sense of life. I remember films using a hand-held camera, shot on the spot, like The True End of the Great War. These films came to Belgrade, but they didn't play for very long . . . Then we were seeing lots of short films from different countries, especially at the Oberhausen Festival in the early sixties.

Wajda's trilogy made a huge impression on me, as did the work of Kawalerowicz. Then came Jules et Jim, and À bout de souffle – freedom of editing without careless editing, plus the casual treatment of the story, with casual dialogue. I liked the dancing camera in Claude Chabrol's À double tour. He was for me probably more important than anyone else in the early days. Some of the images from Les bonnes femmes have stayed with me for forty years.

The thing about the Polish films and then the French films was that they evinced any number of meanings, not just one or two. They recognized that we can bring several complicated emotions to the same subject. In Jules et Jim, for instance, each character carries his own complexes. Endless variations on a theme of being together, of not being together, not being able to be together, wanting to be together, desiring, being afraid . . . In the American cinema, it was traditionally just good guys and bad guys. But then a young American critic, Gideon Bachmann, brought a big package of new American films to Belgrade in the early sixties, including Shadows, The Connection, Hallelujah the Hills and The Brig. There was Bruce Baillie, Bruce Conner, Stan Vanderbeek and Ed Emshwiller – Relativity I liked a lot. We had seen a lot of Russian cinema from the twenties and thirties, even something like Medvedkin's Happiness (1932), years before it reached even France.

I had started making experimental films already in 1955: Amos Vogel of Cinema 16 somehow found out about them, and sent a letter to Jugoslavija Film in 1959, asking about my work. One of my films was screened at a festival of amateur cinema in Cannes in 1957. A group of us film society members travelled with two tents to the Riviera in December, and found a place to set them up in the hills behind the railroad at the back of the town, where the Algerians lived, and for 1 franc a day you could erect your tent! My film, Angela's Broken Mirror, *aroused discussion and a very good review from Simone Dubreuilh in* Libération. *Amateur films in those days in some way were harbingers of new trends to come.*

The Polish cinema that so impressed Makavejev's generation was already in significant transition. In 1962, **Roman Polanski**'s first feature, *Knife in the Water,* reached the West at the Venice Festival, where the critics gave it their FIPRESCI Award. Two years later, it would be nominated for an Academy Award as Best Foreign Language Film. *Knife in the Water* recalls Genet and Kafka in its observation of two men sparring for a woman's admiration, on a yacht in the remote lake district of Poland. Like two birds, the men flaunt their virility and sophistication before the woman, revealing in the older of the two a cynical sadism, and in the younger, a youthful hardness symbolized by his knife. Polanski records his characters' behaviour as he sees it, not straining to stretch their skirmishes out according to a motive, but rather sensing intuitively how they react to challenges within their lives. Shooting in cramped conditions, and almost entirely on location, Polanski confirmed the emergence of a sophisticated visual idiom, at once spontaneous and controlled. His use of silence, creating a mood of uncertainty, set him apart stylistically from many of his peers: his proved a rare gift for trapping emotions in imagery rather than through dialogue.

The inspired **Andrzej Munk** had been killed in an accident in 1961, leaving behind him a legless giant of a film, *Passenger.* It is an often terrifying, sometimes ethereal web of memories, as a German woman recalls her time as an officer in Auschwitz, and her relationship with a Polish girl. The prologue and the epilogue are made up of stills, assembled by Munk's old team at the Kamera studio. The real fibre of *Passenger,* however, consists of the flashbacks, with the director's cool, sombre appraisal of concentration-camp routine resembling a nightmare recollected in tranquillity. Munk's comprehension of the psychological skirmishing between the two female characters is even more remarkable. The German woman regards her *protégée* with a feline sadism mixed with admiration for the nobility and meekness of the Polish prisoner.

Jerzy Kawalerowicz's searing masterpiece, *Mother Joan of the Angels*, appeared in 1961 and gave vivid expression to the conflict between Church and state in Poland. The film drew on the outbreak of demonic possession in a nunnery in medieval France, which had inspired Aldous Huxley's novel *The Devils of Loudon* and John Whiting's play, *The Devils* (in turn brought to the screen in 1971 by Ken Russell).

KAWALEROWICZ: *In* Mother Joan of the Angels, *I used both professionals and very talented amateur actors. Jaroslaw Iwaszkiewicz was a very famous Polish writer, and he adapted the story of the devils of Loudon for Polish circumstances. But it was a problem to make that particular film, because under Communism the state felt that the subject was too religious, while paradoxically the church felt that it was anti-Catholic. I wondered what crime I had committed! A film like* Mother Joan of the Angels *could only have been made in Poland in that particular political framework. The church has to accept the Devil, even in human beings, and the question was, how should the Devil be shown? The Devil is evil incarnate. Even in churches there were posters urging people not see the film, and it was distributed with rather few prints.*

Krzysztof Zanussi was thirteen years younger than Andrzej Wajda, and seventeen younger than Jerzy Kawalerowicz.

ZANUSSI: *When I reached Łódź in 1960, there was a memory of Polanski, who had been the last great product of the school – they were very proud of him. Then there was Skolimowski, who had started his studies two years ahead of me, and so was a model of a successful film-maker. In each course in the Department of Direction there were six students, so around twenty-four in all. There was also a Department of Cinematography, and one of my contemporaries was Adam Holender, who would go on to shoot* Midnight Cowboy *and others.*

At that time Łódź was a totally independent place, and that was important from a creative point of view. Nobody spoke about ideology or Communism; that would have been unacceptable. We talked about Western art and interests and so on and so forth. We had access to what was happening in the West. We were translators to the East, the transformer. The Russians would come, the East Germans would come, to see the new fashion, to listen to the new music, to watch the films, to read the books. Many Russian writers (Brodsky, for example) would learn Polish because this was the easiest way for them to read Camus or Kerouac, whereas English was much more difficult for them.

In 1962 I remember going to Helsinki as a film student for the Youth Festival, and the great Polish theatre director Jerzy Grotowski was there. Before I left I was supposed to meet Wajda, to get instructions from him. And it was amazing that I knew already about the Nouvelle Vague, and I was ready to embrace it enthusiastically, and Wajda said, 'No, we are _against_ it. We don't care, this is a kind of light-hearted, egocentric cinema – we are making cinema that touches the nerve of social life, so don't praise them. Talk about our independent approach to all these issues. We don't forget history, we are a part of history, and we fight against history – but we are not individualists, like those French are.'

In fact, from Helsinki, I hitchhiked to Paris, and there I got interviews with Truffaut, with Resnais and with Chabrol, because I knew Georges Sadoul, and his step-daughter, Yvonne Baby, who wrote about film for Le Monde, introduced me to these directors. I was most disappointed seeing Truffaut shooting Tirez sur le pianiste, because I was sure that this was a nod towards commercial cinema, and I felt that Wajda was right – that this cinema was somehow frivolous, and with an enormous amount of vanity. I loved Truffaut's first film, Les 400 coups, so I was slightly disappointed at his doing something irrelevant. But I respected Resnais, because of his research into film language, and I came back overwhelmed by his work.

Now, from today's perspective, I see that this was an interesting contrast – that we were not attuned to the New Wave. However, I brought from this experience the technique of shooting – no studio crowd, and a hidden camera – and I was kicked out of the film school, because with Adam Holender I made my third-year graduate film and they hated it. I used to make amateur films as a university student, and suddenly the professor said, 'Well, he's incorrigible, he's going back to his origins. Why does he need film school?' He said, 'You're no longer a promising student. Go away if you don't want to learn how to make sets in the studio, how to set the camera in the *correct position.' There was one big flaw in my film, which I discovered later – I had no sync sound, and I was post-syncing improvised dialogue.*

One director in particular exerted a tremendous influence on Zanussi (and on many film-makers of that generation):

ZANUSSI: *Bergman was for me a god. I came to film-making only because I discovered Bergman. He institutionalized auteurist cinema. Renoir, Buñuel and others had occasionally made auteur films, but it was not a rule. Then Bergman came along, and he was making nothing but auteur films. That's what inspired me. I did not want to be a film-maker who did commissioned work, I wanted to make films that were put forward by me and written by me.*

V US INDEPENDENTS

I remember seeing Pasolini's Accattone *in Florence, and thinking, 'My God, the faces! The subject-matter! The camera being there! What an interesting way to tell stories.'*
Phil Kaufman

Although more than two years had elapsed since the first new-look European films had appeared, the vagaries of distribution meant that British and American audiences only became aware of the resurgence across the water during 1960 and 1961. Enterprising distributors like Janus Films, based in Cambridge, Massachusetts, imported Bergman's masterpieces of the late fifties, and in March 1960 the Swede featured on the cover of *Time* magazine. Although *Les 400 coups* had opened in North America in November 1959, *À bout de souffle* did not reach US screens until February 1961, and *Hiroshima mon amour* and *Ashes and Diamonds* three months after that.

Walter Murch began his career in the sixties and would become the most respected sound designer (some would also say the best editor) of his generation.

MURCH: *The impact [of European films at that time] was huge. They all shared that quality that I first noticed in* The Seventh Seal, *of being particularly stamped with an individual sensibility. For various reasons involving the way films were made in Hollywood at that*

*time, or in the fifties, I did not get that from Hollywood pictures.
Starting with* The Seventh Seal, *which was really the film that made
the most impact on me in the late fifties when I saw it in New York, I
wound up at university studying the history of art and Romance languages, and engineered a year in Paris to study these subjects. When I
reached Paris, it was at the height of the New Wave. I had seen* À
bout de souffle *when it came out in New York in the early sixties. I
fell into film, really, during that year in Paris, because of the excitement of being there where all this was happening.*

*So I returned from that trip smitten consciously to a degree,
unconsciously more powerfully, and started looking around in my
senior school at university. Then I discovered that there were such
things as schools of cinema at a graduate-programme level, which I
found remarkable – slightly hilarious because I'd come from an academic background – the idea that you could 'teach' film in those days
was not exactly acknowledged. But I applied to NYU and UCLA and
USC – and I got accepted at USC with a scholarship. I found myself
among a second wave of people such as George Lucas and Francis
Coppola and Caleb Deschanel and Matthew Robbins, who had all
been pushed into film school by the force of, primarily, the French
New Wave, but really the world cinema movement as a whole.*

Kurosawa exerted a huge influence on me when I saw Yojimbo
and then, later on, Rashomon. *I remember vividly seeing* La dolce
vita *in New York in 1960. I was already going to mostly European
films when I was in New York.*

The doughty work of Amos Vogel at his film society, Cinema 16,
ensured that the experimental fringe received continual attention in New
York. Artists like Maya Deren and Stan Brakhage were genuine screen
poets, producing short, evocative impressions of life that were far
removed from the grind of mainstream Hollywood, and for which the
musty, mysterious term 'Underground' was too patronizing. This avant-
garde syndrome persisted throughout the sixties in New York movie circles, most notoriously with Andy Warhol's soporific efforts, like *Sleep*,
and his still interesting *The Chelsea Girls*, and most exhilaratingly with
Jordan Belson, Saul Bass and Ed Emshwiller.

Cassavetes tried to sustain the momentum that *Shadows* had given his
career as a director. But he kept being sidetracked into acting on television and in films. He also procrastinated, and this, allied to a tendency

The Connection (1963): Carl Lee (right) as Cowboy

towards the unflinching optimism of his beloved Frank Capra, softened the heart of his work, especially in the studio production *Too Late Blues* (1962). Cassavetes preferred the faintly sentimental approach of Zavattini and the neo-realists to the anxieties and tribulations of a Bergman or an Antonioni. He regarded *À bout de souffle*, *L'avventura* and *The Virgin Spring* as 'sordid' and even 'negative' – adjectives that paradoxically would be applied to his own work during the seventies and eighties.

Shirley Clarke, who had loaned Cassavetes cameras and sound equipment for *Shadows*, seemed destined for a major career herself when *The Connection*, her screen adaptation of Jack Gelber's play, appeared in 1962, followed by *The Cool World* the following year. She captured the argot of street gangs and heroin junkies in New York, falling foul of censorship regulations but attracting critical admiration for the *verismo* of her vision. Her training as a choreographer led her to experiment with kinetic movement, and her skill as an editor was outstanding. 'I identified with black people,' she said later, 'because I couldn't deal with the woman question and I transposed it. I could understand very easily the black problems, and I somehow equated them to how I felt. When I did

The Connection, which was about junkies, I knew nothing about junk and cared less. It was a symbol – people who are on the outside. I always felt alone and on the outside of the culture that I was in. I grew up in a time when women weren't running things . . . they still aren't.'

Clarke had been profoundly influenced by the work of Rossellini and by the neo-realist movement as a whole. *Roma città aperta* was the inspiration for *The Cool World*. 'That's what I was looking to do in *The Connection* also, but I ended up having to do it in a set. The original idea was to shoot it in the streets of New York, but at that point in time we were scared to shoot 35mm without better sound controls. When it came to *The Cool World*, we developed the radio mike and took it into the streets so the kids could talk running up and down the streets.' *The Connection* won a prize at Cannes and then, almost to Clarke's embarrassment, earned an Academy Award too. *The Cool World* became the first American independent film to appear at the Venice Festival, opening the way for other directors.

Independent Shirley Clarke undoubtedly was, but 'independence' has many faces, and **John Frankenheimer**, a director to whom Clarke probably would not have given the time of day in 1962, has outlasted her as a commercial film-maker. There again, some would say that Frankenheimer made his peace with Hollywood from the start and that therefore his work has remained more accessible through the decades. But Frankenheimer made a dozen features between 1960 and 1970 and remains important to the decade for two basic reasons. Firstly, he dared to question political rectitude in Washington, a suspicion that the 'assassination' of Marilyn Monroe seemed to bear out. Secondly, he responded more eagerly than such mainstream worthies as Martin Ritt and Sidney Lumet to the opportunities offered by new equipment and faster film stock. His background in live television made him aware of the significance of mass communications technology. His masterpiece, *The Manchurian Candidate* (1962), was made with the same freedom as a European director enjoyed in those years. A few years ago, Frankenheimer said, 'When we made *The Manchurian Candidate*, we certainly didn't know we were making a classic. We knew we had an excellent script, we had a hell of a good time making that picture, and I shot the whole movie in 41 days – working with Frank [Sinatra] on the first take . . . We were a group of people getting together at a certain moment in our lives and doing the best work we were capable of.' Laurence Harvey's Raymond Shaw is a GI who has been brainwashed by the Chinese in Korea and must carry out an assassination at the behest of none other than his own domineering mama. Frankenheimer manipulates the tokens of a technological era with remarkable confidence; television sets seem to monitor and then to mock the accusations hurled at suspect Communists by the right-wing Senator Iselin. 'I wanted to do a picture that showed both how ludicrous McCarthy-style far-right politics are and how dangerous the far-left is also,' declared the maverick Frankenheimer, 'how they were really exactly the same thing, and the idiocy of it all.'

Another, even feistier personality emerged in the margins of Hollywood during the Kennedy years. **Sam Peckinpah**'s early westerns, *The Deadly Companions* (1961) and *Ride the High Country* (1962), explored issues no more complex than those of the classic westerns, but did so with such visual assurance and such impeccable control of performances (Joel McCrea and Randolph Scott eclipsing all their previous work) that a new master was clearly on the horizon.

John Korty was destined to become a paradigm for the West Coast independent film-maker, although he spent his formative years in the East. Korty had started drawing and painting with serious intent at the age of nine in Lafayette, Indiana.

KORTY: *In tenth or eleventh grade I had this great teacher, Mrs Vorhees, who did all kinds of things to stimulate art. One day she started pulling the blinds down in the classroom. 'We're going to look at some movies today,' she said. She starts up the projector, and there's this hen hopping around. It was Norman McLaren's* Hen Hop *... And then she showed* Begone Dull Care. *That was it. I was only seventeen years of age, but I thought, 'This is what I want to do. I want to make images, and I want to make them move.'*

At first I thought I would be an animator. I was going to do experimental animation like McLaren. So I had to start working my way through college, and I did some cartoon animation for commercial purposes. So that took me from 1954 to 1959, and I got out of school just before the sixties. Foreign films were just coming in, and I remember seeing them in 1956, 1957 and on. I was hooked on early Bergman and many other foreign films. By the time I reached New York I was watching nothing but foreign films. There were almost no American films of interest to me at that juncture. I quickly heard about Amos Vogel and his Cinema 16 film society, so I joined that.

So on the one hand I was seeing foreign features in the theatres in Manhattan, on the other I was seeing Stan Brakhage and the experimental films of the American underground. Indeed, Stan Vanderbeek and I shared billing on the first programme in America that used the term 'underground cinema'. It was in the Village, one night, and I had just finished what was not really an underground film – a documentary commissioned by the Quakers, called The Language of Faces. *And Stan Vanderbeek had some shorts that he'd done, and there were two or three other films on the programme.*

I was always drawn to the films that surprised and woke me up visually. I saw all the early Bergmans, and as much Fellini as I could, and then I remember Truffaut's 400 Blows. *My friend Bob Hughes had seen* Jules and Jim *at a midnight screening in New York, and he was just blown away – because* The 400 Blows *is a very good film but a documentary kind of film, and* Jules and Jim *to him was the turning point. To me it was just a knockout. In those days, the European cinema was not nearly as frustrated as it is today. There was the political aspect, the artistic aspect. I found that the lighting, the way they shot the films, the character development, everything about those films just spoke to me.*

I got to go to the Montreal Festival in 1960, which was a great experience – only because my film, Language of Faces, *had won a Grand Prize for Documentary at the Bergamo Festival in Italy. So that put me on the map, and I got a nice review of the film in the* New York Times *from Bosley Crowther. Next thing I knew, I was invited to the Montreal Festival as one of six American directors. Truffaut was there that year, and Kobayashi from Japan, and André Martin from France. We had three days of symposia and discussions, held in one of the sound stages at the National Film Board. Everybody was spouting out their frustrations and ideas, and all the feature-film directors were complaining about the frustration of the commercial world, dealing with distributors, trying to get into theatres, all that stuff.*

As an outsider, I raised my hand and said, 'Let me pose a hypothetical situation – we all need money to make our films, and we all have to deal with this commercial world. But what if a very wealthy person contacted you and said, I've seen your films, I love your work, I have a lot of money, and I will finance whatever you want to do next – on just one condition, that you and I are the only two people who will ever see the film.' There was this moment of dead silence, and everyone was looking at everyone else, and saying, Mmm, well, what would I do? What I was getting at was that of course the commercial world is a nightmare, and of course distribution is a problem, but do we want our films to be seen or not seen?

My friend Bob Hughes knew all the people involved with Shadows. *I met Ben Carruthers at a party. But apart from Cassavetes, surprisingly little else was going on in New York. My first marriage was breaking up, and she wanted to stay in New York and be a dancer and I wanted to go west. I had this vision of living on the coast. Not in LA but up here somewhere on the coast, although I had never visited San Francisco. So I decided to live here without having seen it, and that turned out to be the best blind date in my life.*

Phil Kaufman came of age during the sixties, though it would be the 1980s when he established himself as one of the most audacious voices in American cinema, through *The Right Stuff* and *The Unbearable Lightness of Being*.

PHIL KAUFMAN: *I am making films because of the Europeans. I consider myself an American film-maker by background, going to double features every Saturday as a child, as did all my friends. Then in high school, in dark movie theatres in Chicago during my high-school years. Films were less for the watching and more for the fun of hooting at the screen. We'd have fights outside with other gangs. The American films were post-Black List, vapid, big, Technicolor, by and large uninteresting American movies.*

Then, right at the end of the fifties, and into the early sixties, suddenly film was being discussed by myself and my friends. I was at Harvard Law School and saw The Seventh Seal, *and I remember that my friends and I stayed up all night talking about the angles, the people were moving across the screen like the chess game that was being played. When we saw* Les 400 coups, *just the vitality, and the children, and the camera being out in the streets, blew us away. It was the combination of technique and content that was so impressive: that accessibility.*

Then I was teaching at an American school in Italy, and by then I had discovered the Italian new wave. I remember seeing Pasolini's Accattone *in Florence, and thinking, 'My God, the faces! The subject-*

matter! The camera being there! What an interesting way to tell sto-ries.' Also in Florence I watched Cassavetes' Shadows. After about a year we went to live outside Amsterdam, and I remember seeing Shirley Clarke's The Connection. *Those two movies were for me the start of something new here – I could feel the cry of America, the sense of jazz. Then there were inklings of what became known for a brief period of time as the New American Cinema. So I came back to Chicago in 1962 and set about trying to learn as much as I could, seeing every foreign movie I could, especially at the Clark Theatre.*

We came out to San Francisco in 1960, and the beatniks were on the next street, and we were kind of bohemian beatniks, and there was the On the Road *atmosphere, that kind of Whitmanesque spirit that was being revived. I thought that Kennedy was some kind of Boston yuppie, but later I got very interested in the whole Kennedy thing, because the office made the man. It was a spell that was con-stantly filled with a kind of optimism, and I try to keep that opti-mism myself here in San Francisco, with the sense of 'the open road', the frontier feeling. San Francisco was the Barbary Coast: nobody had families here, we all came out here back in the fifties and sixties with no prior attachments, setting up this kind of new way of life. But the minute that family concerns take over, then a sort of bour-geoisie takes over too . . .*

With art-houses flourishing throughout Europe and the United States, and courses in film appreciation beginning to figure in the curriculum at American universities, the European cinema seemed set fair for a decade of dominance. Yet radical change still lay ahead. In Sweden, even as Bergman embarked on his austere, uncompromising trilogy (*Through a Glass Darkly*, *Winter Light* and *The Silence*), Bo Widerberg was chastiz-ing him in the press, dismissing Bergman's obsession with man's place in the universe and deploring his lack of interest in everyday Swedish life.

In mid-1959, with a stream of perceived masterpieces already under his belt, Bergman needed a fresh impetus. It came by happenstance, when his regular cameraman, Gunnar Fischer, was contracted by Disney to shoot a film during the bitterly cold winter of 1958–9, and so Bergman hired Sven Nykvist to work on *The Virgin Spring*. The rapport between the two men changed Bergman's eye on faces and landscapes for ever. *The Virgin Spring* was a transitional film in so many ways, and emblematic of the passing from one mode of cinema to another. Set in the Middle Ages, still coloured by religious angst, it nevertheless had a lean and relentless narrative structure, an economy of means and a naturalistic look that came from using locations in the heavily wooded province of Dalarna.

Bergman's first film of the new decade – *Through a Glass Darkly* – was as austere as a Munch, its gaunt island vistas meticulously limned in Nykvist's lens. Like the Bach cello sonata on the soundtrack, this film dispensed with ornamentation, instead distilling its debate, its dialectic. *Winter Light*, about a pastor's shortcomings, and *The Silence*, set in a murky city on the cusp of war, followed over the next two years. Bergman called them a trilogy on the theme of 'reduction'. 'In *Through a Glass Darkly* the predominant thing is God and love. Then comes *Winter Light*, criticizing this and ending in a bare-scraped lowest level with a prayer to an unnamed god . . . And then *The Silence* – everything is still more bare-scraped, a world utterly without God. In which only the hand – fellowship – is left. And the music.'

Bo Widerberg's own first feature, *The Pram* (1962), about an unmarried mother coping with a rigid social democracy, certainly demonstrated a closer kinship with Godard and Truffaut than with traditional Swedish cinema. Widerberg – along with Bertolucci, Forman, Skolimowski and the quizzical talent of Chris Marker – would be riding the second wave . . .

5 Burying 'Papa's Cinema'

There is no New Wave, there's only the sea . . . We don't form a group, as the surrealists did earlier. We haven't made a revolution. Our movement has merely allowed young directors to get recognition, each with his own style, in a period when the French cinema had grown ossified. Today, it's much easier for a young guy to make his first movie. The second, though, is more complicated . . .
  Claude Chabrol

By early 1963, many of the battles had been won. Orthodox productions had learned from the revolution in technology. More scenes were shot on location. New actors were sought instead of established stars. But the smaller European countries yearned to follow the lead of France, Italy and the United Kingdom, and so a subsidy system of some kind had to be developed.

At that juncture, half a shelf held most of the good books in English available on the cinema. We greedily grasped at the steady flow of titles from neighbouring France – Chabrol and Rohmer's seminal study of *Hitchcock*, for example, or Marcel Martin's useful textbook, *Le langage du cinéma*, Henri Agel's spiritually inclined *Les grands cinéastes* (1960) and everything written by André Bazin (his provocative *What Is Cinema?* appeared posthumously between 1958 and 1962).

In 1963, I published two little paperbacks, one a trio of 'monographs' (a buzz-word of the time) on Antonioni, Bergman and Resnais, and the other entitled *International Film Guide*, the first of what I hoped would be an annual survey of world films and film-makers. I was amazed by the demand for these titles. Zwemmer's, a small art bookshop in the Charing Cross Road, filled the window with copies and sold two hundred in a week. Peter Graham's pocket-sized *Dictionary of the Cinema*, which we published at Tantivy Press the following year, sold out within a couple of months.

At the same time, a new community of critics, journalists and archivists tended to cluster, like crystals, at the ever-increasing number of film festivals. Some, like Louis Marcorelles, proved crucial in their influence on the commercial distribution of European films. Gene Moskowitz, an American resident in Paris, reviewed all the significant new titles in the pages of *Variety*. Richard Roud, a 'genuine Boston Yankee' by his own description, had studied in Paris, made friends with many directors, and founded the New York Film Festival with Amos Vogel. Criss-crossing the Atlantic, Roud soon found himself in an enviable position, persuading Truffaut to show the first, almost dripping print of *Tirez sur le pianiste* at the London Film Festival in 1961. A fresh generation of French critics came to the fore, including Michel Ciment at *Positif*, Claude Beylie and Bertrand Tavernier at *Cahiers du cinéma*, and Pierre Rissient at *La Présence du Cinéma*.

Richard Lester, an American who decided to settle for good in Britain in 1956, had entered the sixties with a bang, his short extravaganza *The Running Jumping & Standing Still Film* being nominated for an Academy Award. For Lester, the great international film festivals played a vital role in bringing directors together.

> LESTER: *If you look at a list of European directors of the early sixties, I would think that one in ten would have known each other in the way that we all did in the sixties. Festivals and festival-going may since have been downgraded – I've been out of the business for ten years, and I may therefore have rather misguided ideas about what's going on today. But I get the feeling that we cared a bit more then about going to the festivals, and meeting and talking. We were thrown together with the passions that existed. It's difficult, thirty years on, to remind people of just what that was like ...*

There were other individuals who combined a passion for resurrecting and preserving older films with a discriminating taste where the new European cinema was concerned: Ulrich Gregor and Enno Patalas from Germany; Aito Mäkinen and Jörn Donner from Finland; and Freddy Buache from Switzerland. Henri Langlois was the granddaddy of them all, but he rarely travelled beyond his lair at the Cinémathèque Française. Directors adored him, however, as they did also Jacques Ledoux, of the Cinémathèque Belgique, who also appeared as a key actor in one of the most haunting films of the period, Chris Marker's *La jetée*.

This medium-length photo-essay charts a nightmarish experiment in the wake of 'World War III'. Paris has been devastated, and a survivor is subjected to the whims of German scientists in the catacombs beneath

Chris Marker's *La jetée* (1963)

the city. As a child, the man had foreseen his own death, and now, impelled by the bizarre drugs of the enemy, he travels back through time to keep a rendezvous on the pier at Orly airport. Marker tells this story with still photographs, blending elliptically into each other like fragments of a story rescued from some archive. The arrested postures seem to radiate more life than the movements themselves. Men's faces become craggy and filled with shadows, like petrified stones. This audacious style gives *La jetée* a degree of elongated emotion that makes the romance at the film's centre appear excruciating in its doomed beauty, and the idea of a voyage through time seem horrific and unfair.

One of the most seething cauldrons of debate in the early sixties was the Oberhausen Festival, where, confined within the ghastly murk of the Ruhrland, festival-goers engaged in debate and passionate acclaim for the adventurous short films emerging from Yugoslavia, Poland and Czechoslovakia. The art of animation flourished in Europe during the early sixties as never before or since. Individual artists such as **Jan Lenica** and **Walerian Borowczyk** emerged to transcend their national boundaries and reach a world-wide audience. Studios like Zagreb Film in Yugoslavia proved to be hotbeds for a remarkable diversity of talented animators. Theirs was an art far removed from that of Disney, and more in tune with UPA or Norman McLaren. It accommodated political satire, avant-garde draughtsmanship, and a vision often so dark that it made contemporary feature films appear tame by comparison. Apparatchiks either could not understand what the cartoons were trying to say, or felt assured that their public would be a minor one. In Lenica's *Labyrinth* (1963), an innocent individual roams through a terrifying, deserted city composed of steel engravings and cut-out figures. Lenica's fellow Pole, Borowczyk, found inspiration in Paris. *Les Jeux des anges* (1964) is an abstract, nightmarish masterpiece. Its foreboding imagery and weird tableaux evoke a universal desolation, and something of what one imagines to have been the atmosphere of the Nazi death camps.

At Oberhausen on 28 February 1962, a group of young German film-makers issued a manifesto, proclaiming that 'papa's cinema' of the post-war era was dead and should be buried. But although the new generation of cinéastes stood ready to assume the economic risks involved in film-making, their early efforts found little favour with either critics or public, and not until the mid-sixties did West German cinema show signs of vigour.

It seemed clear that if a film subsidy system were to function fruitfully, it would require the support of government. When change came about in Sweden, it was initiated not by any one director but rather by an imaginative administrator. Harry Schein, who as a youngster had fled from Austria to Sweden, trained as an engineer and turned his searching mind first to the recycling of water and then to his hobby, film criticism. Writing in the pages of the influential cultural monthly *BLM*, Schein became friends with Bergman and married one of the master's leading actresses, Ingrid Thulin. In 1962, having formed close contacts with the ruling Social Democratic hierarchy, Schein drafted the blueprint for the Swedish Film Institute, a concept that would be emulated in several European countries. By 1963 he was ensconced in an office on Stockholm's Kungsgatan, along with a minuscule staff and a rickety archive outside the city centre.

Schein's idea embraced the best of both East and West. The state (i.e. the Institute) would fund and reward creative film-making. It would also stimulate the role of the private producer, who would be enticed into partnership with the Institute. For the first eight years, most of the money accrued to a film only after it had been released and judged by a jury of critics and savants. Up to three-quarters of a film's budget could be covered by this *post factum* subsidy. 'The Swedish Film Institute expresses in this way the status of a free film production in a modern welfare state,' said Schein, 'in which the government abstains from direct control of production, economically, thematically, or artistically, provided that the film industry recognizes its responsibility not only towards its shareholders but towards the art of film as a whole.' This was, all told, quite a shock for a country that had seen its entertainments tax reach a pinnacle of 37.5 per cent, and where production had dropped from forty features per annum during World War II to a mere dozen in the early sixties.

Jörn Donner, a flying Finn whose mother tongue was Swedish, was among the first to benefit from the Swedish Film Institute's existence – and some fifteen years later he would become head of the Institute itself. A brilliant essayist, he found it hard to adapt his laconic, pungent style of writing to the screen. His early films, made in Sweden, often appeared stiff and pretentious. They starred his partner, the actress Harriet Andersson, who had in 1952 become Bergman's most wilful heroine in *Summer with Monika.*

DONNER: *Bergman used to have a screening every Thursday out at Filmstaden studios, and he invited some friends, including me. He had the opportunity to show the Nouvelle Vague films. It was a time of upheaval and change. During the early sixties Antonioni came to Stockholm, and I brought him to Helsinki. So there was a sort of 'Internationale' of film-makers.*

I happened to start as a film critic for BLM in 1958 or 1959, and in the summer of 1961 I got offered a post as critic for Dagens Nyheter, a position that had been offered to Vilgot Sjöman (but he refused, because he was already into film-making). I started there in that September, and one of my first big reviewing jobs was Bergman's Through a Glass Darkly – and I think I changed film criticism a little, because I wrote more of an essay about it. Then I wrote a book about Ingmar in 1961–2, and in 1963 I had the chance to make my first film, A Sunday in September, starring Harriet Andersson and Thommy Berggren. But then I had the luck or misfortune to get terrible reviews in Sweden. The reception improved somewhat when I won the Opera Prima prize in Venice. Harriet Andersson got the Coppa Volpi (acting prize) in Venice the next year, for To Love.

At the time of To Love, *the United States was very interested in European films, and they were shown commercially, and they made some money. Richard Roud selected* To Love *for the New York Film Festival, and it was sold to the States as well as to several other countries.*

When Donner retreated to his native Finland in the mid-sixties, he felt immediately more at ease with his medium, producing and directing a stream of witty, outrageous and self-mocking movies.

Much impressed by the New Wave and by the lightweight 16mm cameras becoming available, **Bo Widerberg** seized the initiative in early sixties Sweden, chronicling the plight of a single mother (*The Pram*) and an aspiring writer from the tenements of Malmö (*Raven's End*). Like Cassavetes, Widerberg strove to capture the taste and rub of the everyday. At this stage in his career, he was still very much an individualist and a romantic. Anders (Thommy Berggren), the neophyte novelist in *Raven's End*, reacts against his parents in an impoverished Malmö of the thirties. Anders does not want to be dragged down to the same level of humiliation as his parents, but by moving alone to Stockholm he opts for flight rather than fight, leaving behind an unborn child who will presumably encounter the same pattern of life as himself.

Raven's End depicts pre-war Sweden with a verisimilitude far removed from Bergman's world. One believes in the despondency that hangs over the community. A propaganda broadcast from Nazi Germany booms stridently over the radio as Anders walks home in the opening scene. A reference to 'the war in Spain' only prompts a neighbour to ask if the Christmas supply of oranges will be affected. Wintry games of soccer in the fields and visits to the amusement park break the monotony of working life. 'If you shout loud enough someone's bound to hear you, but they're too far away to understand what you're saying,' is Anders' term for his frustration.

Jerzy Skolimowski had enrolled at the Łódź school in 1960, and a year or so later collaborated with Polanski on the screenplay for *Knife in the Water*. In 1964, he made his first feature, *Identification Marks: None*, a quirky début by any measure. It's a film in the J. D. Salinger tradition, a question mark in every sentence, and Skolimowski gives his anti-hero the same mournful idiosyncrasies as does Olmi in *Il Posto*. The subjective camerawork may owe something to Godard, but the film is both too dour and too bitter to be French, while Skolimowski's own performance in the main role carefully avoids magniloquent gestures and makes no appeal to sentimentality. In *Walkover*, made the following year, Skolimowski develops the autobiographical element by playing the role of Andrzej, approaching his thirtieth birthday and eager to score a success as a boxer. Midway through the film, Andrzej pronounces his own ambivalent epitaph: 'At thirty a president's a kid, but at thirty a boxer's finished.'

The mid-sixties for British cinema were also a spell of extremes, in terms of both budget and subject matter. On the one hand there was *Lawrence of Arabia*, which still appears in many a director's all-time top ten and which marked the apogee of David Lean's career. Of course, it was produced by an expatriate American, Sam Spiegel, and of course Columbia's money cushioned its epic budget. But Robert Bolt, the screenwriter, was one of the most dazzling of British playwrights, and Peter O'Toole proved an authentic discovery in the title role. Where the film seemed moored in an earlier period was in its romantic sweep and its orthodox technique – however brilliant the cinematography by Freddie Young. The success of *Lawrence of Arabia*, however, demonstrated the pluralism of British cinema in the sixties.

On the other hand, there was the little miracle of *It Happened Here*, directed by Kevin Brownlow and Andrew Mollo in 1964 on a shoestring budget of £7,000. 'Easily the bravest and most original film made in Britain for the past five years,' I wrote in the *International Film Guide* in 1965. The originality of the idea – Britain supposedly occupied by the Nazis and then overrun by Fascist methods until the inevitable reprisals occur – was at once both monstrous, and exciting. The film follows a district nurse, Pauline, who is compelled by circumstances to enrol in an 'Immediate Action Organization', before being posted to a euthanasia centre, disguised as a harmless country hospital.

The most controversial chord struck by *It Happened Here* was that British people, for whom law and order have been a lodestone, were shown as espousing militarism with hardly a murmur of protest. Thus the tone of the film seemed resolutely anti-Fascist rather than anti-German. The entire film was *created* (no library footage – and yet what a stunning *tour de force* the newsreel is, worthy of *Citizen Kane*), using authentic uniforms, wartime buses and newsreaders. As a result, the location sequences carried immense conviction. Kevin Brownlow was just twenty-six years old when he made the film with his friend Mollo.

He went on to make a couple of further features and many television programmes, but since then his career has been devoted to championing the cause of the silent cinema, and his other claim to fame is the restoration of Abel Gance's *Napoléon*.

Another low-budget film, Anthony Simmons's *Four in the Morning*, launched the screen career of Judi Dench, offered a sombre, uncomfortable image of London's docklands, and deservedly won the International Confederation of Art House Theatres Award in 1965. At dawn, a nightclub singer is met by a new boyfriend, and they wander along the Thames, circling each other with emotional wariness – unwilling to fall in love and yet eager to sleep together. Simultaneously, a young mother (Judi Dench) is quarrelling with her husband (a superb portrait by Norman Rodway), who has blundered home with a drunken friend and woken the baby. The film is clipped together with realistic shots of a girl's corpse being recovered from the river and taken to the mortuary. The implications are clear: each relationship represents a further stage in the death of love, until suicide is the only solution.

The arrival of a new Labour administration in 1964 did not bring the radical improvements so eagerly anticipated by film-makers in Britain. The National Film Finance Corporation's budget remained small, and indeed crippled with interest payments. Even a paltry £5,000 grant to the National Film Theatre was refused by the government. Independent production was still not as prolific as in France, Italy, or the United States. The quality of British cinema tended to be obscured by the tremendous financial success of a few productions (some of them only nominally British). *Tom Jones*, *A Hard Day's Night* and *Goldfinger* all earned high profits around the world in 1964–5. At the time, such productions were dismissed by many critics as being too commercial; but they have stood the test of time better than many more pretentious films of the period, such as Losey's *The Damned* or Finney's *Charlie Bubbles*.

Long before John Lennon bid fair to become the Jean-Luc Godard of popular music, one of the deftest and most idiosyncratic directors of the period had transplanted the magic of the Fab Four to the big screen. The appeal of the two features Richard Lester made with the Beatles lay as much with the engaging personalities of the four Liverpudlians as with the songs they sang during the movie. *A Hard Day's Night* in particular was a goldmine of editing tricks, zany jokes and cultural references that still work when the film is shown on video or DVD today. This can be explained by Lester's background as a musician and a co-creator of the

Richard Lester

television comedy series, *The Goon Show*. But he found the way to his profession by a long and winding road.

LESTER: *As a child, I never saw films. We didn't have a car, and we lived in a very rural area outside Philadelphia. I was taken by my parents to see* Fantasia *when it came out. But really I saw nothing until I was in my third year at university in America – then I saw Keaton's films, Ben Turpin's films, a few of Chaplin's, and Alexander Mackendrick's pictures.*

I came to Britain in 1955, not because I particularly wanted to come here – in fact, I didn't come for a year. I left in early 1954 and wandered around Europe. But I ended up in England because I realized that I was speaking with the wit and ability of a five-year-old, because these were not my languages. Sooner or later, I wanted to bring myself up to my nine-year-old standard – and I have to work in my own language!

When I came over, I assumed all British films were Ealing comedies, and they weren't. I immediately started going to the National Film

Theatre, and saw absolutely everything. I was impressed by Resnais and Truffaut and Renoir, and I gradually built up a small base ...

The biggest blow that I felt in the early years was the British inter-vention in Suez in 1956, which to me was a monstrous conceit, of three nation-states behaving very badly. In fact, after Suez, we then decided to leave England and found ourselves among queues miles and miles round! Canada House and Australia House – you couldn't get within three blocks of those buildings for the queues. And so we emigrated to Canada, and then to Australia, and then thought, 'Enough of this nonsense.' So we came back within a year, with no money, and started again. But we were not alone. I think that way of thinking – getting rid of Anthony Eden and the memory of Suez – paved the way ...

Lester's *The Running Jumping & Standing Still Film* was made in 1958 and nominated for an Oscar in 1959.

LESTER: *It's very dangerous to be credited with originality. I'd argue that I wasn't doing anything that Buster Keaton hadn't done, or that Jacques Tati had not done in* Jour de Fête *and* M. Hulot's Holiday. *There's nothing new, but there is a re-adaptation of ideas, and we all just grab whatever it is that we can take from the others, and move it on a little bit. And then it gets stolen from us, and it moves on to someone else. It's just progress ...*

After documentaries and commercials, Lester made his first feature in 1961, *It's Trad, Dad.*

LESTER: *I've never been an assistant, I've never set foot on anyone else's sets, not even Joe Losey's, with whom I was close friends. I started at the top. I didn't know how people made films. So I took ten years of live television, and purely live television experience, on to a film stage. And my first feature film,* It's Trad, Dad, *had to have been made that way because we had two and a half weeks to shoot it. I had to use multiple cameras, and I was accustomed to doing it, and I had to work out of my head – I couldn't write down lists, or pre-plan anything, and I just had to wing it. And I did that for twenty-five films.*

Then came *A Hard Day's Night*, and the opportunity to see if the Beatles could be as appealing on screen as they were on disc.

LESTER: *In those two films, we didn't do an injustice to what the Beatles did. The screenplay for* A Hard Day's Night *was all down on paper, except that there were huge gaps – for example, where it would be written 'The boys escape, through a fire door, and play in a field', for the 'Can't Buy Me Love' sequence. Or in* Help!, *with 'Ticket to Ride' – 'The boys learn to ski'. So there I had to sort of ad-lib it with the boys.*

From the start with A Hard Day's Night, *we said we wanted a fictionalized documentary. Alun Owen, the screenwriter, and I went with the Beatles when they played Paris, stayed in the same rooms at the Hotel George V. And the film wrote itself. What we'd planned emotionally was that they were told what to do, and put upon, in low corridors, low rooms, low ceilings – they were hemmed in and oppressed by people telling them what to do. And at a certain point they break out, and say 'Sod this'. Then that leads to something else, and that in turn leads to a final concert. In essence, therefore, we had a very strict emotional spine where the film was going.*

On the sets of both films, the Beatles were very trusting. I think they were careful in two or three major decisions in their life, and left all the rest to George Martin, Brian Epstein and a few other people. We asked them to say things that we thought they would understand, put them in scenes where it was logical that they would have been before, and allowed them no long sentences – because if it all went wrong, I could say the line to them, and they could say it back. And that was pretty well planned in the script. Then, as we saw that they could indeed act, the rules of the game were relaxed. In fact, not only could they do it, they could do it with élan.

Lester was ideally placed to witness a new ebullience in the British scene that encompassed the local film industry, itself given fresh assistance by way of the EADY fund, a levy on cinema income that was used to support the production of indigenous British films.

LESTER: *Harold Wilson was the first person who produced the EADY Fund when he was at the British Board of Trade, and there was a relaxation in the way that films could be taxed and the way they could be set up. And that ran through Wilson – he was a film enthusiast. Then of course once you have the* Time *magazine cover, then you walk down Wardour Street and Paramount will offer you a three-picture deal! Woodfall was wonderful, and had the great engine of the Tom Jones profits, which they were then cross-collateralizing over eight or ten features.*

But amid all the exuberance, there was always a very healthy cynicism, thank God. I couldn't have had three years with John Lennon, seeing him on an almost day by day basis, and not felt that! When the Peace Corps started going out, I remember, we thought, 'They're all bloody spies, aren't they?'

Looking back at the early sixties, there was a sense that there was a US President who was awake, and that was fairly rare, if you looked at what had been going on since Roosevelt. The cult of the aggressively enthusiastic amateur took over. All the fifties music was polished and honed and orderly. Not for nothing were there a lot of 'close harmony' groups, where you have to get the notes right, and you have to rehearse a great deal to make sure that the balance is correct. Even the silliest musical songs, the Jerry Lieber and Mike Stoller songs done by the Platters, they worked on their act, there was none of the rawness – in the sense that John Lennon said to Stuart Sutcliffe, 'You'll be the bass player' and Stuart replied, 'I can't play a bass', to which John said, 'Doesn't matter. We need somebody. Here, learn it!' And within three weeks, they were playing in Hamburg. John Lennon was the epitome of a 'I'm damned well gonna do this' spirit. 'There's no point in telling me that I will never learn to play the guitar like Andrés Segovia. It doesn't matter. This is what I'm gonna do.'

A show like Beyond the Fringe *or the* Establishment Club *had a huge theatrical audience, but it was tiny in the context of the country as a whole. When we put John Lennon into prescription granny glasses, within three months every kid in Argentina was wearing those same glasses! For all Peter Cook's and Alan Bennett's skills, it would never have happened that way. Everything was happening at once – hairdressers, night-clubs . . . It was optimism, it was 'Let's do it, let's go for it.'*

By the time Lester had directed Lennon in the dark World War II satire *How I Won the War*, some were comparing his style to that of Godard. What, though, did Lester himself think of the French director?

LESTER: *In a way, his style was more deliberate, and he chose, I think intellectually, to produce a certain kind of shock in a certain way. Mine was instinctive – I didn't know what I was doing!*

On location for *Pierrot le fou* (1965), Anna Karina and Jean-Paul Belmondo place their trust in director Godard

During 1963 and 1964, the French New Wave continued its momentum, and Godard's *Alphaville* was a terrific notion – a sci-fi thriller featuring that icon of French *série noir*, Eddie Constantine, abetted by other cult actors such as Akim Tamiroff and Howard Vernon. However, it ground to a halt about midway through, with Godard, one felt, trying to stretch a sketch into a feature. But his masterpiece in the eyes of many of his fans proved to be *Pierrot le fou*, with Jean-Paul Belmondo devouring the title role, travelling south with Anna Karina to his inevitable demise in a Provence that dazzled with kaleidoscopic colours. ('There's a good deal of blood in *Pierrot le fou*,' commented one interviewer, to which Godard replied, 'Not blood, red.') Unveiled at the Venice Festival in 1965, the film is an audacious mating of Lionel White's psychological thriller, *Obsession*, with Rimbaud's poem, *Un Saison en enfer*. The protracted conversations between Belmondo and Karina in the car would influence several directors, not least, in due course, Abbas Kiarostami in *Ten* (2002).

In *Le bonheur* (1964), Agnès Varda again gambled on the wit and wisdom of her audience by justifying not only infidelity but also the

Jacques Demy and Agnès Varda together at a Cannes première in 1965

abandonment of family – two pillars of the social temple that few dare to challenge. A young carpenter, François (Jean-Claude Drouot), happy with his wife and young children, meets another woman and falls in love with her. Transparently honest, he tells his wife, who says little but then drowns herself during a picnic excursion to the Ile de France. No problem for the carpenter, who lives with his paramour. Together, they care for the children and go out for another picnic – in the autumn. Varda adopts no moral pose in *Le bonheur*. Instead, she emphasizes the tactile, sensual pleasures of life in the tradition of Renoir and the Impressionist painters. Life may be cruel, but its terrible beauty transcends the moral structures so carefully (and often hypocritically) erected by human society. The notion of sin does not belong to *Le bonheur*; in its place resides a wonderful clarity, a sumptuous palette of colours that may appear superficial but are none the less ravishing.

In *Les créatures*, released the following year, Varda continued to speculate with disarming candour. A novelist and his wife, who is dumb, live in a world of quiet understanding. The people they encounter gradually become the inspiration for a new book. At the same time, their love seems nurtured and even enriched by the absence of dialogue. Varda must have smiled when she read Henri Langlois' letter to her about *Les créatures*: 'Your film is as stupid as Jean Renoir, as bad as Rossellini, and as unpoetic as Méliès . . .'

Although he adored the American musical genre, Jacques Demy proved capable of reconciling the brash colours and snappy dialogue of Hollywood classics such as *Singin' in the Rain* and *On the Town* with the more restrained, often subtler approach of the French cinema. In *Les Parapluies de Cherbourg*, which won the Palme d'Or at Cannes in 1964, Demy again ponders the vagaries and transfigurations of time, referring to *Lola* at numerous moments, so that the film almost seems like a sequel to his maiden feature. The dialogue is sung throughout, from the most casual phrase to the most ardent expression of love or despair. Debussy had conceived *Pelléas et Mélisande* in this idiom, but in 1964 it came as an utter surprise to the cinema. Michel Legrand's music builds on five essential phrases, and links people, places and situations in a wholly original way. The central threnody is particularly successful at under-scoring the grief of first Geneviève (Catherine Deneuve) and then her lover, Guy (Nino Castelnuovo). 'Why is absence so hard to bear?' sings Geneviève. The answer may be that all Demy's heroines, even the fading Jackie (Jeanne Moreau) in *La Baie des Anges* (1963), offer their heart with a romantic intensity at odds with the modern world they inhabit.

Both in *Les Parapluies de Cherbourg* and his next film, *Les demoiselles de Rochefort*, Demy ranges through the spectrum, concentrating on subtle colours – indigo, saffron, olive, aquamarine. In every shot, the colours are matched imaginatively with the décor and even the locations (certain streets in Cherbourg were painted so as to achieve additional harmony).

Truffaut, if no longer so angry about life, continued to pursue new idioms. *La peau douce* (1964) thrived on a series of contradictions. When a sober literary lecturer, Pierre Lachenay (Jean Desailly), embarks on a precipitous affair with an air hostess (Françoise Dorléac, sister of Catherine Deneuve), he unleashes one minor apocalypse after another, culminating in his being gunned down in a restaurant by his vengeful wife. 'What interested me about *La peau douce*,' recalled Truffaut, 'was to show an anachronistic character. In reality I was thinking all the time, "It has to be a character from the nineteenth century and what is furthest from a nineteenth-century character? It's an air hostess, because she's on these Boeings." It's this opposition that pleased me. That's why when [Pierre Lachenay] talks about Balzac in the restaurant, he speaks in the present tense ... The other notion is that uttered by Duvivier in *La règle du jeu*, when he says, "It's possible to cross the Atlantic by plane, but not the Champs-Élysées at the pedestrian crossing."' *La peau douce* feeds on friction and *faux pas*: the nerve-wracking rush to the airport at the beginning, the tension between Lachenay and his wife, the delays that punctuate a lecture trip to Reims, the explosive temper of Nelly Bénédetti as the wife ...

The greatest exponent of *cinéma-vérité*, and a portal figure in the history of sixties cinema in his own right, was **Chris Marker**. This unobtrusive figure, who would supply magazines and friends alike with photographs of cats instead of himself, had served during World War II with the French resistance (and even parachuted into occupied territory with US forces). *Le joli mai* (1962) took the temperature of Parisian opinion at a critical moment in French history, with people reacting to the loss of Algeria and to new movements in art.

Marker could make searching studies of remote peoples (such as *Lettre de Sibérie* and *Dimanche à Pékin*), but he could also transcend the boundaries of documentary to arrive at a poetic form of cinema unequalled before or since. He was close friends with Alain Resnais, and the two innovators share not just a massive intelligence, but an instinctive flair for editing, for the *rubato* of a sequence, that embellishes even the most mundane of subjects. *Le mystère Koumiko*, made during Marker's trip to Tokyo for the 1964 Olympic Games, exemplifies his ability to use narration to enhance images of the everyday. As always with a Marker film, one is fed gobbets of arcane information, but these are sprinkled in the background of a human portrait that goes beyond the picturesque. The Japanese tour guide Koumiko, whether giggling or serene, represents a new generation unsullied by war or even its guilt.

In Italy, Rosi, Pasolini and Bertolucci all strengthened their position in the vanguard of Italy's film renaissance. Uniquely among major directors of the sixties, Pasolini expressed his ideas through the life of a primitive society – his Jerusalem is situated in a straggling Italian hill town in *The Gospel According to Saint Matthew*, just as Thebes in *Oedipus Rex* is re-created in the guise of a barbaric Moroccan fortress.

Like all milestones in sacred art, *The Gospel According to Saint Matthew* (1964) is both self-confident and full of humility. Enrique Irazoqui's Jesus projects purposefulness, deliberation and – finally – resignation. His career is set firmly in its historical context. The authorities regard him as a meddlesome agitator, all too well versed in the Law. This saviour, like the film as a whole, is free of the effete glamour and bogus solemnity attaching to most of Hollywood's New Testament spectaculars. Pasolini looks unflinchingly at the Agony in the Garden and the Journey to the Crucifixion; and at Pilate's mock trial, the camera peers over shoulders and between heads like a shocked witness. The high priests resemble Renaissance princes, shrewd and fleshy, with hats shaped like baskets as in Rembrandt's religious paintings. But a majority of the cast consists of simple, unadorned folk who gape and smile and somehow sniff the importance of this prophet's unequivocal demand for faith.

In *Oedipus Rex*, the 'Son of Fortune' moves in a doomed circle from birth to death, and only as a blind and haggard outcast does he at last retrieve the 'fields of Asphodel' – a meadow where his mother suckled him and where the plane trees still shiver enchantingly. Franco Citti's performance as Oedipus reminds one constantly of this cyclical progression. He wheels through the plains and over the scalding tracks, his eyes ranging anxiously in search of some relief from his destiny. The rocky expanse of this pre-classical, almost prehistoric wasteland gives a physical cast to the distress and desolation of Oedipus's soul. His roar of agony on finding that Jocasta has hanged herself is merely the climax to a film so bursting with animal vigour that it marks the *fortissimo* moment in Pasolini's career.

Bernardo Bertolucci, the youthful protégé of Pasolini who had assisted him on *Accattone*, now hit the ground running with his own directorial career. Before he was twenty-two years of age, Bertolucci had completed a startling first feature, *La commare secca* (1962). The dance-hall references that identify the killer in this complex Italian film noir would recur in several Bertolucci works.

BERTOLUCCI: *I was a film buff. I was full of La Cinémathèque Française in Paris, where I had been during my holidays. I was unhappy because the power of neo-realism was fading into* la commedia italiana, *which was very popular abroad. But what I liked in those days was the Nouvelle Vague. I felt much closer to the French. I saw* À bout de souffle *during the early summer of 1960 in Paris, and I had the feeling that something was starting from zero there, that all the films I had seen up to then constituted the cinema* <u>before</u> À bout de souffle.

Bernardo Bertolucci

By 1964, Bertolucci had made the first of a dazzlingly polemic series of films, *Before the Revolution*. Set in its director's birthplace, Parma, the film takes its title from the famous dictum of Talleyrand: 'Only those who lived before the revolution know how sweet life can be.' The reference seems, in retrospect, to have been ironic. 'Those who live before the revolution,' said Bertolucci, 'experience not so much the sweetness as the anguish of existence.' Fabrizio (Francesco Barilli), the fastidious young hero of *Before the Revolution*, makes a half-hearted attempt to shake off his patrician pedigree. He believes himself to be a Marxist and learns by slow, painful degrees that he is not. He dallies with ideology much as he flirts with his beguiling aunt Gina (Adriana Asti) from Milan, and his marriage to a local girl is as predictable as it is frustrating. Bertolucci regarded the film as more than just autobiographical. 'It was a way to exorcize my own fears. Because to be like that character is almost a destiny for all bourgeois young Europeans.'

BERTOLUCCI: Before the Revolution *was screened at the Critics'*
Week in Cannes in 1964, and after the projection there was a little
discussion with the audience. Who should come on the stage but
Jean-Luc Godard, who had seen the film and loved it. I had met him
previously, in London, when my first feature, The Grim Reaper, *was*
shown at the Film Festival there. I remember that Richard Roud
introduced me to Godard in the lobby of the hotel where all the
directors were staying, and I was so emotional that I almost fainted!

Shamelessly eclectic and supremely confident, Bertolucci could not
have survived without the examples of Visconti, Pasolini and Godard.
Bertolucci shows his talent in various virtuoso passages – the lament of
the aristocrat Puck (Cecrope Barilli) for the passing of privilege and
landed wealth, or the climactic scene between Gina and Fabrizio at a
performance of Verdi's *Macbeth* – and while the style is sometimes deriv-
ative (jump-cuts from Godard, 360° pans, irises, zooms, etc.) it remains
convincing because Bertolucci so obviously *believes* in the grandilo-
quence of his characters. The Italian public disdained the film, however,

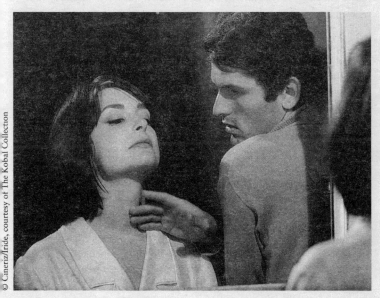

© Cineriz/Iride, courtesy of The Kobal Collection

Gina (Adriana Asti) and Fabrizio (Francesco Barilli) in Bertolucci's
Before the Revolution (1964)

and Bertolucci had to wait until 1968 before he could release another feature.

To some extent, all **Francesco Rosi**'s major films have been concerned with idols, good or bad – the heroic Salvatore Giuliano, the villainous Nottola and the matador Miguel (played by the famous Miguel Mateo Miguelin) in *The Moment of Truth* (1964). 'What interests me passionately,' said Rosi while shooting the film, 'is how a character behaves in relation to the collectivity of society. I'm not making a study of character but of society. To understand what a man is like in his private drama you must begin to understand him in his public life.' *The Moment of Truth* ends with Miguel's death in the arena. The king, like Giuliano, has fallen – but not, Rosi would seem to suggest, without reason.

ROSI: *On* The Moment of Truth *I wanted to bring the bullfighter to the public, so I used a real matador, because I did not like the idea of doubles and stuntmen in the action sequences. I chose a 300mm lens that was in service rarely at that time, apart from covering football matches. We succeeded in making the colour softer, more hazy and less startling. Pasqualino de Santis proved a master at handling that lens, because with the movements of the torero and the bulls, it's very difficult to control the focus and the framing.*

Our generation was impressed and dominated by the camera, because the camera was the means of expression. Nowadays, with digital cameras and very small cameras, it's all changed – young directors are much more casual in their attitude to the camera. At that time, the camera was a mystery, and had to be wielded with great skill. The choice of composition, or movement, was very important.

Phil Kaufman managed to make his first feature, *Goldstein*, outside of both Hollywood and New York during the same year – 1964 – that found Rosi in Spain on location for *The Moment of Truth*. *Goldstein* typified the laid-back quality of the sixties, with its disconnected observations of life in Chicago, punctuated with hilarious, zany antics.

KAUFMAN: *I had been reading a lot of Martin Buber, a Jewish, mystical philosopher, who did a number of powerful books – Norman Mailer wrote a great deal about him. So Goldstein was combining some of that mystical stuff with the everyday life of the streets and the world I was living in in Chicago. And there was a comedy group*

that became pretty well known in Chicago, called Second City.
Earlier, they had Mike Nichols and Elaine May. Nelson Algren tells a
story, as Nelson Algren, in Goldstein, *and so we shot that in 1963.*

When we had finished the film, the very first screening took place
in Chicago at the Coronet Theater on a Saturday morning, and who
should walk in but François Truffaut. He was in town visiting
Alexandra Stewart, who had a relationship with him and was shoot-
ing Mickey One *for Arthur Penn. Right in the middle of the screen-*
ing, Truffaut leaped to his feet and started applauding. Afterwards,
we had a party on the west side of the city, in Nelson Algren's house,
and I chatted with Truffaut. He didn't speak any English, but my
wife spoke a little French. We said how much we loved his first three
movies, and he exclaimed that they no longer interested him. I think
he was entering his Hitchcock phase . . .

We went to Cannes in 1964 and a few of the French critics like
Georges Sadoul and Robert Benayoun were in the audience.
Benayoun was a big champion of Goldstein. *Then Jean Renoir saw*
the picture in Los Angeles – I wasn't at that screening, but a friend
told me – and he declared that it was the best American film he'd seen
in twenty years. 'I want to show this film to René Clair,' he stated.

Goldstein *had a very limited release, because it had a comic abor-*
tion scene. That actually caused a little bit of commotion at Cannes.
A couple of nuns suddenly got up and started screaming. And then
some people got up and started screaming back at the nuns!

An early indication of the influence of European cinema on
Hollywood could be discerned in *Seven Days in May* (1964), John
Frankenheimer's intelligent thriller about a Pentagon plot to overthrow
the President and assume military control of the United States. An underlying issue of the film recalls Antonioni's concept that Sixties Man would
find it easier to communicate through technological means than through
a familiar emotional approach.

But as the sixties reached their midway point, a host of new directors
– disciples of the World According To Godard – were surging forward
with their breakthrough pictures.

6 Towards a Fresh Aesthetic

We were very interested in what cinema is, so our movies were kind of thinking about cinema itself. You know, there were many mutations, if you look back at cinema history: first it was silent, then it started to speak, then it started to think, in the sixties – about the nature of itself.
 Bernardo Bertolucci

The search for a new aesthetic around the midpoint of the sixties began with a vengeance in Eastern Europe. Political pressure obliged artists to find a language that could satisfy government apparatchiks while presenting intelligent audiences with a transparent critique of contemporary society.

VOLKER SCHLÖNDORFF: *The Czech films were very important. When we saw* Loves of a Blonde *at the Berlin Festival in 1966 ... Wow! I felt that the German movement was rather late by comparison with the Czechs and the French. But they all shared the same aesthetic, which was a revolt against the old-style 'quality' film-making of the Establishment. Not so much in terms of Left and Right – more in terms of one generation against another.*

MILOŠ FORMAN: *I was lucky because my films were considered comedies. It was easier for those who were on our side and yet had some power to defend films such as mine or Ivan Passer's. Evald Schorm, or Vera Chytilová, or Jan Němec – they had a more difficult life ...*

Forman's work still demonstrates, unobtrusively and with great charm, that comedy has been invented to delay the moment of despair, to offset the waste of emotion. *Loves of a Blonde* (1965) and *The Firemen's Ball* (1967) touch a universal chord because they care for their characters rather than exploiting them. 'All the most important and immediate conflicts in life,' he noted, 'are between different, well-intentioned people's conception of what the best is.' Set in provincial towns and communities where everyone knows everyone else, Forman's films appear to

Miloš Forman sports the Golden Sail of the 1964 Locarno Film Festival, awarded him for *Peter and Pavla*

embrace the principles of *cinéma-vérité*. Beneath their informal surface, however, they are carefully structured (Forman actually graduated from film school as a screenwriter rather than a director), and also free of the often cold, objective interview tactics of *cinéma-vérité*.

A key actor in Forman's early work was Vladimir Pucholt, whose antic mournfulness lights up both *Peter and Pavla* (1964) and *Loves of a Blonde*. He plays the archetypal youngster disconcerted by adult life, always being confounded by those more experienced than himself. When he goes to a dance (in *Peter and Pavla*), he practises his steps in a corner and earnestly drinks some liquor to give him courage. But by the time he returns to the floor, his girlfriend has been whisked away by a rival.

For Forman, life is a cycle; we begin and end at the mercy of a complex code of social behaviour. When we are in our prime, said the director during the sixties, 'we pursue our professions, go after money, after women, after position, and we mercilessly spin the wheel of society which carries both young and old in its whirl, whether they like it or not, because they cannot protect themselves against it – they have neither the sense nor the strength necessary'. That is why, in *The Firemen's Ball*, it is so wrenching when the weary but stiff-backed Brigade Commander opens his presentation box and sees that the gilt axe has been stolen. A brief scene like this, or the one in *Loves of a Blonde* when Andula simply abandons her composure and weeps against the bedroom door, surely refutes the charge that Forman is a shallow director.

In Poland, Jerzy Skolimowski spun engaging variations on Godard's style. *Barrier* (1966) and *Le départ* (1967) abandon the subjective, almost myopic vision of Skolimowski's apprentice work. The narration is objective, the tempo livelier, and the cutting becomes ever more hectic. *Barrier* champions a young student outsider, and dares to question the hallowed status of the generation of the Warsaw Uprising. Sombre, menacing scenes tip over into comedy at their last gasp. *Barrier* resembles a piece of avant-garde animation where one has time only to respond, Rorschach-like, to the welter of images and not to reason out their larger meaning. *Le départ*, shot in French, in and around Brussels, charts a young man's frustrated desire to participate in big-time motor racing, and Jean-Pierre Léaud brings his cheekiness and mordant humour to the main role. In 1967, Skolimowski's fifth feature in four years, *Hands Up!*, fell foul of the Polish authorities: it was banned for some months, then passed with a few cuts, and finally proscribed once more. Five doctors in their forties meet for a reunion and are trapped in a railway coach which, as Polish critic Boleslaw Michalek noted, has by a weird association of ideas become a replica of the wagons in which their older brothers and fathers were consigned to the Nazi gas chambers.

Godard was not the only influence at work in the Communist bloc. **Andrzej Wajda** would make one of the finest of all Eastern European films, *Everything for Sale* (1967), a year after Bergman's *Persona*. It would revive his career, and yet it was inspired by the director's acute sense of loss at the death of Zbigniew Cybulski, the iconic star of *Ashes and Diamonds*, who had died in a needless accident in Wroclaw a few months before shooting began. Cybulski had been dashing to catch a train and had fallen beneath its wheels. 'The death of Cybulski was a real story that I didn't want to tell directly,' recalls Wajda. 'It was a tragedy, but in a way Cybulski was looking for it.'

Like Bergman's masterly speculation on his medium, *Everything for Sale* – a rebarbative title that barely hints at the film's profundity – communicates the mercurial, ambivalent quality of film. An attempted suicide and the hero's train accident, for example, are unexpectedly revealed as staged scenes. The director himself takes pictures of his bleeding face after a minor car smash. Such moments demonstrate Wajda's moral distrust of the cinema's obligatory deception. Clearly the film developed into a tribute to Cybulski – 'I think I'll be crying at the end of this film,' conceded Wajda on location – but despite the banalities of show business, and the anguish that fills the dead man's colleagues, Wajda's style sings of hope, discovering a final release in the huge tele-photo close-ups of Daniel Olbrychski in pursuit of stallions in the snow. It is an exultant conclusion to a challenging, painfully intimate film.

> WAJDA: *We were able to use more real locations, to use direct sound, and to shoot outdoors a lot more thanks to the improvement in sound recording and film stock. Our style changed, until it was simi-lar to the Nouvelle Vague. Gradually we didn't use the studios so much for black-and-white. But we returned to the studios when colour came in.*

Throughout the late fifties and early sixties, vibes extended not just from film-maker to film-maker within a single country, but reached across national borders as well. The Hungarian **Miklós Jancsó** probably had scant access to Western films during the mid-fifties, but he began to forge a distinctive style that seemed in sympathy with Antonioni's. In Jancsó's cinema, the camera wheels and glides, and peers through doorways like a threatening *deus ex machina*. The human beings involved in Jancsó's stories of nineteenth-century perfidy and intimidation move with bowed heads through a hostile landscape. Men on horseback assume a particu-lar significance, rounding up their prey like collies in the sheep-pen. In many films, Jancsó uses the vast Hungarian Plain to suggest isolation, even agoraphobia. His soundtrack swarms with sibilant murmurs of wind and the occasional burst of gunfire.

The absence of verbal communication enabled Jancsó's films to breach the borders of Hungary and its language. Costumes speak vol-umes about the soldiers and fugitives who wear them. People often run naked through the landscape, preparing to enter some obscure infinity. Bareness is all. Although many of Jancsó's films concern crucial moments in Hungarian history, one does not need to know their context in order to appreciate the director's supremely rigorous art. The tech-nique is mesmeric. 'I work very fast,' said Jancsó in the late sixties. 'I usually shoot a film in fifteen, sixteen, or seventeen days . . . I shot *Sirocco* in eleven days. I used very long sequences. For instance, there are

Jancsó's *The Round-Up* (1965)

only about twelve sequences in *Sirocco*, so that some go on for ten or eleven minutes.' One learns to relish the self-denial of Jancsó's style, as one appreciates the poet who works in the sonnet form, or the composer who resorts to the tightly strung concision of a quartet.

The Round-Up, released in 1965, offered Jancsó a subject and a milieu in precise accord with his cinematic vision. A group of brigands is herded into a stone enclosure set in the Hungarian Plain. They are the remnants of the anti-Habsburg revolutionaries of 1848 who were led by Governor Lajos Kossuth. Now they must pay for Kossuth's bravery, and Jancsó watches their resolution crumble before a series of insidious questions and confrontations. The guards remain inscrutable; the film's groundswell of tension derives from their fiendish subtlety and also from the prisoners' fear of their own weakness. The sly camera movements encompass the topographical signs of distress – the spotless white buildings, designed to harbour beasts, not men; the black cloaks of the inquisitors; the unnerving absence of walls or fences (when one man tries to flee, he is, swiftly, scornfully, outflanked by guards on horseback). Someone, allegedly Godard, has said that Jancsó would be the ideal director to make a film about the Nazi concentration camps . . .

As the years passed, Jancsó's language grew more self-referential. He tried to develop characters of flesh and blood, but they were two-dimensional. With hindsight, one can see his films of the sixties as one man's way of analysing the ruthlessness and obduracy of old-style Communism. How ironic that, like so many directors in Central Europe (for example, István Gaál, András Kovács and Pál Sandor in Hungary), Jancsó's star diminished as artistic liberty became commonplace.

István Szabó contributed a discreet, contemplative film to the decade with *Father* (1966). This delicately woven pattern of memories, dreams and illusions illustrates how a young boy's image of his father undergoes a gradual change. Its warmth of observation, its flashes of humour and, above all, a sense of man's emotional vulnerability set Szabó apart from his Hungarian contemporaries.

Animation in Eastern Europe also criticized the totalitarian way of life. In Zagreb, Nedeljko Dragić made a wholly different animated paradigm on misguided oppression – *Tamer of Wild Horses* (1967), all flowing movement and twilight colours. From the same studio came Aleksandar Marks and Vladimir Jutriša's *The Fly* (1967), about a man haunted and chastized for his arrogance in stamping upon a winged insect. By 1969, Dragić's talent had reached a peak. His *Passing Days* is a masterpiece of black humour, a spare yet devastatingly eloquent study of the disasters that overtake the individual throughout his life. The animation in the best of the Zagreb cartoons achieved a kind of short-hand brilliance and concision. The studio's first muse, Dušan Vukotić, won the first Academy Award ever given for animation outside the United States, with *Ersatz* (1961). Plastic beach toys assume a wriggling, jerky life of their own, their angular shapes and primary colours intermingling to hilarious effect.

Of course, Eastern Europe had nourished quality animation since the end of World War II, but the Poles and the Yugoslavs of the sixties reacted sharply to the world in which they lived, and to the expanding medium of television, which offered a home for their short, waspish jokes. In Britain, animators such as Bob Godfrey, Richard Williams and George Dunning would build on the beachhead established by John Halas and Joy Bachelor, and churn out witty, imaginative commercials for the agencies that sprang up throughout Britain, Germany and France. Mainstream acceptance for the 'new look' in animation came in 1968 with *Yellow Submarine*, which grasped something of the surrealist brilliance of the Beatles' lyrics.

Volker Schlöndorff, having for so many formative years been immersed in the French New Wave, surfaced in his native West Germany in the mid-sixties and immediately made an impression with his adaptation of Robert Musil's rites-of-passage novel about German private schools, *Young Törless,* which effectively underlined the dangers of standing idly by in the face of Fascistic behaviour.

SCHLÖNDORFF: *During the sixties there was a huge loss of film audiences to television. In Germany, attendances fell from 700 million a year to 110 million; television was all the rage. And that is why subsidy laws were then brought in, to protect national film-making.*

In France, the traditional style of film-making was dead – the New Wave and the film critics had seen to that – and also the New Wave directors were dominating all the commissions who granted money. All my French friends urged me to go back to Germany and make German movies. 'There are enough French film-makers,' they said – and I must admit that there was quite a crowd!

As I knew very little of contemporary Germany (I'd lived in France from the age of fifteen until I was twenty-five), I thought that doing a literary adaptation, set in the past, was something I could do without committing a lot of mistakes. On the one hand, I carried that influence of the New Wave, in terms of camera and sound and non-professional actors. On the other hand, I was very much influenced by the German silent movies I had seen at the Cinémathèque, such as The Student of Prague, *the Stroheim movies, all those uniforms! So I thought I knew how to do* Young Törless. *Mathieu Carrière had appeared in a film that had been shot in his hometown of Lübeck – they had recruited some boys from the local school. My producer had also produced that film, and he told me, 'We have this fantastic boy' . . .*

In Munich I met up with Enno Patalas and Ulrich Gregor, who ran the magazine Filmkritik *and had come to Paris to do interviews with directors like Louis Malle. They put me in touch with Alexander Kluge, from whom I rented an apartment, and Werner Herzog, who was working in a basement on Leni Riefenstahl's Steenbeck editing table. Herzog had just made a short documentary, and he told me about a fabulous location in Austria that seemed exactly right for* Young Törless. *So* Filmkritik, *you could say, was the hub of film activity in Germany.*

I had the feeling at that moment in Munich that everything still remained to be done, which the French already for five or seven years had achieved. Indeed, Kluge started to prepare his first movie, and Herzog started to write a script called Signs of Life. *They were not so much under the influence of the French New Wave; they came from short films, and they were much more involved with German questions, like 'Daddy, what did you do in the war?' and the Nazi generation. I had been an assistant on numerous films in Paris, but these Germans of my generation were autodidacts without special training. Even their cameramen were not professionals. So they discovered the technique, and the way to use it, at the same time. Then there was Ulrich Schamoni, whose* Es *came out the same time as* Young Törless; *we shared the director's award here in Berlin in 1966.*

Schlöndorff did not share the passion for theoretical concepts that obsessed many of his contemporaries in Germany during the mid-sixties.

SCHLÖNDORFF: *All I wanted to be was a professional film-maker! That's why I always said, 'I'm a craftsman, I'm not interested in your auteur theory!' And that was a label that stuck to me for ever – just a craftsman – something I had created to distance myself from the theoretical side. I thought this was something one could just learn – and the fact is that I learned it in the New Wave, where we were all against the old craft. We didn't want to be amateurs, we just wanted to revolutionize the craft – a different way of storytelling, a different and more inventive way of using actors and also the technical resources. So we did not want to ignore professionalism, we wanted to improve it! The older generation said that Godard didn't know how to edit pictures, but that was all a big misunderstanding – Godard just edited his films in a different style, and today nearly every film is edited in the way that Godard cut* À bout de souffle. *Godard invented the craftsmanship of the future. He didn't light up the dark spots, but he left the bright spots bright and the dark spots dark, and went for contrast rather than levelling everything off.*

Already, while driving to the set of Young Törless, *we were always listening to Bob Dylan, the Stones and Jimi Hendrix. We felt somehow uneasy about making* Young Törless, *because it seemed so old-fashioned given what was going on in the world at that moment. So we were eagerly waiting for the next one, when we could be in sync with our time.*

But at the same time I sort of was paying my dues to the silent movie, and also to this Nazi thing, this idea that in this small world one is the witness and the other is the victim (the Jewish boy called Basini), and the idea that a group needed to have one as an outsider and that this would create the unity within the rest of the group against that one, and how he was then eliminated.

But it was not really the kind of movie that I would have gone to see as a spectator, you know – I would have rushed to the next Godard! But I thought that it was also a way of revolutionizing the technique, by going back to the black-and-white style of the silent days, and with non-professionals for the adults and boys alike.

Volker Schlöndorff and Anita Pallenberg on location for
A Degree of Murder (1966)

The sight of Rolling Stone Brian Jones and the band's most famous groupie, Anita Pallenberg, sunbathing beside the pool at the Majestic Hotel in Cannes in 1967 attracted large crowds in the days before security took over at the world's most glamorous festival. They were in Cannes for the screening of Schlöndorff's second film, *A Degree of Murder*, starring Pallenberg and with music composed by Jones.

147

SCHLÖNDORFF: *I already knew that I wanted to make* A Degree of Murder *after* Young Törless, *and that would be the real one, based on a true incident. In* A Degree of Murder *we deliberately tried to avoid making the colour photography beautiful in the old Technicolor way. Plus, Anita Pallenberg had a white-painted face, just some beauty cream on it. A lot of it was shot in the fall and in winter in the outdoors, in the woods and the rain. She was living with Brian Jones at the time, and so he did the music, a beautiful score with a lot of help from Keith Richard – who then later took Anita from him as well!*

Although the distinctive national atmosphere of European film-making dominated the sixties, some directors made a courageous leap into the chilly waters of another culture. British cinema certainly drew nourishment from the work of, for example, Michelangelo Antonioni and Roman Polanski.

Polanski, who had attracted a world-wide art-house following with *Knife in the Water* in 1962, came to Britain three years later at the behest of the Compton Group, which, under Tony Tenser and Michael Klinger, specialized in what the skin trade called 'daring' films. Polanski's contract called for two feature films to be made on location in the UK. *Repulsion* (1965) was the first and less successful of the two, because Polanski had not yet assimilated the niceties of the English language or the geographical significance of the London locations he used. Catherine Deneuve was imported to play a Belgian manicurist, Carol, whose sister treats her like a chattel and makes audible love to her boyfriend; and so Carol deteriorates into a schizophrenic delirium while alone in her South Kensington flat. Polanski's eye for the disquieting symbol and his flair for defining the sinister elements of physical objects are uncanny, and redolent of his work in Poland. But the mechanics of madness are illustrated too crudely. *Repulsion*, however, remains a gripping film. The use of wide-angle lenses and Deneuve's startling performance remain its most remarkable characteristics.

In *Cul-de-Sac*, gangsters take refuge in a castle on a lonely island off the coast of Northumberland. Polanski pries open their various personalities, ranging from the insensitive arrogance of the chief villain, Richard (Lionel Stander), to the effeminate, ineffectual behaviour of Albie (Jack MacGowran), his comrade in arms. The castle, like the boat

TOP *Repulsion* (1965): Roman Polanski filming with Catherine Deneuve

BOTTOM *Cul-de-Sac* (1965): Polanski directs Lionel Stander and Donald Pleasence

in *Knife in the Water*, becomes a trap in the surrounding sea. It is fowl-infested by day and owl-ridden by night, decaying in sync with its occupants, whom it releases only in the aftermath of violence. The film's bloody, fiery climax crowns its grotesqueness and gives it the durability of a nightmare.

Hercules Bellville, who worked on *Cul-de-Sac*, recalls how the long six-to-seven-minute scene on the beach, with Françoise Dorléac swimming and a plane flying past above her, was shot in a single take by Polanski. 'Normally, we'd have needed some three days to shoot a scene of that length,' recalls Bellville. 'So at a production meeting one night, when the matter was raised, Roman declared, "OK, I'll do it all in one take!" But during the next couple of days there were mutterings among the crew about the rehearsals that would be needed, and how the lights would have to be moved about, and so on. So Roman then announced that he would film the scene on a tripod – tilting, panning, but not moving the camera. And so we did the whole thing in a single take, with the plane flying through precisely on cue!'

Richard Lester's most spectacular success came with *The Knack*, which in 1965 won Britain its first Palme d'Or at Cannes for sixteen years. The plot is flimsy, and emblematic of Swinging London. Two young guys, Tolen (Ray Brooks) and Colin (Michael Crawford), live in a Victorian house in Shepherd's Bush, west London. Tolen is very adroit with girls, whereas Colin, a schoolteacher, is hopelessly shy and gauche. When a provincial girl (Rita Tushingham) crosses their path, she gives Colin an unexpected chance of turning the tables on his suave, arrogant companion. Lester saturates *The Knack* with his ebullient personality, so much so that it now seems unbelievable that the film derived from a stage play. The dialogue remains deadpan, but the London locations and the breezy editing transform the material into a ribald, rambunctious mêlée reminiscent of the Marx Brothers. The influence of Godard is felt in this film more than anywhere else in British cinema.

Three years later, in 1967, Joseph Losey reached a crest of achievement with one of the period's most subtle analyses of social behaviour. In *Accident*, Losey and his screenwriter Harold Pinter deploy the surroundings of Oxford University to convey a sense of pressure gathering beneath the pastoral calm. The film penetrates the reticent academic routine to find in its hero, Stephen (Dirk Bogarde), the frustration and pettiness that stem from the don's incipient middle-age and the arrival at the university of an attractive Austrian girl. Like *The Servant*, the film revolves around class etiquette. *Accident* strains to demonstrate that professors and aristocrats commit the same mistakes as their less clever and less privileged colleagues.

Michelangelo Antonioni continued to speculate in his films on the emotional and ethical dilemmas confronting youthful, well-heeled individuals. In *Blow-Up* (1966), shot in English and in south London, an aggressive young photographer of the David Bailey type, played by David Hemmings, finds himself contemplating a sinister mystery. As would Harry Caul in Coppola's *The Conversation* (1974), Thomas tries to exhume the figure in the carpet, the kernel of truth in the surrounding banality. Antonioni's moral revulsion in the face of affluence manifests itself in the reduction of the Hemmings character to a cipher, a phantom who loses touch with reality. 'All these people who amuse themselves at parties are smiling cynics,' the director commented at the time. 'Young people who are against order because they want a greater emotional happiness than in the past – who try to live a freer life than before and are therefore against everything, even against love.'

Although he himself spoke poor English, Antonioni located the pulse of contemporary British life while at the same time retaining his own distinctive and mysterious *Weltanschauung*. At the end of *Blow-Up*, Thomas withdraws to a safe distance, so that the clues of potential murder are buried once more in the mass of forms before him. He has learned that contemporary life is 'against interpretation'. The spontaneous reaction and the 'happening' are all that count – and all that *did* count for a generation growing up between 1960 and 1970. *Blow-Up* accommodates a dormant violence, but its symbolism is never crude – it is linked to the pattern of the film, a pattern of abstract suspense.

Despite the startling rigour of *Through a Glass Darkly* and *Winter Light*, **Ingmar Bergman** still smelled musty to many a mid-sixties intellectual. Few realized that he was an obsessive viewer of films, ancient and modern. When *Persona* appeared in 1966, it took Bergman once again to the head of the line, and showed that he had absorbed the best innovations of the New Wave. Just eighty-one minutes in length, *Persona*'s audacity of expression makes it the most visually exciting – and disturbing – of all Bergman's films. Alma, the nurse (Bibi Andersson), and Elisabet, her patient (Liv Ullmann), meet and commingle, like the Yin and the Yang, the id and the ego, Doctor Jekyll and Mr Hyde. Through a scintillating stream of sounds and images, Bergman explores in *Persona* the nuances of

Bibi Andersson, Liv Ullmann and a shyly smiling Bergman on location for
Persona (1966)

time and memory with a skill worthy of Resnais and (many years later)
Kieślowski. He takes risks he would never have dared to take pre-New
Wave: staccato editing, whole sequences repeated with subtle variations,
even a moment when the film itself burns up in the projector as though
unable to bear the anguish and guilt imprinted upon it.

Courtesy of The Kobal Collection

Political reality intervenes in *Persona* in a wordless scene where Elisabet recoils, aghast, from television images of a monk's immolation in South-east Asia. Two years later, in *Shame*, Bergman would manifest his confusion in the face of the Vietnam War, as troops overrun a village on the island of Fårö, and a violinist and his wife are humiliated and interrogated in a brutish wave of violence. Bo Widerberg had accused the *maestro* of being out of touch with current affairs, but in his 'island' films of the late sixties, Bergman proved sensitive to his political environment. Nor should one forget Bergman's roguish side. In *The Virgin Spring* and *The Silence*, he challenged the tolerance of his contemporary audience with explicit scenes of rape and sex – as well as the almost subliminal shot of an erect penis during the credits of *Persona*.

An impassioned analysis of *Persona* appeared in one of the decade's seminal works of criticism – Susan Sontag's *Against Interpretation*, published in 1966. Sontag fused her profound knowledge of Greek drama and literature with an awareness of sexual metaphors in the art of the sixties, and especially in films by Bergman, Antonioni, Godard and Truffaut. She even dipped her toes into film-making herself, travelling to Sweden to make two features for the ambitious firm of Sandrews. *Duet for Cannibals* starred Adriana Asti, the heroine of Bertolucci's *Prima della rivoluzione*, and Lars Ekborg, Harriet Andersson's ill-starred lover in Bergman's *Summer with Monika*. Released in 1969, this smug, hermetic film sank without trace, as did its successor, *Brother Carl* (1971).

The influence of Richard Lester and the Beatles, allied to the intellectual drollery of Jean-Luc Godard, surfaced in Jonas Cornell's *Hugs & Kisses* (1967), which cast a surrealistic and sardonic eye over the foibles of the Swedish bourgeoisie. Equally sardonic, yet lacking in humour, the directorial début of Mai Zetterling (*Loving Couples*, 1964) inaugurated this former ingénue's long campaign for women's rights. *Night Games* and *The Girls* anticipated much feminist debate, some years before *Ms* magazine and Germaine Greer gave it the seal of approval.

The decade's most impressive Scandinavian co-production was *Hunger*, directed by a Dane (Henning Carlsen), starring a Swede (Per Oscarsson), in an autobiographical study of a starving Norwegian writer (Knut Hamsun). When Oscarsson won the Best Actor award for this role at Cannes in 1966, the mood in the press room was one of exhilaration, because for the first time in many years it had been demonstrated that acting of such intensity could be found outside Bergman's domain. A documentarist by training, Carlsen already had a respect for plastic

Per Oscarsson in Henning Carlsen's *Hunger* (1966)

beauty. His best work was characterized habitually by a fervent devotion to individual human beings, whose faces loom out imploringly from the anonymous mass like those frantic sufferers in the woodcuts of another Scandinavian artist, Edvard Munch.

The following year, Cannes again crowned a Swedish performance – by Pia Degermark in Widerberg's *Elvira Madigan*. As in Varda's *Le bonheur*, the cloying, lush surface-texture of the film proved deceptive. Widerberg's screenplay ran to just twenty-five pages, and both Degermark and Thommy Berggren were encouraged to improvise before the camera. Elvira Madigan and her lover, Count Sixten, are hopelessly impractical – so impractical, said Widerberg, that they cannot survive. They retreat from the world into an idyllic pastoral bliss, and the film communicates their joy as it registers the dwindling of their funds. Elvira and Sixten feel afraid of their own identity; they are the individuals who feel persecuted by an amorphous society. *Elvira Madigan* derives strength from the remorselessness of its narrative. Sixten has abandoned a wife and children. He has betrayed his background and he cannot return. He must accept the consequences of his flight. Compromise is out of the question. He can see nothing beyond the blade of grass before his eyes. 'But without grass,' he tells a friend, 'the world would be nothing.'

In the space of twenty-six months – from March 1965 to May 1967 – Widerberg had managed to work through his *Sturm und Drang* spell. *Love 65* (1965) and *Thirty Times Your Money!* (1966) had allowed him to discuss his craft (and his pretensions), as well as satirizing a society that, with the advent of television, fell prey to the siren call of the ad agencies. The inchoate texture of both films had certainly not prepared one for the piercing shock of *Elvira Madigan*. The intensity and conviction of Widerberg's vision carries the film beyond romantic concoctions such as Lelouch's *Un homme et une femme*, which had won the Palme d'Or at Cannes in 1966. Like Bonnard's canvases, the film communicates an intimate bliss, a sensual affection for natural light and objects. Its textural grace is tinctured with Scandinavian premonitions of death – the wild strawberries signalling happiness, the spilled wine prefiguring the final loss of blood and vitality.

Jan Troell, the Swede whose limpid style flowed unmistakably from the sixties, insisted on handling the camera himself (and, in post-production, on cutting the film too). The only thing he could not do was write, and he was fortunate to find Bengt Forslund as producer and co-screenwriter. The peak of their collaboration came on a spring evening in 1973 in Los Angeles, when *The Emigrants*, directed by Troell and produced for Svensk Filmindustri by Forslund, was nominated as Best Picture alongside *The Godfather* and *Cabaret*.

Troell's two major films of the sixties, *Here Is Your Life* (1966) and *Eeny Meeny Miny Moe* (1968), boast a supple, fluent, soaring quality, as though the camera were mounted on the wings of a bird. Troell studies his actors in immense close-ups, and a few minutes later gazes down on them from high above the land and the water. *Here Is Your Life* charts an orphaned teenager's journey through northern Sweden in the early twentieth century, as he drifts from job to job and meets some weird and wonderful characters *en route*. *Eeny Meeny Miny Moe* deals with a teacher's woes in a Swedish state school. Again, Troell the operator accompanies his characters into the most intimate of situations, like a newsreel cameraman, but with much more subtlety. And this almost thirty years before Lars von Trier and his friends devised the Dogme 95 manifesto, restricting film-makers to the most unpolished and naturalistic of techniques. '*Eeny Meeny Miny Moe* is a pure Dogme film!' exclaimed Troell recently. 'There were five of us in the crew and most was shot on hand-held camera with only natural sound and natural light. It is laughable how they've managed to blow up this whole Dogme thing and even create a set of rules. Even having no rules is to have a rule. You can't use a tripod! Tripods save on sea-sickness pills for the audience.'

In the Netherlands, too, the new aesthetic had influenced even **Fons Rademakers**, a member of the older generation.

> RADEMAKERS: *For* The Spitting Image *(1963), I hired Raoul Coutard, who had photographed so many Nouvelle Vague films. This was because I heard that he could have just a row of flood-lights reflecting on to the set, and that was sufficient – and that he was very fast as a result. We had been used to waiting for the cameramen to finish setting up all the lights. But as soon as I had finished rehearsing with the actors, Coutard was always ready. Then, for* Dance of the Heron, *made in Dubrovnik, I used Sacha Vierny, who of course had been Resnais' cameraman.*

Other Dutch directors alert to new developments included George Sluizer, whose haunting short, *Clair Obscur* (1963), looks in retrospect like the harbinger of his much later masterpiece, *The Vanishing* (1988). None was more talented than Adriaan Ditvoorst, who made *Paranoia* (1967) from a claustrophobic story by W. F. Hermans before committing suicide in the prime of life. Frans Weisz seemed at the time the likeliest to last. His films, such as *The Gangster Girl* and the short *A Sunday on the Island of the Grande Jatte*, exuded an energy akin to Godard's. The influence of Truffaut could be glimpsed in the sensitive, lyrical films of Nikolai van der Heyde. The spirit of the American Underground inhabited the bizarre cinema of Frans Zwartjes. Paul Verhoeven, who caught the eye with short films such as *Feest* (1963), would become the most prosperous and famous of all Dutch directors in the United States, bringing his subversive, satiric eye to bear on American institutions as sacrosanct as the army (*Starship Troopers*), Las Vegas (*Showgirls*), and the police force (*RoboCop*).

At the Hyères Festival of Young Cinema of 1966, I met a diffident Belgian who was presenting his first feature, with the intriguing title of *The Man Who Had His Hair Cut Short*. **André Delvaux** had become a movie buff almost by sheer practice – he had served for several years as a piano accompanist for silent films at Jacques Ledoux's celebrated Cinémathèque in Brussels. Charming, and concealing his roguish mind behind an academic exterior, Delvaux instantly beguiled us with his bizarre, compelling portrait of a lawyer and teacher who may or may not have killed a female student, and when his film reached Britain it won various awards. *Un soir, un train* (1968) underlined Delvaux's gift for grasping the twilit world between fantasy and reality, as a stage producer comes to terms with his wife's mysterious disappearance from a train. The influence of Antonioni was palpable in Delvaux's films of the sixties.

John Cassavetes found his soul mates in Europe, and in 1964 he attended the ill-fated première of Carl Theodor Dreyer's last film, *Gertrud*, in Paris. Cassavetes stayed until the last disdainful Parisian had filed out of the cinema, when he was delighted to see Dreyer 'give the finger' to his perfidious audience. The incident strengthened his refusal to compromise, and *Faces* (1968) would justify its long gestation. A slice of Californian life on the turn, *Faces* blooms with brilliant close-ups, and its individual sequences (improvised, as ever) are more valuable than the whole.

In *Seconds* (1966), John Frankenheimer's most personal work of the decade, technology assumes the dominant role. Wealthy individuals, Faust-like, trade their souls to 'The Company' for a second chance at life in the physical form of whoever it is that they would most like to be. Thus does middle-aged New York businessman Arthur Hamilton (John Randolph) become Californian bachelor and abstract painter Tony Wilson (Rock Hudson). But this Faustian bargain is ultimately not at The Company's expense. James Wong Howe's fish-eye lens gives an unnerving menace to the opening and closing sequences of a film that, alas, represented Frankenheimer's last stand as an innovative director.

Compared to the abrupt transition from silence to sound in the late twenties, the displacement of black-and-white by colour during the sixties was less dramatic and yet almost as significant. *Seconds* may have revelled in its monochrome photography, but Columbia's *In Cold Blood* (1967) would be the last major studio picture released in monochrome for some years; while in the same season Arthur Penn's *Bonnie and Clyde* brought the spilling of blood and guts to the screen in colours that were romantic yet never garish. The decade, paradoxically, produced some of the most imaginative examples of black-and-white photography alongside stunning essays in colour. If Marcel Camus's *Black Orpheus* had closed the fifties with a riot of kaleidoscopic pigmentation, Agnès Varda's *Le bonheur*, Jacques Demy's *Les Parapluies de Cherbourg* and Fellini's *Juliet of the Spirits* used a palette of pastel hues in altogether

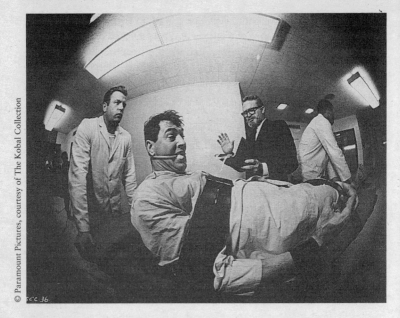

Arthur Hamilton/Tony Wilson (Rock Hudson) *en route* to his fate in John Frankenheimer's *Seconds* (1966)

innovative fashion. Kodak's Eastmancolor prevailed over Technicolor tripack stock.

Like Frankenheimer, Arthur Penn worked in as personal a vein as he could while striving to produce films for a wide audience. David Newman and Robert Benton's original screenplay for *Bonnie and Clyde* had been written with Truffaut in mind. Midway through 1964, Truffaut dithered over the project, finally suggesting that Godard should do it. 'Of all the scripts I have turned down in the last five years,' wrote Truffaut to Elinor Jones, the screenwriters' agent, '*Bonnie and Clyde* is by far the best.' When *Fahrenheit 451* was again postponed, Truffaut embraced the Benton and Newman screenplay once more, asking for a salary of $80,000 plus 10 per cent of the profits. But at last he opted for *Fahrenheit 451*, which was shot in 1966 in London; and it was Penn who happily inherited the Newman/Benton script.

Bonnie and Clyde broke new ground in the gangster film genre. It romanticized where the more familiar model was sleazy; it humoured where other gangster movies condemned; and it inspired Warren Beatty and Faye Dunaway to act with a heart-rending brilliance never found in the performances of Muni, Raft or Robinson. Penn noted that, during the Great Depression, 'Young people felt excluded from a society that seemed to be destroying itself economically.' Perhaps a similar feeling explains the enormous popularity of his film among the young generation of the late sixties. Stylistically, too, *Bonnie and Clyde* exerted a forceful influence on American cinema, with directors like Sam Peckinpah, William Friedkin and Francis Ford Coppola soon describing violence in similar detail and manner.

During the mid-sixties, **Monte Hellman** made some films for maverick producer Roger Corman that caught the attention of film buffs fortunate enough to see them. *The Shooting* and *Ride in the Whirlwind* were shot back to back in Utah in 1966. Both westerns featured Jack Nicholson, and the combined budget came in at around $150,000. Hellman (along with future directors such as Coppola, Bogdanovich and Scorsese) had served his apprenticeship in Corman's company, acting as second-unit director on *The Terror* in 1961, two years after making his début with *The Beast from Haunted Cave*. These early efforts helped mould a distinctive Hellman style that would reach its peak with the richly textured road movie, *Two-Lane Blacktop* (1971), in which the director followed a vogue of the time by casting pop stars James Taylor and Dennis Wilson.

Some British directors made their début on home soil before responding to the siren call of the Hollywood studios. **John Boorman** made an off-beat musical, *Catch Us If You Can*, in 1965, starring the Dave Clark Five. Then, while researching a television documentary on D. W. Griffith in Los Angeles, he found himself courted by MGM. As a result, he made the admirable *Point Blank*, a dark, ominous film that, along with *Bonnie and Clyde*, helped to rejuvenate the gangster movie genre. Boorman recalls that stylistic change arrived in Hollywood from Europe and not vice versa.

JOHN BOORMAN: *The studios were very studio-bound. Griffith had wanted to make films about the wind on the wheat, and he shot his films largely on location. But then, when sound came in and the camera became so cumbersome, they had to shoot everything in the studio. Gone With the Wind is a story about the love of the land, and you never see any land because it was all shot on the back lot!*

The blimped Mitchell, a big camera, was being used at that time. I used an un-blimped Arriflex to shoot a lot of scenes on Point Blank, *just for the mobility of it. But I remember one day when the heads of the studio were coming to visit the set, the cameraman, Phil Lathrop, said to me, 'If I were you, I'd use the Mitchell tomorrow rather than the Arriflex. Because if they come down here and see all that money disappearing into that tiny camera, they are going to get really nervous.' They always referred to the Arriflex as a 'combat camera', which of course it was – it used to be strapped to the underside of a German fighter plane! We all rebelled against that notion, and got out into the streets, which spun off very much from the French New Wave.*

Colour came in on a major scale during that time. Only the really expensive films were being made in colour in the early sixties. But once colour was in, all the great cameramen, like, say, Jack Cardiff, lit colour films in the way they had lit for black-and-white. To light black-and-white you need a lot of direct light and back light, to separate the various planes. And you rely on light to mould and shape the objects, otherwise they blend into each other and become murky. When you apply this to colour – particularly early colour, which was very heavily saturated – it becomes very garish.

One or two cameramen, like Geoffrey Unsworth, began to understand that you didn't need these shafts of light. If you went on a stage in Hollywood at that time, you would see a forest of flags and 'gobos' or shields slicing the light so that little shafts of light hit various objects. You won't see that at all today. Geoffrey in particular started using only soft reflected light that softened the colour so it wasn't so harsh. And you relied on colour to separate the objects – you no longer needed to define them by light. Geoffrey used fog filters and a lot of smoke, and this soft, impressionistic colour, which completely changed everything. Much, much simpler. And much easier to light. Saved a lot of time. Gave much more freedom to the directors and the actors. It had a very liberating effect. He brought that style of lighting to its peak in Cabaret, *with its very soft, diffused style.*

'Scope in a sense had a bad reputation. I embraced it and have used it for most of my films. Although it creates problems for subsequent media, such as television, it attracted me and others with its largeness – it was seen as an antidote to television. You would come

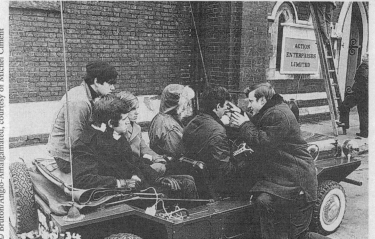

John Boorman directs the Dave Clark Five in *Catch Us If You Can* (1965) . . .

. . . and (third from right) keeps an eye on Lee Marvin in the making of *Point Blank* (1967)

into the cinema and you would see something on a huge scale that you couldn't see on television. I was attracted by its spatial possibilities – you could put all kinds of varying distances between the actors, to express how close or how far apart they were.

Many neophyte directors and technicians in the US felt that film-making could be practised in San Francisco more intimately and less expensively than in Hollywood or even New York. They sought to model their fledgeling, alternative facilities on establishments such as Denmark's Laterna Studios.

John Korty, whose quirky humour and independence of mind made him a figure to be admired during that heady period of the mid-sixties, moved to Stinson Beach (north of San Francisco) in 1963. The story of how he made three features without recourse to traditional sources of film finance illustrates the temper of the sixties – the feeling that anything is possible, and that, aesthetically, anything goes.

JOHN KORTY: *We made* The Crazy Quilt *in 1964–5, followed by* Funnyman – *and in those three years Stinson Beach, a town of 400 people, was more productive than Manhattan. When Francis Coppola and I finally met, he said that he and George Lucas had been hearing about what I'd been doing through the grapevine. When they came to see my studio in Stinson Beach, Francis looked around and said, 'God, if you can do it, we can do it.' And we had done it on the most elementary scale. We rented this old barn for $105 a month. We got two old art projectors. We built an editing room out of plywood. After we'd received some money and were doing* Funnyman, *we bought the first flat-bed editing table on the West Coast, the first Steenbeck. In those days, that was really radical.*

Almost every year there was a blossoming of cinema in a different place. One year it was Czechoslovakia, another year it was Poland, another year it was Japan. Everything was bouncing off of everyone else, in the best way. I'll never forget the first time I saw Billy Liar, *the first shot of Julie Christie, the scene when Tom Courtenay seems to be shooting everyone with a machine-gun, and then he's not – playing with reality. And the pacing. One of the films that I loved was* The Knack *by Richard Lester. I'd seen the Beatles films and they'd succeeded because it was the Beatles, but when* The Knack *came along, that pacing and looseness and lightness I loved.*

Far from the traditional sources of film finance, Korty found himself spending as much time raising money as writing scripts.

KORTY: *It was enormously time-consuming to raise the money. We chose a very inefficient way to do it, on the advice of a young lawyer who didn't know what he was doing. I wanted to start a limited partnership, because I heard that was the way to do it. But this guy, fresh out of law school, said no, you want to start a corporation. Corporations are really clean, and clear, and all that stuff. So I started this corporation, and it proved ten times more complicated than anything else, and got me into all kinds of problems with the corporations commissioner in Sacramento. We couldn't even take the money from the investors after they had invested it, until everything had been approved.*

So I had to raise a further $20–25,000 separately as loans against the money I had already raised from investors, promising the loan people, 'As soon as I get that money, I'll pay you back.' We didn't get the actual cash in our bank account, the cash we needed to make Crazy Quilt, *until two weeks before the answer print was ready. We spent $43,000 on* Crazy Quilt, *and that was 35mm, black-and-white, with an original music score by Peter Schickele, which was cheap but it was still an original score.*

Crazy Quilt *was shot partly in the city of San Francisco, partly in Stinson Beach, which is where I was living, and partly in other parts of Marin County.*

After a screening of one of Korty's features at the New York Film Festival, Amos Vogel, co-founder of the event, told him that he was 'America's only indigenous film-maker, the only film-maker who's identified with one particular region that's not Hollywood'.

KORTY: *It was necessity – even had I wanted to, I could not have afforded to make the film anywhere else.* Crazy Quilt *came from a story by a psychiatrist-cum-writer named Allen Wheelis, published in the May 1964 issue of* Commentary *magazine. I asked him why he wrote this comic fable, and he replied, 'Well, as a psychiatrist the bottom line seems to be that most people manufacture their own misery out of the difference between what they expected life was going to be and what it turns out to be.' So I created two characters, one a man who believes in nothing, who has no illusions, and another, a*

163

woman, who believes in everything and is always positive about life. So the film was a comic fable about these two extremes.

The film didn't make much money, but the reviews were very good and I had the three biggest talent agencies in Hollywood trying to sign me up. Rightly or wrongly, I declined. I wanted to do two or three films up here in the Bay Area, in my way, before I hooked up with anything in Hollywood. At the back of my mind I was thinking, if I'm successful enough up here, I will never hook up with Hollywood!

Having worked with actors a little bit, my first question was, 'Acting is really interesting and I admire people who can do it, but how do they know when they are not acting?' And that became the theme for Funnyman *in 1967. I took the idea to an improvisational theatre group called The Committee, which was operating in North Beach at that time. Peter Bonerz was a member of that group – not only very funny and talented, but you could communicate with Peter a lot more easily than with some members of The Committee, who were extremely talented but off in their own zone. So I cast Peter as the lead, and essentially as a co-writer. The script was never written down – it was a bunch of 3 x 5 cards on a poster board.*

Although some festivals in America liked Korty's maverick approach, his work attracted most sympathy outside his own country. *Funnyman* enjoyed a lengthy run at London's Academy Cinema, and *Riverrun* played for twenty-two weeks in Stockholm.

KORTY: Funnyman *taught me a lot, because as great as improvisation is as a technique, it tends to unravel the story. You try to keep the story going in a certain direction, and every actor in every scene tends to get ideas that start to unravel the story. I could not write a screenplay until I'd done both* Crazy Quilt *and* Funnyman. *By the time I reached my third film, I thought OK, I want to control this one, I don't want to depend on last-minute inspirations, from actors or anything else. So I wrote the screenplay for* Riverrun *quite quickly.*

Of my early films, Riverrun *was probably the least successful. I was very influenced by James Joyce, in a rather pretentious way. I was trying to get over the multi-layered sense of reality and symbolism that Joyce dealt with. I was trying to make a movie about life and death and birth and the natural world, and the civilized world, and everything all at once, a very ambitious undertaking. It was my first* *screenplay, and was shot up the coast from here at Point Reyes, right on the edge of Tomalis Bay. We had a crew of nine people (on Crazy Quilt there had been three maximum, and Funnyman five!), and it was made for $150,000 cash. We got that as an advance.*

It was about a young couple going to a farm and wanting to have their baby at home ... Dealing with the land, etc. I was very influenced by still photography, by Edward Weston and Ansel Adams and those people, their attention to detail in rocks and trees and so on. The director I felt closest to was Jan Troell, and I think that explains Riverrun's popularity in Sweden.

Dan Talbot's New Yorker Films decided to distribute *Funnyman* in the United States, alongside the work of Bertolucci, Bellocchio and Oshima. For Korty, to have earned his place among such newly exalted company was perhaps the ultimate accolade.

7 Commitment Comes in from the Cold

What has happened to the cinema is that it's gone and got itself a morality. It has finally mustered enough courage to say that it's only film. Nothing else. Godard says that a film is the truth twenty-four times a second. He can't bind himself further. And for Antonioni the choice of every camera angle is a question of ethics. You can no longer make two-hour films with a beginning, a middle and an end.

Keve in Bo Widerberg's *Love 65*

As the sixties reached their midway point, the notion of commitment was, like the cinema, changing in both form and content. Young people reacted against Third World poverty as much as they did against the earlier bogeyman of nuclear holocaust. America's involvement in Vietnam could no longer be dismissed as the legitimate protection of US interests. Apartheid in South Africa and the white regime in neighbouring Southern Rhodesia brought demonstrators on to the streets of Stockholm and London alike. In Greece, the armed forces were already wielding power behind the throne and would assume full power in April 1967. Poverty in British cities had provoked the so-called 'kitchen-sink' dramas of Arnold Wesker and Shelagh Delaney. Yet one man's cause could be another's burden. Marxist ideals lingered in many circles in France, Italy and Spain, while film-makers in Eastern Europe found it hazardous to express their feelings about the Communist regimes that controlled them.

There was another kind of commitment, too – to cinema. Behind the success of so many European films stood the enterprising distributors and exhibitors, who took personal financial risks to import films. One saw them at festivals like Cannes, Berlin, Venice and Oberhausen. They sought one's company because they relied on the critical reaction that could acclaim or condemn a picture. George Hoellering, of London's Academy Cinemas, Charles Cooper of Contemporary Films in Britain, Leo Dratfield of the same-named company in New York, William Becker and Saul Turell of Janus Films, Tom Brandon, Line Peillon of Studio

Ursulines and Yvonne Decaris from La Pagôde in Paris, Dick Vriesman from Amsterdam . . . None had the luxury of major studios to bankroll their gambling on talent, as a Miramax does today.

Promotional gimmicks were generous and imaginative. When Bo Widerberg's *Elvira Madigan* came to Cannes in the spring of 1967, Europa Film issued pastel-hued umbrellas to the entire press corps. Two years earlier, Hanns Eckelkamp of West Germany's Atlas Film spent an extravagant sum on offering gold scarab brooches to stars such as Monica Vitti and Jeanne Moreau on each day of the Cannes Festival, in honour of the closing night film, *Pharaoh* by Jerzy Kawalerowicz. (Not long afterwards, Atlas stumbled into an economic swamp, having over-reached its resources in financing art-house films at home and abroad.)

The metaphor and the parable became ever more frequent ingredients of mid-sixties cinema: the metaphor of the Neapolitan Camorra in Rosi's *Hands over the City* that had so infuriated the Italian establishment when the film appeared in 1963; the parable of Greek tragedy in Pasolini's *Oedipus Rex*; the metaphor of Dostoyevsky's 'double' in *Partner*, which would mark the return of Bernardo Bertolucci in 1968 after four years away from the commercial cinema.

Pasolini's work would become increasingly a blend of realism and parable, as manifest in *The Hawks and the Sparrows* (1966), *Oedipus Rex* (1967) and *Theorem* (1968). 'Instead of trying to reconcile the myth with modern psychology,' said Pasolini of *Oedipus Rex*, 'I took the Oedipus complex and projected it back into the myth.' His device of locating the birth and death of Oedipus in modern Italy makes the dramatic gulf between myth and reality even more striking.

While the harsh, ochreous summer dictates the mood of *Oedipus Rex*, the sad, autumnal tones of Giuseppe Ruzzolini's photography in *Theorem* build a climate of emotional misery. The visit of the Jehovan Stranger (Terence Stamp) arouses a violent mutation in a rich Milanese household. The mysterious power radiated by what Pasolini termed 'this apparition from beyond the earth' works deep within each personality, just as the Delphic prophecy stirs within Oedipus. All of them suffer the humiliation and shame of the Fall, the sense of paradise lost. For Pasolini, bourgeois man is unworthy of such a divine presence. 'These people are offered real love,' he noted, 'instead of mere material gifts,' and the experience strikes them as so new that, like Oedipus beneath the eye of the sun, they are dazzled, and retreat into madness (the daughter, Odetta), nymphomania (the mother, Lucia) and the uttermost reaches of

Theorem (1968): Terence Stamp as the stranger

art (the son, Pietro). The final shots of the father, Paolo, as he lurches naked through the desert and bellows out his anguish, constitute a message of despair from an artist terrified by the exclusive materialism of sixties man. The Canadian director Atom Egoyan has written: 'The film is shot with a plaintive simplicity which I find very moving. As the Terence Stamp character places the father's legs on his shoulders in an attempt to comfort him, as the maid tearfully lifts her skirt for the

strange intruder's pleasure, as the son urinates on his empty canvas
. . . so many moments of this film are overwhelmingly powerful for
me.'

While Rosi was fortunate enough to find Franco Cristaldi as an enterprising producer, other young Italian film-makers were obliged to work
outside the system. **Marco Bellocchio** was just twenty-six when he created a picture as revolutionary as any in the mid-sixties: *Fists in the
Pocket* (1965). No documentary about epilepsy could be quite as dis-
concerting as the fiction Bellocchio made. A blind widow lives in a villa
near Piacenza with her four children. Three of them are epileptics; only
Augusto is 'normal'. Sandro claims to have been free of fits for more
than a year; but in Lou Castel's defensive performance, he oscillates
between rational behaviour and snarling, convulsive outbursts. He
wants to relieve Augusto of responsibility by driving his mother and the
others over a precipice. But his resolution fails, and though he does murder the helpless woman and drowns his younger brother, he cannot act
against his sister, to whom he finds himself more and more attracted.

Anxious to earn recognition from 'normal' society, Castel's Sandro
spills over with unexploited energy, and the climactic fit which strikes
him as he mimes gleefully to a Verdi aria is, in its ironic way, both a con-
summation and a solution to his life. The two extremes in his emotional
make-up – agony and rapture – have fused. Bellocchio observes all this
with such intensity and sensitivity that the film throws off a kind of elec-
tric tension. Even the aggravated editing, with sequences jerking spas-
modically from one to another, is like the manifestation of epilepsy itself,
while a mood of isolation creeps up from the wintry Po Valley to pene-
trate the lives of Sandro and his family.

China Is Near, made two years later (and, incidentally, produced by
Cristaldi), also focuses on a family riven with strife and spiritual sickness.
Moreover, the film revealed Bellocchio's obsession with political militancy.
Mao's Cultural Revolution of 1966 had impressed many film-makers, and
the *Little Red Book* could be seen in many apartments and luxury villas
alike in Italy. Bellocchio turned his back on the commercial cinema, and
joined a co-operative movement for the production of propagandist short
films. At heart, however, he remained a prisoner of his own bourgeois,
conventionally religious background, and in the years to follow he wisely
opted to criticize society through the milieux he knew best.

While the Algerian War of Independence, from 1955 to 1962,
embroiled half a million French soldiers and brought anguished debate

The Battle of Algiers (1966): Gillo Pontecorvo directs Brahim Haggiag
(Ali La Pointe)

to every French household, the struggle did not produce films of such
power as the Vietnam War did in America. Many a great French director
had made subtle reference to Algeria, from Agnès Varda in *Cléo de 5 à 7*
to Chris Marker in *Le joli mai*. But it required an Italian vigour of voice
to create the definitive film on the issue – *The Battle of Algiers*, directed
by **Gillo Pontecorvo**. For most foreigners, and not merely the French, the
kasbah was nothing more than an exotic location in films of the thirties
like *Pépé le Moko* or *Algiers*. In Pontecorvo's influential masterpiece,
however, the mood of risk and tension in these tumbled alleys and pas-
sageways is every bit as authentic as Rosi's images of Sicily in *Salvatore
Giuliano*. Marcello Gatti's hand-held camerawork persuaded us that we
were watching a documentary, not a reconstruction, and the acting, in
particular by Jean Martin as the French colonel and by Brahim Haggiag
as the revolutionary Ali La Pointe, presented both sides of the conflict in
tones of unprejudiced, unvarnished plausibility. The fanatical efficiency
of the female bombers still shocks an audience at a time when suicide
attacks are a regular occurrence in the Middle East.

Born into a prosperous Pisan family in 1919, Pontecorvo was over-shadowed for many years by the celebrity, and then notoriety, of his elder brother Bruno, a scientist whose political commitment led him to spy for the Soviet Union. Gillo, feisty to his fingertips and reluctant to remain in the margins of a cinema dominated by the glossy names of Visconti, Fellini and Antonioni, had already shown his skills in *Kapò* (1960), which resurrected the shame and horror of the Nazi concentration camps.

PONTECORVO: *At that period in the sixties, political films did much better than today. There was a trend towards change throughout society as a whole. There was a necessity for change. It ripened throughout the decade until the explosion in '68. It was there in the heads of intellectuals.*

Franco Cristaldi, who produced Kapò, *immediately agreed to help. Personally, I have more affection for* Kapò *than for my other films – perhaps because it was my first real feature. I know there are more faults and weaknesses in it than by comparison with* The Battle of Algiers. *But emotionally, and even where the search for language is concerned,* Kapò *contains more. It only succeeded in two countries, Japan and France.*

I would have liked to have been a composer, but when I was very young there was an economic crisis in Italy and my parents didn't have a penny. I can whistle the music I dream up, but I need others to write it down for me, and so I did that for all my early documentaries. My most cherished award is for doing the music in The Battle of Algiers, *a prize handed out by the National Union of Film Critics in Italy!*

On Battle of Algiers, *we spent seven months in Paris before commencing the shoot, recording interviews with the commanders of the French parachute regiment. Then we went to Algiers and talked to people in the kasbah, because we wanted to get a whiff of reality, and also with the heads of the FLN. Before shooting a single line, we spent at least six months studying the situation. The Algerians put no obstacles in our way because they knew that I'd be making a more or less objective film about the subject. They were pleased that we would be discussing the revolution, and the inhabitants of the kasbah were happy that it would involve them, so they talked freely to us. We chose lenses that would give the impression of real-life happenings.*

We did hand-held camerawork whenever it seemed likely to produce better results.

Screenwriters contributed fundamentally to the power and density of Italian cinema of the sixties. Suso Cecchi d'Amico had worked on the scripts of some of the crucial achievements of neo-realism – *Bicycle Thieves*, *Miracle in Milan*, *Bellissima* – and then helped Antonioni to enunciate his subtle analyses of love in *La signora senza camelie* and *Le amiche*. Her credits include the greatest work of the fifties and sixties in Italian film – from *Senso* to *Rocco and His Brothers* to *Salvatore Giuliano* and *The Leopard*. Almost everyone turned to her, officially or unofficially, in the way that the Movie-Brat generation in America would turn to Robert Towne for advice on intractable scenes.

Franco Solinas, whose credits included Nicholas Ray's *Savage Innocents* and collaboration on *Salvatore Giuliano*, dealt trenchantly with controversial themes until his death in 1982. He could veer from one genre to another – from the spaghetti western, *A Bullet for the General*, to Costa-Gavras's *State of Siege*, and from Pontecorvo's extravagant *Burn!* to Losey's ice-cool *M. Klein*. No doubt Pontecorvo wanted him to impart to *The Battle of Algiers* the same compulsive narrative drive, the same incisive dialogue, that had marked *Salvatore Giuliano*.

PONTECORVO: *Franco Solinas had written two novels, and also worked as a journalist. He loved writing for the cinema, and was extremely committed. He even used to reproach me for being less committed than him!*

The press has written, wrongly, that the French government banned The Battle of Algiers *for four years. In fact, the French authorities, who were very sensitive on the Algerian issue, banned the film for three months. They sabotaged it, in effect, because although it was announced as playing at four big cinemas in Paris, the Fascist organization, OSS, let the exhibitors know that they would be bombed if they went ahead with the screenings. After four years of this, Louis Malle and a group of French directors who adored the film said we must fight for this film. I made an agreement with various youth organizations, and some thirty of them maintained a round-the-clock watch on three cinemas where the film was screened – discreetly, of course. Nothing happened, and the film was released throughout France. In fact, there was only one incident, when someone threw ink at the screen in Lyon.*

So *The Battle of Algiers* finally found its French audience, though it should be said that in the interim years, the events of 1968 and the death of General de Gaulle had changed the circumstances fundamentally – and psychologically – in France.

Czech cinema matched the French and the Italian stride for stride throughout the mid-sixties. The range of talent was extraordinary. Vera Chytilová explored women's issues with a sensitive if zany brilliance in films like *Daisies* and *Something Different*. Evald Schorm veered to the dark side of the spectrum with *Everyday Courage* and *Return of the Prodigal Son*. Jiří Menzel and Ivan Passer preferred the slow-burning tragicomedy, and Žbynek Brynych resurrected the terror and shame of the Nazi Occupation of Prague in ... *And the Fifth Rider Is Fear*. Add the names of Antonín Masa, Karel Kachyna and Voytech Jasný to their Slovak colleagues Juraj Jakubisko and Stefan Uher and one has a formidable line-up of directors.

Jan Němec's second great feature, *The Party and the Guests*, waited two years to be screened in public, and finally found a slot at the ill-fated Cannes Festival of 1968, while Czechoslovakia was basking in its brief Prague Spring. Němec suggests, in his now familiar staccato style, how easily people may be led, how easily they settle for the safe passage through life, and how the nonconformist is hunted down. The villainous 'Host' at this alfresco 'Party' bears a close resemblance to Communist leaders of the post-war era. Shot from start to finish in relentless close-ups, the film breathes an atmosphere of impotence and claustrophobia, cleverly suggesting the myopic stupidity that restrains all but one of the guests from leaving the ominous gathering. Harsh tones in the black-and-white cinematography lend menace to every stone and tree. The slow descent of dusk over the forest is a reminder of the Satanic control that the Host exerts over his guests.

The man whose ironic approach to the erotic and political caused most controversy, however, was **Vilgot Sjöman**. At first a teacher, novelist and then acolyte of Ingmar Bergman, this ostensibly shy, grave Swede began his feature-film career with a worthy if somewhat stilted study of frustrated romance – *The Mistress* (1962), starring two of Bergman's regular actors, Bibi Andersson and Max von Sydow. Thereafter, though, an innate obsession with taboos began to take hold of Sjöman. He directed a screen version of Lars Görling's *491*, about a group of juvenile delinquents and their clashes with the police and probation authorities.

Courtesy of The Kobal Collection

Vilgot Sjöman

Bestiality and homosexuality were not usually on the average Swede's film-going menu, but few could deny the documentary realism of Sjöman's approach – or the performance of an impudent, chubby young actress named Lena Nyman. *My Sister My Love*, made two years later, strengthened Sjöman's reputation as a foe of hypocrisy whether ancient or modern. The incest between siblings in *My Sister My Love* is set in the eighteenth-century reign of Gustaf III, but seems likely also to have been inspired by the Elizabethan playwright John Ford and his *'Tis Pity She's a Whore*.

But none of these films had the sledgehammer impact of *I Am Curious Yellow*, released in 1967 and followed the next season by *I Am Curious Blue*, a companion piece. A massive hit at the Swedish box-office, seen by 1.3 million people out of a population of just over 8 million, the *Yellow* version found itself banned in neighbouring Norway and Finland, and then seized by the US Customs. Freed after a protracted struggle in the law courts, *I Am Curious Yellow* became the most successful foreign film in US history, taking more than 20 million dollars, a figure not exceeded for almost thirty years.

SJÖMAN: *I had followed what was going on in European cinema. A Swedish film-maker goes to see films, and I had also been seeing some French films and wrote about them. I was past thirty before I walked out of my ivory tower, so it started with France, and then also with a year in the States in 1955–6. When I went to Paris to file some stories for* Dagens Nyheter, *I saw things that were quite new to me – for example, the work of Jean Rouch. The journalist in me was awakening, albeit rather late. I was middle-aged and trying to catch up when the music of the Rolling Stones and all the new clothes fashions exploded.*

The novelist in me was already quite developed at that time (my first book had appeared in 1948). The whole idea of French cinéma-vérité *was how you catch and relate how you deal with reality. I went with Ulla Isaksson and her family to Paris and ended up writing the last sequence of* The Mistress, *trying to get hold of Jean-Luc Godard, to get some material for my articles.*

Then someone said, 'There's a new film being shown this afternoon in a small screening room off the Champs-Elysées – I can get you tickets if you'd like to see it,' and it happened to be Hiroshima mon amour. *I was open to new kinds of ideas, and I loved the mixture of documentary and fiction in Resnais' film. Also, Godard continued to fascinate and stimulate me, with his extreme freedom in telling stories.*

The influence of Bergman was decisive, especially after the two men had spent several months together during the making of *Winter Light* in 1961 (Sjöman kept a diary about the shoot, which later appeared in book form).

SJÖMAN: *In my personal life, there were two things. One, Bergman told me how to write screenplays, and I was a good pupil in his master school. It ended up with* My Sister My Love, *and it happened to be a very personal, very emotional film. There's a scene in* My Sister My Love, *when Bibi Andersson and Jarl Kulle are getting married, and Per Oscarsson is with a fat woman and a rather nice young woman, and they are just in bed. That scene was added, there was no dialogue in it, everything is very well calculated, so it's an idea that came up during the Freudian psychoanalysis I was involved with at the time. I also wrote a play about two lesbian women, and I started that already in 1949! It opened in 1964. That shows my attraction to difficult themes, to taboo subjects.*

The second thing was the journalistic impulse within me. For 491,
I brought in real guys who knew the kind of juvenile crime life
depicted in the film. So I thought, 'Let's improvise a bit.' And we suc-
ceeded in doing one improvisation, one story that's not in the script,
but I felt so strongly . . . If you try to improvise within a written
screenplay, it's very difficult, it's a collision. So that was my first taste
of it, in the spring of 1963 when we made 491.

Then I did some improvisation in an episode of Svensk's portman-
teau production, Stimulantia *('The Negress in the Cupboard'). So I*
was tasting improvisation while I was completing my last year, as it
were, in the Bergman 'school'.

Ingmar read in a newspaper that I was going to improvise I Am
Curious *totally, and invited me to dinner. 'I would like very much', he*
said, 'to be with you when you do this.' He looked serious, so I said,
'Why?' And he replied, 'Because I don't believe in the method.' His
rationale was that if you invite actors to take part in creating the
film, they take things out of their own lives – they get a little bit
inhibited by that, and they are much freer if they have a good, won-
derfully written part, because then they can project themselves in
another way than they do in everyday life.

When Bergman eventually saw I Am Curious Yellow, *along with*
Liv Ullmann, he turned around to me afterwards and said how
impressed he was by the improvised nature of so much of the film –
and in Shame, *he improvised the brunch scene involving Liv and*
Max von Sydow. He had two cameras going, one on Max and one on
Liv, and he ended up using only the one on Liv's face.

During the late sixties, Sjöman gave the impression of being Sweden's
most committed film-maker. Looking back more than thirty years later,
however, he confesses that he actually suffered from a lack of conviction.

SJÖMAN: *During the Vietnam debate, I was so afraid of taking sides,*
and I relate that to my childhood. While we were improvising in the
beginning on I Am Curious, *I did push Lena Nyman into a demon-*
stration that was going on in the streets . . . So instead of tackling the
Vietnam War as a theme, I turned instead to the sentimental Spanish
Civil War. Later on, it was easy to take sides, because everything was
so clear, but in the beginning, I wondered what Stalin and the
Russians were doing in Vietnam, even if I knew what the Americans
were doing.

The only way in which I related the film to the fashion explosion of the sixties was my making Lena wear different glasses in every scene, so we got a huge box containing all sorts of pairs of glasses.

The working title of the film from the beginning was Yellow and Blue, *because it was meant to refer to Sweden.*

It became so difficult to improvise things, because you had to present your ideas in some form to the various funds that handed out government money via the Swedish Film Institute. So there were a lot of problems in the period 1963 to 1972, the first decade of the Institute's existence. But with I Am Curious, *I could go to Göran Lindgren at Sandrews and say, 'I want to improvise the whole film,' and after some discussion he allowed me total freedom, and he never interfered with the rushes or anything.*

The first part of I Am Curious Yellow *is comedy, which was a new development for me. I happened to have two actors who were very gifted and also real comedians. We started the first love scene in the apartment, and that's my idea. They shocked me by going right to the wall and started . . . well, not fondling, that's too nice a word. Then the idea of the mattress being drawn out, that's my idea.*

The publication of the books in the States proved to be a weapon for Barney Rosset at Grove Press in his fight against censorship, and when we saw each other twenty-five years later he admitted that only then was he seeing the film for the first time!

From a commercial point of view, I Am Curious *was such an exception, and I guess the movie people in Hollywood, who never made me any offer to work there, felt that the film's success was all due to the trial, and the sex, and the free publicity the trial had given me.*

We should not avoid saying that the reason for politics in I Am Curious *is because of the clash between the Social Democratic government and 491. That had provoked a storm in the media, and that in turn had provoked the religious groups. And it became a problem for the government headed by Tage Erlander. For the first time, I was in touch with political reality. I was forty! It's funny, because Kenne Fant, the head of SF, was in fact able to save 491 in its entirety except for a few seconds of dirty dialogue, and I'd been so hurt and humiliated by somebody interfering with my film.*

I wanted Lena to have three heroes in I Am Curious, *one Russian [Yevtushenko], one American [Martin Luther King] and one Swedish*

One of the moments that made an immediate *cause célèbre* of *I Am Curious Yellow* (1967)

> *[Olof Palme]. I met Martin Luther King a month or so before start-*
> *ing to shoot, and he was in Norway to receive the Nobel Peace Prize*
> *and came on to Stockholm, where I had a chance to interview him.*
> *In June 1966, I met Yevtushenko, when he was performing at the*
> *Club T, which was a very leftist organization.*

I Am Curious remains a conspicuous peak in the sixties landscape because it combined sex and politics with such provocative flair. Sjöman did not flinch from (indeed he relished) showing a girl nuzzling a man's penis as they lie together in the grass; nor did he swallow the complacent Swedish attitude towards social democracy. Lena Nyman charges around Sweden in a state of barely controlled fury, interviewing upright citizens on everything from non-violence to women's rights and the separation of church and state. Lena despises her bibulous father, who fought against Franco and then chickened out of the Spanish Civil War, and she soon starts jousting with her boyfriend, the pliable Börje. The sheer vigour of the film-making, as informal as Godard, as intimate as

Cassavetes, triumphs over the often childish narcissism of Sjöman himself as the ubiquitous 'Director' of the movie.

The most eloquent disciple of Godard in West Germany was **Alexander Kluge**, a brilliant thinker and a Professor at the Ulm Academy of Design. In the early sixties, he appeared at the Oberhausen Short Film Festival with documentaries like *Brutality in Stone*, a study of Hitler's architecture that he co-directed with Peter Schamoni. Politically astute, Kluge stood at the centre of the revolt by younger German film-makers against 'Bubis Kino' ('Papa's Cinema'), and helped draft the Oberhausen Manifesto that crystallized their dissatisfaction.

'The situation here is different from what it is in France and Italy,' Kluge told me when we eventually met during the Oberhausen festival in 1967. 'The German film has been more provincial and degenerate in the past twenty years than that of any other country. Despite Fascism in Italy and the Occupation in France, there is a distinct tradition dating from the twenties in the Italian and French film, whereas the normal growth of German cinema was interrupted from the time when Geheimrat Hugenberg, leader of the German Nationalist Party and later a minister under Hitler, purchased UFA; and Goebbels used the cinema almost like a state industry. It became virtually impossible to get into the industry – it was like a gigantic syndicate.'

In 1966, Kluge finally made his first feature, *Yesterday Girl*:

KLUGE: *I had to wait four years to get a grant from the 'Drehbuch Prämien Kommission' of the Federal Republic for the actual script, and in the fifth year I managed to shoot the film. I received 200,000 DM from the Drehbuch Kommission and 100,000 DM from the Kuratorium 'Junger deutscher Film'. The Kuratorium draws its income from the government – it's a sort of cultural grant – and if the film proves successful, I have to pay it back, with reasonable interest. I have already done so with* Yesterday Girl. *This money can now be given to another new director and his project. Foreign profits go to me and the Kuratorium, and therefore one can make more pictures.*

There is therefore a tendency for young directors to become also the producers of their films. This is good because one's given more responsibility. I don't believe in the 'free artisan' in cinema. I think it is necessary for a young director to consider the economic factors involved. Of course, one needs a good production assistant and

Alexandra Kluge as 'Anita G.' in her brother's *Yesterday Girl* (1966)

accounts administrator. Freedom requires more responsibility, and you only enjoy sufficient freedom if you also have economic control. The cinéma des auteurs *is not merely a question of new style and content – it may also be a different economic approach to the making of films.*

Aesthetically, *Yesterday Girl* owed much to Godard: indeed, the director's own sister, Alexandra Kluge, who plays the young heroine, could as well have strayed from a Godard picture. Her 'Anita G.' flees from East Germany and finds herself confronted by misunderstanding, hostility and emotional betrayal. She struggles to retain some individuality in the strait-laced bourgeois society of sixties West Germany. Anita G. is a creature of circumstance. She steals at random, and becomes pregnant by a government functionary, who promptly washes his hands of their affair. The men and women who enter her life talk with maddening irrelevance: the teacher who babbles of Max Weber's theory of popular sovereignty, and the civil servant who feeds her on Kafka and Verdi. *Yesterday Girl* castigates the contemporary, complacent world while at the same time dazzling with its innovative technique and its persuasive acting. There is one improvised scene – when a dog-training demonstration drifts into farce in the rain – that justifies Anita G's distrust of order, and that belongs unmistakably to the anti-heroics of Godard, Skolimowski, Pasolini and Bertolucci. Kluge would make one further fine film in the sixties (*Artistes at the Top of the Big Top – Disorientated*), but did not recover his momentum until the late seventies.

The Netherlands had long been considered the home of well-crafted documentaries: illustrious exponents of the genre included Joris Ivens and Bert Haanstra. When I was first invited to visit Holland in 1964, I was a guest of the Netherlands Information Service, and they would drive me to the homes of one documentarist after another. But that was not the whole picture. The mood of the sixties wafted infectiously across the tulip fields from France and Germany, and a fresh generation of film-makers emerged, many of them in tune with the 'Provo' protest movement that filled the streets of Amsterdam with demonstrations during the decade. Two fast friends, **Pim de la Parra** and **Wim Verstappen**, led the charge, churning out films with facility and nonchalance, many of them naïve to a fault; they showed, however, that feature films could be made inexpensively in Holland, in English, and could attract a large local audience. In 1967, Verstappen's *Joszef Katús* was invited to the Critics' Week at Cannes. 'He returned to Amsterdam to die,' says an off-screen narrator as Joszef Katús arrives in Holland on his birthday. Verstappen shows, in a pre-credits sequence, how his anti-hero will die, coughing blood in a fœtal crouch, left to expire in the shabby streets like Michel in *À bout de souffle*. Katús foolishly cheats an old acquaintance over a drugs deal, and treats the Provo movement with an ill-disguised scepticism. The Provos, long forgotten, were the true harbingers of the student protests of May 1968. During the mid-sixties they were publishing clandestine notes on how to make explosives. They even founded a quaint and alternative transport system by offering free bicycles, painted white, to the people of Amsterdam.

The spasmodic, off-the-cuff style of *Joszef Katús* reflected the anxieties and uncertainties of the period, when an upheaval in Dutch society seemed possible and idealism collided with tradition. Verstappen ignores all conventions. Sunlight spills repeatedly into the frame, often reducing the tonality to a milky grey. Pedestrians stare at the camera with embarrassing concern. The noise of aircraft drowns many an exterior conversation. The music of Aram Khachaturian threatens to shatter the primitive sound equipment. Yet, as so often in the sixties, the very crude-ness of the technique gives birth to a new dimension of realism. There is no doubt that the filming of *Joszef Katús* took place in Amsterdam in 1966; the Provo rallies were not staged. The film is wilfully coarse, but never artificial; banal, but never mendacious.

The man whose company I enjoyed most over dinners in Amsterdam in the sixties was **Fons Rademakers**. Eternally young, buoyant of spirit, and a superb observer of the human animal in darkness and light, Rademakers had studied acting and made many friends across Europe in the theatre world.

RADEMAKERS: *I had the privilege of working with Vittorio De Sica in Rome, with Jean Renoir in Paris (on* Eléna et les hommes) *and with Charles Crichton – on* Man in the Sky *in 1956 – in London. De Sica was a marvellous director of children, but his way of making people in the street act was not my cup of tea, and it always took a lot of time to set up.*

My maiden feature, Village on the River *(1958), started because there was a banker, who also loved theatre, called Van Hall, who later became mayor of Amsterdam. He knew me as an actor, and had read in an interview that I wanted to make a career as a film director. He said, 'If ever you do, I will finance you.' I said I wanted to go abroad first and see how some of the master directors worked – so he made that possible too (and I also got some help from the government). So in my mid-thirties, I was more than a year abroad, in Rome, Paris and London.*

When I came back with the idea for my first film, Van Hall lived up to his promise, but just before we began production he said, 'Don't you think you should have a supervisor of some kind, someone with experience who can help you on what is after all your first foray into the cinema?' So I said that I'd opt for either Jacques Becker (I loved Goupi mains rouges *and* Casque d'Or) *or Ingmar Bergman.*

I had seen two films by Bergman, Sawdust and Tinsel *and* Smiles of a Summer Night, *and both appealed to me immensely. Becker was very nice about the screenplay, but Bergman said that he was starting a film at that time and so could not help. I persisted and Hugo Claus, who wrote the screenplay, came with me to Malmö to meet Bergman at his offices in the Municipal Theatre. He was very nice and said, 'I know how to work this – I will gladly furnish you with a letter saying I will act as your supervisor. Then you tell me the date of shoot-*

ing, and two days before you start shooting I'll send a telegram saying I'm confined to hospital and cannot come to Holland!' It worked like a dream. We did the film, and when it was in the can I thought it would be a good idea to go to Stockholm and work with Oscar Rosander (Bergman's editor) and cut the film in Sweden.

The first people to see the film were Bergman and his actors, because they were making The Magician *at the time. He embraced me and said he loved it. But he took me aside later and pointed out that the scenes with the peasant who has been saying bad things about the doctor's wife needed to be cut, because the audience would end up disliking the doctor. When I protested, Ingmar said, 'Listen – kill your darlings!' He then showed me some scenes he had cut from* Smiles of a Summer Night *because they slowed up the narrative. So that convinced me and I cut out the scenes. Hugo Claus was furious, and when I tried to replace them after about six months, the negative for those shots had vanished.*

Rademakers turned to black-and-white 'Scope as a format well suited to his pictorial approach to cinema. Both *The Knife* (1961) and *The Spitting Image* (1963) tell their story with cool verve. Neither made any concessions to mainstream commercial cinema, and the intricate structure of *The Spitting Image*, as a man finds himself being shadowed by a 'double' during the wartime occupation of Holland, gives off a whiff of mystery much beloved of Rademakers.

Born, like Truffaut, Malle and Oshima, in the magic year of 1932, **Carlos Saura** attended film school in Madrid and in 1959 made *Los golfos*. The film tracks the rough and ready progress of a wannabe bullfighter, relying on improvisation in the Cassavetes idiom, and on undressed locations *à la* New Wave. Five years later, Saura wisely established a partnership with the young producer Elias Querejeta. Together, they would make more than a dozen films, many of them hostile to the Falangist government but most too subtle and too metaphorical to provoke an outright ban, and all representing Spain's Nuevo Cine. *La caza* (1965), like Skolimowski's *Hands Up!*, uses the device of a masculine reunion to unleash a dramatic and jagged-edged assault on the legacy of Fascism. Veterans from Franco's army gather for a rabbit-hunt in a valley that two decades earlier had resounded with the guns of the Civil War. As Rob Stone has noted, 'In his innovative use of high-contrast film

Violeta García in Saura's *La caza* (1965)

stock, Saura evokes the bleaching heat that keeps an overpowering sense of menace and tension simmering until the violent impulses of each man are ultimately directed against each other.'

Saura enjoyed experimenting with film form, searching out different ways of expressing his outrage at his country's regime. Whether it was freeze-frames, blunt cutting between shots or feverish camera movements, his style would become distinctive, some would say hermetic. A weakness for melodrama, as in *Peppermint Frappé* or *La madriguera*, prevented Saura from scaling the heights of the greatest European directors of the period. His commitment to the undermining of Franco's dead-handed regime, however, ensured him a place in Spanish cinema history.

Yugoslav cinema oscillated between the sinister and the profane, between partisan atrocities and jet-black comedy, underscored with an ethnic pride (one that endured into the nineties with Emir Kusturica's *Time of the Gypsies* and *Underground*). The pungent ironies of the Zagreb Studio's cartoons embodied much of the Yugoslav attitude to life in those days. Looking back, the more sombre directors – Živojin Pavlović, Puriša Djordjević, Matjaž Klopčić and Miloš Radivojević – failed to reach a wide public beyond the borders of Yugoslavia. Aleksandar Petrović won the Palme d'Or at Cannes with *I Even Met Happy Gypsies* (1967) and would attract support for future projects in West Germany, and Zvonimir Berković's allusive, richly modulated *Rondo* (1966) enjoyed a lengthy run at London's Academy Cinema.

But the most charismatic director at work in Yugoslavia during the mid-sixties was **Dušan Makavejev**. One met him constantly at festivals: he would talk in his husky voice until late in the night, his anarchic humour embodying the essence of a schizophrenic Yugoslavia:

MAKAVEJEV: *My maiden feature,* Man Is Not a Bird, *was chosen for the Critics' Week in Cannes in 1966. It all started when I was in school, in 1949, and we organized an excursion with our chemistry teacher to the copper mines in Bor, a backward region in the mountains near the border with Bulgaria (where* Man Is Not a Bird *would take place). So, as sixteen-year-olds, we went to see how it worked. We'd been told how Socialism was building for the future, but when we arrived in Bor we saw how people were living in wooden barracks and eating miserable food in their cafeterias. I remember we came to a special department where they processed the ore in furnaces, and it was horrible, with sulphur in the air, and you could scarcely breathe – it looked like Hell. Despite their protective dress, the men were sort of smouldering themselves. I remember having read that the most famous shock-worker of Yugoslavia, named Jovanović, worked in the Bor copper-processing factory. And there he was, right in front of me! Soon afterwards, I directed my chemistry class in a kind of dramatic presentation of that trip to Bor.*

I was supposed to make my first feature film about this theme in 1959, but then I made a short film entitled Parade, *which created such a splash that I could not work for another few years, and* Man Is Not a Bird *was postponed until 1964.*

I spent a month in Bor preparing Man Is Not a Bird, *and we talked to doctors and priests, policemen and football coaches and social services people, and we collected all the real stories they told us, and then I and my co-writer concocted the story, a kind of distillation of all we had seen and heard, maybe half as bad as the real thing, and we kept in mind the real location.*

Dušan Makavejev (standing left behind camera) directs *Switchboard Operator* (1967)

The title *Man Is Not a Bird* comes from a peasant saying implying that man should not dream too much. Makavejev's maiden feature revolves, like all his work, around various seemingly unrelated matters. A much praised 'heroic' factory worker is unfaithful to his wife, and an engineer visiting the provincial town of Bor falls for his landlord's daughter.

MAKAVEJEV: *One of the stories we heard in Bor while researching the film was about a teenage girl hairdresser who had been murdered in the salon where she worked; she had got involved with a lame, forty-two-year-old newspaper seller. She found someone else, he got jealous and killed her on the spot while she was in the salon. But I dropped that. One thing came out of my talks with the judge and those involved with the real case, however. The guy had been obliged to pay the girl's parents a huge amount of cash to 'compensate' for the fact that this fifteen-year-old minor had lost her virginity. Your films can never be as absurd as life itself is!*

We had a smart production manager, who knew we would have problems with the local police and the local Party organization, and he brought in some incredible cartoons. When asked what they were for, he said they were props for decorating the office in the film. He approached the local Party secretary and persuaded him to loan us a wonderful carpet from his office. So whenever anyone visited him during the thirty-odd days of the shoot, he would say proudly, 'My carpet is appearing in this film!' We weren't troubled by the studio executives, who had no wish to spend a day travelling over the mountains in the early snows of October, and spending the night in some badly heated hotel . . .

For Man Is Not a Bird, I had chosen a copper mine because officially we were supposed to be living in a working-class society, so I thought, let's see how they live! So when I decided to shoot in the factory in Bor, they could not say, don't go there, because it was very 'positive'. So I managed to produce a kind of political film that makes its own statement, nicely disguised within an amusing story and discreetly confrontational.

Critical acceptance for Man Is Not a Bird *was very good in Yugoslavia, and it had an excellent reception abroad. But it did not win the top awards of its year. It was invited to the Mar del Plata Festival in Argentina, so that was my first trip outside Europe. I met Vilgot Sjöman there, among others. Then it was screened at the*

*UNESCO Building in Paris. One year later, it was taken by
Mannheim, and then one year later by the Semaine de la Critique in
Cannes – the same year as Evald Schorm's* Courage for Everyday,
*which had made a major impact on me when I saw it in
Czechoslovakia.*

In early 1967, I attended the Belgrade Short Film Festival.
Makavejev suggested I come to the lab where he was editing his second
feature. We racked our brains for an English-language title. Trying to
blend what I saw as the film's oscillation between infatuation and
clinical detachment, I came up with *Love Dossier*. Makavejev loved it,
but although still referred to in some magazines and cinémathèque
programmes by this title, the film soon became better known as
Switchboard Operator.

MAKAVEJEV: Switchboard Operator *was good-natured, with nothing
to offend anybody politically. But there was one very strong moment
when the authorities set fire to the dead rats they have collected. The
battle between mankind and rats is not finished. We still don't know
who will run Earth in the future – people or rats. But in the background, in the middle of the shot, you see the building of the Central
Committee of the Communist Party of Yugoslavia!*

Switchboard Operator brims with ideas but not with didactic solutions.
It starts with a bland dissertation on sexual customs by a genuine professor of sexology, and then launches into an affair between a girl tele-
phonist and a middle-aged civil servant, a former revolutionary of the
pre-1948 period who is now only good for killing – of all things – rats.
As the couple live together in the first flush of pleasure, Makavejev flips
forward in time to the autopsy on the girl's body after it has been
retrieved from an old Roman well in Belgrade. Thus, as in *Four in the
Morning* (the Anthony Simmons film so admired by Makavejev), there
are overtones of death that endow the affair with extremes of severity
and exuberance.

In conversation, as in his films, Makavejev adores to digress – but with
such captivating conviction that one follows him down every byway.

MAKAVEJEV: *Rats are very vital and energetic animals. They are more
numerous than us, and outnumber man by three to one. Some scientists think that they are even more intelligent than man. During my
army service, I was serving in a psychological department in the*

central army hospital in Belgrade. This department was at the very, very end of the whole complex – across the street from the morgue. Next door was a kind of 'educational hygiene' building. I asked them what they did there, and they found some American military films that came as a leftover from the end of the war when Tito's army was being helped by the US forces. There were three half-hour films on rats and how they can enter any building and how you have to sink some steel walls into the ground, some metres deep, to prevent them getting through. There was one image that I shall never forget – a street in New York with a telephone wire from one building to another across the street – and there was a rat crossing the street on that high wire – and that was not staged, it was a real shot. They can eat steel, film stock, they can eat corpses from morgues. So this con-tributed to my image bank, if you like. And in Switchboard Operator *the rats were not a negative force, rather a vital one.*

I wrote a twenty-four-page outline. The beginnings of the story were coming through that outline, but the producers said, 'Mmm, can you write a little more?' I knew there was not much money avail-able, and so I tried to devise something that would cost even less than Man Is Not a Bird *– which was not very expensive anyway.*

I went to the central police station and I asked for the boss in charge of serious crimes, and I said, 'What is the problem in the city, what is the biggest type of crime, and what are you the most proud of?' And he replied, 'The Case of the Severed Head.' (Actually, this is the case I used later for WR Mysteries of the Organism.) *Then there was the body in the Roman well. They were fishing this boy out, and discovered a woman's body that had been there for three months. In the cold water, the bodies don't decompose. The police let our make-up woman study the photographs taken of the faces of these corpses after immersion in water. How do you reconstruct an identity from a refrigerated corpse? This particular woman came from another part of the city; she drowned when her husband pushed her. They finally tracked down the murderer, who was a seasonal construction worker, and he had in his overcoat two ticket stubs for the zoo (where the Roman well is located), even though he denied that his wife had been with him in the summer.*

I wanted my villain to be a puritan guy, very clean and neat, so I had him working in the sanitary department. Very poor, too, from the south, so he is not as urban as she is. He's a little shy, he's not very

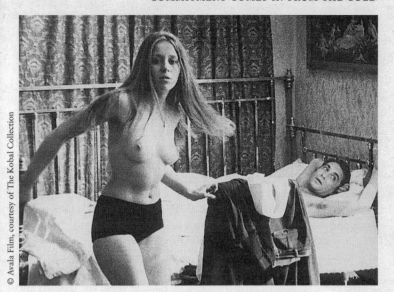

Switchboard Operator (1967): Eva Ras and Slobodan Aligrudić

*open – you know, he was in the army and had been an orphan. I
liked the idea of his meeting a warm woman, who would be the ini-
tiator in opening him up. But her reward for bringing him to life, for
loving him and making a home, is death.*

Part of the story for Switchboard Operator *was constructed in the
editing. But the shooting was based on these little written scenes, and
on the reconstruction of documents I learned about from the police.
So it was all kind of a staged documentary. I had my leading actress
[Eva Ras] in these scenes, but I had a real policeman sitting at the
typewriter, and a real doctor working on the corpse in the morgue.*

British commitment, so fierce in the dawn of the decade, grew flaccid.
There was Schlesinger's *Darling* (1965), based on an original, if meretri-
cious, screenplay by Frederic Raphael. Julie Christie's shallow, brittle
and eventually vulnerable young model turned actress represented the
most obnoxious aspect of Swinging London. *Darling* demonstrated that
beneath the veneer of liberation there lurked an empty void, in which
greed and selfishness ran rampant. Ironically, the cover girl of the title,

everybody's 'darling', finds herself at the end a prisoner in a gilded cage, the wife of an Italian prince, condemned to a life of infinite boredom.

Frederic Raphael also provided the satirical, waspish screenplay for *Nothing But the Best*, directed by an energetic young talent, Clive Donner. Unlike Joe Lampton in *Room at the Top*, Jimmy Brewster in *Nothing But the Best* is unashamed at the end of the film. He begins as a clerk in a Mayfair estate agent's office and by his unscrupulous forgery of patrician behaviour (mostly taught him by a *roué* who gets strangled for his pains) and a marriage to the boss's daughter, he hoists himself up to the board room. The merits of *Nothing But the Best* stem from Donner's astonishingly imaginative direction. He repeatedly realizes in visual terms the film's twin themes of acquisitiveness and the danger of accepting material things at face value. The jaunty pace of his direction, matching the mood of the hero and his time, confirmed Donner's experience in television, and also proved him capable of a much wider range of expression than his previous film – an adaptation of Pinter's *The Caretaker* – would suggest.

Another potentially corrosive vision of London town failed to live up to expectations. *The Pumpkin Eater*, scripted by Pinter from a novel by Penelope Mortimer, was directed in 1965 by Jack Clayton, who had attracted so much praise for *Room at the Top*. The American actress Anne Bancroft was imported to give bite to the role of an over-fecund woman and her marital problems. Clayton clearly responded to the experimental mood of the sixties, merging delirium and reality in a way that tipped its hat to Antonioni. The music by Georges Delerue also paid lip service to the French New Wave. But as in *Darling*, these bored and spoilt denizens of a moneyed generation were just not viewed with sufficient detachment.

British television did not dwell in such a comfortable cocoon. One Briton alone provides a bridge between the sixties and the first years of the new millennium, **Ken Loach**. He had cut his teeth on docu-dramas for British television, including the popular police series, *Z Cars*. In 1967 he began shooting *Poor Cow*, a gritty, unrelenting study of a young woman left with a baby after her violent husband is imprisoned. Carol White and Terence Stamp were encouraged by Loach to improvise their dialogue in the Cassavetes or *cinema-vérité* idiom, and the authentic locations added a remarkably authentic feeling to sound and image in *Poor Cow* – produced, incidentally, by Joseph Janni, who had backed the first films by John Schlesinger. Less inspired, less imaginative than

Lindsay Anderson, Loach still possesses an innate passion and a refusal to espouse the fashionable cause.

Many directors of the New Wave, among them Godard and Varda, were impressed by *cinéma-vérité* and incorporated elements of it in their work. This interrogatory form would reach its apogee in 1970, with Marcel Ophüls's prodigious exposé of wartime France, *Le chagrin et la pitié*.

Prolific himself as a documentarist, Chris Marker also contributed a lyrical commentary for Joris Ivens's ode to Chile, *À Valparaiso*, and co-directed an animation film with Walerian Borowczyk, *Les astronautes*. Towards the end of the decade, he devoted himself full-time to left-wing causes, mustering several talented directors to produce the angry *Loin du Viet-Nam*. Shot in 1967, this portmanteau film brought together the diverse gifts of Resnais, Godard, Varda, Demy, Lelouch, Joris Ivens, William Klein and Chris Marker. Joris Ivens shot a lot of footage on location in South-east Asia, and Marker was, by common consent, in charge of the final cut. Angry, didactic and poignant by turns, this quasi-documentary represented a gesture rather than a threat. Godard's contribution, for example, shows him behind a movie camera, telling us how he tried, and failed, to get permission to visit North Vietnam because he was not considered politically correct. Varda, whose episode was not used in the end, expressed reservations: 'Strong, intelligent personalities grouped together are obviously not the most suitable means of expressing an emotion, nor the most effective for signalling awareness.' *Loin du Viet-Nam* does, however, mark a step towards open militancy in French cinema, a kind of prelude to the attitudes of 1968.

Across the Atlantic, San Francisco was becoming the equivalent of Paris or Rome. The Bay Area sympathized with the political and ethical stance of students in France, and with the brightly-spangled music and fashions of London. Charles Burress recalled the roots of protest in an article for the *San Francisco Chronicle*: 'The Free Speech Movement [in Berkeley] began in September 1964 when the campus revoked permission for tables and advocacy for off-campus political movements, which had been centered at the campus' south gate at Bancroft and Telegraph Avenues. Former student Jack Weinberg was arrested for defying the ban by setting up a table for civil rights, and when he was placed into a squad car on Sproul Plaza, the car was surrounded for two days by thousands of students.'

Protests erupted, and Sproul Hall itself was occupied. Berkeley was forced to concede and, as Burress says, 'the image of resolute student protest' was branded into the public consciousness. There is little doubt that the Free Speech Movement led directly to a right-wing backlash and the election of Ronald Reagan as Governor of California. The heavies who harass Clint Eastwood's cop in Don Siegel's *Coogan's Bluff* (1968) were dropping acid and fulfilling Middle America's image of the 'love children' of San Francisco. For Phil Kaufman, the counter-culture seemed to efface the past and its artistic legacy.

KAUFMAN: *We came into a little coffee shop in Haight-Ashbury, and as I looked behind the counter, there was a letter from Anaïs Nin saying, 'Congratulations, there's a new movement afoot, all of this is wonderful.' And I said, 'Oh and you've got Anaïs Nin?' and the guy behind the counter said, 'Who's she, man?' And I realized that the culture was going to stop, and drugs and whatever else were going to wipe the slate clean. It was a tragedy in a way that we lost any memory of, for example, the thirties: we had to rebuild in a way. Everything came tumbling down in that kind of feel-good blur that suddenly entered, and came from England in a way. The past was forgotten.*

It wasn't until 1967 or so that you could say that films were tied into politics, when the Vietnam War reached its height. I lived in Haight-Ashbury before the summer of love. We came back out here, and I remember that they were going to round up the hippies. The Berkeley contingent purposely started throwing stones at the cops to get riots. But the Haight-Ashbury thing was not that; it was a sort of extension of the Allen Ginsberg beatnik thing – at least they thought it would be.

The true harbingers of May 1968 reside in the abundant output of Godard during 1966 and 1967. In the space of almost exactly a year, he released four features (plus his contribution to *Loin du Viet-Nam*). Beneath the complex frivolity of these films runs an ominous bass chord of pessimism about the future. *Made in USA*, for example, seeks to probe the murders of both President John F. Kennedy and Mehdi Ben Barka (the Moroccan radical politician who 'disappeared' while living in exile in Paris in October 1965) and presents the viewer with a seemingly chaotic collage of information and illustration. *Deux ou trois choses que je sais d'elle* discusses, in essay form, issues even closer to home – prostitution and urban development. Godard's view, commented Richard Roud, 'is that under the pretence of reforming and modernizing social structures in France, the Gaullist regime is only trying to regularize, to standardize the natural tendencies of capitalism'. *La Chinoise*, which appeared in late August 1967, offers an eerie foretaste of the events of the following year, even down to the dialogue, which uncannily enunciates the entrenched attitudes of both the old-style French Communist Party and the Maoist tendency among the student ranks. Although restricted to the form of a series of conversations, *La Chinoise* gave vent to a harshness that had not been discernible in Godard before.

Finally, in December 1967, *Weekend* emerged. Replete with images of rape, death and cannibalism on the crowded roads of France, it concluded with the line: 'The end of the story. The end of cinema.' Mireille Darc, until then a sex symbol in much lesser films, plays the bourgeoise who's converted to the Maoist cause. A traffic jam serves as an admirable metaphor for the fatal indigestion afflicting consumer society. In a brilliant travelling shot, almost a reel in length, Raoul Coutard's camera gazes dispassionately at men playing cards beside the road, a cart-horse deep in its own mire, lorries filled with animals for some zoo, overturned cars and even one vehicle facing the wrong way, rammed up against a petrol tanker. Off-screen proclamations mingle with the din of crashing dustbins, in characteristic Godardian dialectic. *Weekend* pulls no punches, anticipating the outrageous work of Marco Ferreri (*La grande bouffe*) and recognizing the imminent conflict that would engulf France – indeed Europe – the following year.

8 1968 and All That . . .

Violence and revolution are the only pure acts.
    Mick (Malcolm McDowell) in *If . . .* (1968)

The year 1968 began on an auspicious note in Czechoslovakia, with Alexander Dubček replacing Antonín Novotný as first secretary of the Communist Party on 5 January. This would lead to the so-called 'Prague Spring', with political prisoners released, reputations rehabilitated and much greater freedom for the press. But only twenty-five days later, in Hué and around Saigon, the North Vietnamese and Viet Cong launched the ferocious Tet Offensive. The journalist I. F. Stone could be heard declaring to a massed outdoor audience in Washington that American imperialism was the true enemy, and in private most Americans conceded that the war was effectively lost. Phil and Daniel Berrigan, Jesuit priests in Maryland, burned piles of draft records in public. Campus rioting began in earnest.

Although Miloš Forman's comedies had been popular in Czechoslovakia, and even more acclaimed on foreign soil, the director himself still found his path obstructed at every turn.

FORMAN: The Firemen's Ball *had a very dramatic career. I finished the film in late 1967. The Communist apparatus functioned similarly to Hollywood: it took for ever to get a project approved, but once the project was approved, nobody dared to meddle with it – to look at the dailies, or try to figure out how the film will be. Then you delivered the final film. Usually it was immediately screened for a censorship commission, and normally the next day you heard whether or not the film was accepted – they might love the film, or they might press you to make some changes, or whatever.*

But The Firemen's Ball *was screened, and for several days I did not hear anything. Then I was told that it so confused the censors that*

*they asked the cultural department of the Communist Party to see it
and say what they felt. Then I was told that it was screened for the
Politburo members. I was not there of course, but I was told by
someone who was that the Secretary-General of the Party, and the
President of the Republic, Antonín Novotný, 'climbed the walls' . . .*

*Later, I learned that they assumed the whole film to be a satire on
the Politburo, with the firemen's committee a parody of the top eche-
lons of the Party. There were lines there that incensed them. For
example, after the thefts from the tombola, the fire chief is asked if
he wouldn't return stolen goods, and he says angrily, 'Never, never –
because the reputation of our brigade is much more important than
any honesty, pighead!' That was the nail in the coffin. But . . . still
nothing happened yet, because the film was a co-production with
Carlo Ponti. He had paid $65,000, and if they did not give him the
film, they would have to pay back the dollars – which of course had
long disappeared in a Communist country! Ponti arrived in Prague
and I thought, 'This will save me and shield me from further attacks.'
But Ponti saw the film, didn't say a word, left, and asked for his
money back because he hated the film as much as the Party did! I
received an official letter from the studio stating that I would be
accused in court of sabotaging the Socialist economy – because they
had to repay $65,000. That was not funny, because in those days sab-
otaging the economy carried a prison sentence of ten years.*

The Firemen's Ball *reached Cannes in May 1968 because the selection occurred at exactly the time of change in power in Prague, from
Novotný to Dubček. Fortunately, Jan Němec smuggled the print out,
so it could reach Cannes. I was able to take the film to Paris, where
Truffaut and Claude Berri put up the money to buy out Ponti.*

VOLKER SCHLÖNDORFF: *In December 1967 I went to Prague, and
stayed until August 1968 – a week before the Russian tanks rolled in
– making my adaptation of the Kleist novel,* Michael Kohlhaas. *So I
spent those months in Slovakia, and early in the morning, when we
were driving to the location, and then at night on the way home, we
would listen to the French long-wave news broadcast about what
was going on in Paris and we couldn't believe our ears!*

*Generally, the students were not all that interested in our movies
and we more or less loathed the students! We thought they were
stupid and couldn't react spontaneously to films. Which is funny,*

because when May 1968 happened, we had the sensation, 'But we've done this already in the cinema five or six years ago.' Now finally the rest of society was catching up, and all of a sudden it became a general condition.

KRZYSZTOF ZANUSSI: *In 1968 there was a spirit of protest in the air, but the target was different in different countries. I remember at that time in Poland that we felt that French students were striking to oust their professors, while we were on strike to defend our professors, to protect them. So the aim was different. We were with our professors, against the populist wave of reaction in our society that kept crying 'Enough with education, we are fed up with culture!' – something which comes back nowadays as a kind of echo. The Party was trying through populism to regain some popularity, so it turned against culture and anyone who made life difficult.*

We heard some revolutionary tunes, and there was a lot of Marxist rhetoric. We all admired Charles de Gaulle, and we thought what a terrible thing it was that the élite was against him, and we all wanted him to emerge victorious. But at the same time there was some satisfaction that there was a voice apart from that of the establishment. So we had split feelings.

At Cannes in 1968 we had a marvellous film by Witold Leszczyński, The Life of Matthew, *with its wonderful baroque music, and this film has never enjoyed a world career – which it would have done had the festival come to a proper conclusion . . .*

Although, to the outside world, Daniel Cohn-Bendit's occupation of Nanterre University with a mass of students on 22 March may have been the bullet that launched the 'events of May '68', it was the expulsion of Henri Langlois from his post as head of the Cinémathèque Française on 9 February that had stunned the Paris intelligentsia. André Malraux, de Gaulle's Minister of Culture, had himself taken the decision. Dubbed 'the dragon who guards our treasures' by Jean Cocteau, Langlois appeared pig-headed to the authorities, yet in the eyes of directors, critics and film buffs alike, he was a much beloved figure. Pierre Barbin, who replaced him, may have done a decent job as head of the Tours and Annecy Film Festivals, but he stood no chance against the will of the film community – even if Langlois did indeed treat the preservation and classification of films with an idiosyncratic laxity.

Huge demonstrations came out in favour of Langlois, with personalities like Catherine Deneuve, Jean-Paul Belmondo, Simone Signoret, Alain Resnais, Jean-Luc Godard and François Truffaut standing in the chill spring winds outside the Palais de Chaillot where the Cinémathèque had one of its screening rooms (the other being in the rue d'Ulm). Gilbert Adair evokes the mood of the demonstrations in his novel, *The Holy Innocents*, describing 'actor Jean-Pierre Léaud, who, like a wilder-eyed and more demonic Jesus, was declaiming in a hoarse voice the text of a muddily photocopied tract that was simultaneously being distributed among the demonstrators below'. With the police in rampant form, many demonstrators suffered injuries, among them Truffaut, Godard and Bertrand Tavernier.

> BERTOLUCCI: *The whole '68 protest movement, including Berkeley, including Chicago and Columbia University – everything started in February when Langlois was fired, and for the first time the police attacked a group of peaceful demonstrators who just wanted 'le père Langlois' back at La Cinémathèque Française. And this attack, this violence was the trigger – so cinema was involved from the beginning.*

In Bertolucci's adaptation of *The Holy Innocents* (entitled *The Dreamers* and released in 2003), the director notes that 'There is a moment in the beginning of the film where Jean-Pierre Léaud and Jean-Pierre Kalfon are reading this little tract, this very manifesto that they were reading at the time in '68.'

By 21 April, the government had lost the battle, and Langlois returned in triumph to his lair in the rue d'Ulm. On 2 May, the Cinémathèque reopened its doors, and the following afternoon – 'Red Friday' – the first of the 'May '68' battles took place between students and police in the Quartier Latin, following a swoop on militants inside the university buildings. On 10 and 11 May, the violence accelerated. Cars were burned, police in riot gear stormed the barricades. Officially, 367 people were injured and 460 arrested on 10 May alone.

By early 1968, French cinema had lost its unquestioned leadership of European cinema. But the Cannes Film Festival, quintessentially French, continued to play a dominant role. Everyone went to Cannes – and still does. But during the sixties it had not yet become a frenzied marketplace. I remember a typical 'press lunch', held at nearby Mandelieu, with Orson Welles holding court on a rough-hewn bench as Truffaut and others sought his company.

The Festival President, Robert Favre Le Bret, was an avuncular individual, gracious and obstinate by turns. Although the ex-editor of *Cinémonde*, Maurice Bessy, was the 'Délégué Général' – in other words, the chief selector of films – behind the scenes, the influence of Favre Le Bret remained imposing. The consummate cultural functionary, Favre Le Bret would cling to the presidency of the Cannes Festival until 1984.

On 13 May, students occupied the Sorbonne and the unions declared a general strike throughout France. The same day, at the demand of a majority of those critics present, the Cannes Festival stopped for twenty-four hours. In the morning, students from Cannes and Nice gathered in front of the Palais des Festivals. In the afternoon, some festival participants went to a protest in Nice while others remained to demonstrate in Cannes itself. At the Free University in Berlin, meanwhile, students were marching into the offices of the rector, declaring him to be redundant. The belligerent Daniel Cohn-Bendit, leader of the protests at Nanterre University, debated the protest movements in France and Germany with other students and journalists. (Thirty years later, Cohn-Bendit would become a member of the European Parliament, representing the Greens.) On 17 May, in the Paris School of Film Technique, thousands of demonstrators from various sectors of the film world had massed to show their solidarity with the striking workers and students. They demanded that the Cannes festival be brought to a halt.

Everything was to be decided on 18 May. At 10.30 a.m., in the Salle Jean Cocteau, the '*p'tite salle*' so beloved of Cannes regulars and the home of the Critics' Week, a meeting took place of the Committee for the Defence of the Cinémathèque. Jean-Luc Godard and François Truffaut, in the name of the Etats Généraux du Cinéma which had met the previous evening in Paris, put to the vote a motion demanding 'all directors, producers, distributors, actors, journalists, and members of the jury here in Cannes, to oppose – in collaboration with their colleagues abroad, and by appropriate means – the continuation of the festival in order to show solidarity with the workers and students currently on strike'.

The main figures on the stage in the Salle Jean Cocteau included Truffaut, Godard, Lelouch, Dominique Delouche, Polanski, Malle and Henri Alekan (representing the technicians). Miloš Forman announced that he was withdrawing *The Firemen's Ball* from competition, while Lelouch said he was cancelling the screenings of two films he was involved with – Michel Cournot's *Les Gauloises bleues* [in competition] and *Treize jours en France*, the documentary on the Grenoble Winter

Olympics slated for the closing night. When the theatre grew full to over-flowing, it was announced that everyone should move to the Grande Salle. There, Truffaut asserted that 'It is inconceivable that people should be seeing films down here when there's blood being spilt in Paris.' Godard, ever the sourpuss, retorted to one critic who dared to ask him something about his own film-making: 'I'm talking to you about soli-darity, and you talk about tracking shots. You're a bastard!'

Gradually, other films were withdrawn by their directors from the competition: Richard Lester's *Petulia*, Jan Němec's *The Party and the Guests*, Carlos Saura's *Peppermint Frappé*, and Salvatore Samperi's *Grazie, zia*. Louis Malle sided with the demonstrators without a moment's hesitation, and called for a meeting of the jury behind closed doors. Robert Favre Le Bret put up a fight, arguing in the Grande Salle that France had no greater rights at the festival than other countries, and urged that the foreign films in the official selection be screened. Following a show of hands in favour of screening, the cinema lights went down and the first shots of *Peppermint Frappé* appeared on screen. Saura could be distinguished, almost in tears, pleading for the screening not to take place. Godard shouted: 'This film is being shown against the will of its director. Films belong to those who make them . . .' Scuffles ensued, with someone wresting the mike from Godard, and Truffaut was surrounded by various people. After a couple of minutes, the chaos seemed to have been quelled. But the demonstrators – including Geraldine Chaplin, star of *Peppermint Frappé*, and Saura's partner – grabbed the curtains and pulled them across the screen to block out the image. Eventually, Carlos Saura and his producer prevailed, and the pro-jection came to a halt.

Early the following morning, Favre Le Bret threw in the towel, declar-ing above the din of an impromptu press conference that, in view of the current events, 'the jury says that it can no longer carry out its functions'. And he closed the competition. Four jury members had already resigned in support of the protesters: Monica Vitti, Louis Malle, Roman Polanski and Terence Young (ironically, they were the only professionals on the jury). Seventeen films in the competition would not unspool at Cannes that year.

Penelope Houston, editor of the British quarterly *Sight and Sound*, recalled later: 'The saddest figures in this boisterous political carnival were the doormen of the Palais, stern disciplinarians who could spot a gate-crasher across a cinema foyer. They watched in shock, in one case actually in tears, as the invaders barged through the doors marked "Jury", put their feet on the seats and ate sandwiches in the stalls. These were the people whose world really turned upside-down.'

FORMAN: *That day in May 1968 in Cannes was the most absurd day for me, because here I am at the festival with the film-makers who I not only admired but respected. And suddenly I see these same film-makers trying to put up a flag which all the young intellectuals in Communist countries were trying to tear down! My French at that time was very poor, and there were a lot of speeches, and yelling and shouting, and I didn't understand 90 per cent of it. So finally I raised my hand and said, 'Listen, I don't understand a word you are saying, I don't know if I agree with what you are saying, but because I admire and respect you very much, I am joining you.' So* The Firemen's Ball *was not screened.*

RICHARD LESTER: *The funny thing is that I wasn't in Cannes when* The Knack *won the Palme d'Or in 1965, because I was shooting* Help! *I had been a great fan of Cannes, because it represented all the best of the people whose work I had begun to admire – Truffaut and Resnais, and Fellini and Bergman. So naturally to me it was much more important than an Oscar – and remains so, to this day.*

Lester, clad in a kaftan, was one of those directors prevailed upon to withdraw his film from competition, and watched as the police began to engage with the more aggressive protesters in what was rapidly becoming a chaotic situation around the Palais.

LESTER: *I had been invited by a chap I did not really know, the director Conrad Rooks* (Chappaqua), *to stay on his enormous yacht. We moored just off Cannes, and he had Baccarat crystal glasses lined up everywhere, and we were sitting down, and there was a piano on board the yacht, and we could suddenly see this screaming baton charge, the first one that happened, along the Croisette. I turned to him and said, 'Conrad, do you think we could get the piano player to play some revolutionary songs? I'd like to feel a part of this!' As we sipped our champagne!*

I think it was Louis Malle who approached me about withdrawing my film. A tall, beautiful press officer, Louisette Fargette, was acting as the go-between. I was alone, there was nobody from Warner Brothers. Finally, I was told – and it was probably not correct – that everyone was withdrawing their films. I said, 'Quite apart from the politics of this, I don't want to be in a competition where all the players have gone home. I will come out with you because I think that to carry on under these circumstances would be a nonsense.' Only afterwards did I listen to Roman Polanski, who said the equivalent of 'I'm not having any of this. I escaped from Fascism, and I disagree with this kind of ordering people around, and you can go screw yourselves.' Certainly my withdrawing Petulia *didn't do me any favours when I tried to get finance and, as you know, I did not work for five years. But partially that was my own fault, because I didn't want to.*

I was due to start shooting The Bed Sitting Room *on the following Monday, and we got out of Cannes on the Thursday. We found a car and then took a train and reached Genoa.*

ALAIN RESNAIS: *I was in Paris, then travelling down to Cannes on the train for the official screening of* Je t'aime je t'aime *when I heard the news about the demonstrations in Cannes in support of the French workers and students. So I admit I was very torn and upset, and I was not happy to show a film in Cannes in that atmosphere. I much preferred to stay in Paris. Truffaut reported from Cannes that we had to stop the plans for the screening, which made me happy in a selfish way because* Je t'aime je t'aime *did not correspond to people's tastes at the time, which leaned more towards the action and thriller genre. In my film, the provocation lay within my main character, who does not want to do anything, has no ambition. So halfway down to the Riviera, in Lyon, I decided to return to Paris. Just as well, because Cannes must have been rather stifling in those circumstances compared to Paris.*

'Is this a revolution?' asked one excitable British distributor, as festival veterans sat around at the various bars still open for business. George Hoellering, Hungarian-born proprietor of London's Academy Cinemas, answered crushingly and accurately: 'This is *not* a revolution. I have *been* in revolutions.'

With the festival effectively dismembered, the exodus from Cannes began. Rumours had reached absurd proportions. One French colleague assured me that bands of peasants had cut off the road to Nice and were brandishing scythes at any foreigner who dared to flee to Italy. Banks had closed. So, too, had the airport, to all intents and purposes. No trains were running. One checked one's wallet nervously every few hours. Maximilian Schell, among others, was rushing round the lobby of the Carlton Hotel, asking if anyone could lend him – perhaps even sell him – a car.

In company with a Swiss journalist, Felix Bucher, and a British critic, John Gillett, I cadged a lift in the ancient Chevrolet of an exhibitor from Lucerne. We set off in the late afternoon, fortunately with a reasonable supply of petrol in the tank. Our Swiss host regaled himself with swigs from a large jar of *marc* which he kept lodged adroitly between his legs as he drove. He chose the old 'Route Napoléon', to avoid roadblocks. As darkness closed in, we were on some escarpment not far from Grenoble when a loud crack could be heard above the noise of the engine. A rear tyre had burst. The only light available was a pocket torch used by Gillett for taking notes during screenings. Somehow the wheel was changed, and we trundled down into Grenoble. Sharing double-bedded rooms with the utmost fastidiousness, we survived to reach the Swiss border the following day.

On 29 May, just ten days after the closure of the Cannes festival, with ten million workers on strike and even *lycée* students occupying their school premises, President de Gaulle disappeared from the Élysées Palace. For a few ecstatic hours, students and workers alike thought he had fled from power. But the following day, his staff conjured up an anti-Communist demonstration, with between 400,000 and – according to some reports – one million people marching up the Champs-Élysées. The left had not given up. Daniel Cohn-Bendit continued to harangue the media in the lecture theatre in the Sorbonne. Then de Gaulle made a radio broadcast, announcing fresh elections for late June. The President would win a substantial victory at the ballot box, but when in April 1969 he called for the support of the French in a referendum, he was rejected and retired in high dudgeon to Colombey-les-Deux-Églises.

JÖRN DONNER: *The events of '68 took all the business away from the cinemas – because of the political content, people were not so interested in paying to see that kind of film.*

In the summer of 1968 I was in Copacabana, and could not get home directly via Paris because of the upheavals in France. I had to fly to Rome to get back to Finland. But then came Czechoslovakia in August of '68; that changed a lot of things. You had one youth revolutionary movement that had very little to do with Socialism, mainly it was a revolt against an older generation – but then on the other hand there were many people who were frightened by the Russian invasion of Czechoslovakia. It's strange that this whole leftist movement of the late sixties in Western Europe was anti-authoritarian. Some of them even became terrorists, and in Finland they turned into Stalinists – don't forget the Vietnam War issue – and some into Maoists. And so instead of taking the Russian side on Vietnam, they took a pro-Chinese stance, waving the Little Red Book *and so on.*

ANDRZEJ WAJDA: *We had a '1968' here in Poland, and they had one in Czechoslovakia, and there was France – three entirely different things, almost a coincidence. The student movement that started in Poland was used by the other wing of the Communist party that wanted to get rid of the men in power and take their place. The students at the university in 1968 were the children of those who had been in the Uprising. When I and some colleagues created Unit X in Łódź at the turn of the seventies, we were convinced that it would be a unit composed of the best directors. But I realized that my reputation as an overwhelming man was inhibiting people from joining my group. Still, Wojciech Has did so, despite this, and then the generation of '68 started to join up, too – Agnieszka Holland, Feliks Falk and others. But our rules dictated that to make a theatrical feature a director had first to make a short film for television. I said, 'No, these kids are not going to make anything for television,' so for the first two years I thought we would go bankrupt. We also made films that were made up of shorts directed by different individuals.*

Wajda's work underwent a significant change during the seventies, influenced by the writing of the young Agnieszka Holland, who was very much part of the '68 generation.

WAJDA: *Later, when I was shooting* Man of Marble, *I wanted to take Agnieszka Holland as my assistant. The minister said, 'No, you can't, because she has a very bad influence on you.' She had been in prison in Czechoslovakia for smuggling copies of the underground newsletter. In the seventies, after Gierek had come to power, the situation changed. Things were more liberal, more open.*

Throughout the year, violence had punctuated public life. In April, Martin Luther King had been assassinated in Memphis; in August,

Robert Kennedy met the same fate in Los Angeles; and the same month, Warsaw Pact tanks had rumbled into Prague, bringing to an abrupt end the dreams of liberty in Czechoslovakia. The 'Summer of Love' of 1967, captured in spirit and music in Pennebaker's *Monterey Pop*, became a nostalgic memory.

> RICHARD LESTER: *The emotional impact of what had happened – that destruction . . . I said at the time, and I think it probably still holds, that if you put a bomb under an establishment, it's like putting a bomb under a Doric temple: the columns will collapse but the fluting that makes them Doric will be broken yet unchanged. For all the explosion of energy and anger, it's all going to turn around and nothing will happen. We wrote the end of* Bed Sitting Room *to imply just that! In other words, of these twenty people still left alive in Britain, once they heard that life was resuming, they immediately started assuming exactly the same posture they had done before the Bomb . . .*

Ironically, quite possibly the most important film of 1968, Kubrick's *2001: A Space Odyssey*, had appeared in New York cinemas in April. It was met with a cool reception from mainstream audiences, but was then saved by teenagers who embraced the epic as something mysterious, compelling and vibrant, with respect for the universe in which we lived. Everyone had been so possessed by the chaos of the moment: to see beyond the next demonstration took considerable courage and foresight.

9 Aftermath: The Impact on Hollywood

Looking back, I suppose we can say that we were lucky in that the studios didn't understand enough about their audience in the sixties and early seventies.
   John Boorman

The world did not lurch to an end in the wake of May 1968 – although, for just about twenty-four hours, some of us trapped in Cannes thought that the earth might indeed halt on its axis, and that never again would men in black ties and women in long gowns stroll up those fabled steps within the old Palais des Festivals. But they still do, just as opera-goers still descend on Glyndebourne in evening dress in the heat of a summer's day. *Plus ça change . . .*

Perhaps Chabrol's suave satires of French bourgeois life were more lethal than the din of the demonstrations. *Les Biches* (1968) and *La Femme infidèle* (1969) luxuriated in the feline skills of the director's wife, Stéphane Audran, as the quintessential spoiled woman. The aroma of decadence clinging to these and subsequent Chabrol thrillers had something in common with the novels of Patricia Highsmith, with dark passions at work beneath a heavily lacquered surface of deceit.

Deceit also governed *Z*, an unexpected masterpiece from **Constantin Costa-Gavras** about the junta's take-over in Greece (although the setting was an unidentified Balkan country). Based on a novel by Vassili Vassilikos, *Z* had been inspired by outrage at the murder of left-wing Greek politician Gregory Lambrakis during a visit to Thessaloniki in 1963. By 1967, those responsible for covering up his assassination, the notorious Generals, had seized power in Athens. Greek by birth, trained in France, Costa-Gavras shared Rosi's flair for dissecting the mood of paranoia that always surrounds a totalitarian regime, with each level of authority living in dread of its superiors. Like Rosi, he shot on location (using Godard's favourite cameraman, Raoul Coutard), set prominent actors alongside non-professionals, and left his audience dangling in uncertainty.

In fact, 1968 had yielded some of the decade's most pugnacious and rewarding films, while others, inspired by the upheaval, went into production for release in 1969. Bernardo Bertolucci's *Partner* appeared during 1968. The story has tenuous links with Dostoyevsky's *The Double*, but *Partner* seems disturbingly of its time, with student demonstrations against war and everything else colouring the life of its much perplexed central figure, Giacomo (played by an iconic actor of the period, Pierre Clémenti). The film takes place in contemporary Rome, where Giacomo teaches at a drama college. The radical, violent side of his personality (Giacomo I) seeks to pursue the doctrine of the Theatre of Cruelty to the brink of revolution; while the obverse side (Giacomo II) takes a more diffident approach to sex and politics. As the two characters blend and blur with events, the film develops into an excursion into the surreal, with – outstandingly – Clémenti seducing a girl and then drowning her in the suds of a washing machine. Shot with extravagant camera rotations in colour and 'Scope, *Partner* is confusing in its effort to equate art with politics, and to distinguish revolutionary theory from practice. Once again, Bertolucci bowed to the innovations of Godard – though the two men would soon part company on ideological grounds.

> BERTOLUCCI: *Jean-Luc and a few other friends had this kind of revelation in 1968, and became pro-Chinese and so on. I said I was a Communist, and they accused me of being a 'revisionist'. And so there was this debate. And I became a member of the Italian Communist Party in fact because of this very, very violent quarrel with Godard, Bellocchio and other friends.*

Nevertheless, Bertolucci recovered from the chaos of 1968 to make two magnificent films in the following year: *The Spider's Stratagem* and *The Conformist*. The first of these, financed by RAI Television, recalls Visconti's *Senso*, and not just because a principal role is played by Alida Valli. The young Athos Magnani's visit to Tara (really Sabbionetta, in the Po Valley) wears the trappings of a psychological thriller. But Magnani's discovery that his much-revered father ('Hero, vilely murdered by Fascist bullets' says the inscription on his bust in the town square) had in fact betrayed his friends' plot to assassinate Mussolini in 1936, becomes entwined with his own journey through the past. By the end, Athos is drawn relentlessly along by his dead father's instincts, climbing to the fatal box at the opera only to be confronted by the old men who, so long

Athos Magnani (Giulio Brogi) in *The Spider's Stratagem* (1969)

before, had concealed Magnani's treason in order that the people might mourn their hero.

Bertolucci side-steps the temptation to use flashbacks. The film follows such a linear course that the closing shot – tracking along the rails until they are buried in the undergrowth – comes as an exquisite shock, sealing one's complicity in Magnani's disgrace and also throwing into question the substance of the entire episode. Thanks to sterling work by young cinematographer Vittorio Storaro, *The Spider's Stratagem* exudes the hot, glaring yellows and browns of Parma and the Emilia-Romagna countryside. The film may also be adduced as a metaphor for 1968 itself, which had failed to engender the revolution that students and workers had yearned for.

The Conformist, shot through with subdued, steely blues and greys, would prove as influential on the US 'Movie-Brat' band of Coppola, Scorsese and Spielberg as *The Seventh Seal* had on the previous generation. (Paul Schrader adored the film to such a degree that he hired its designer, Ferdinando Scarfiotti, to work on his *American Gigolo*.) Marcello (given a zombie-like charisma by Jean-Louis Trintignant) suffers from none of the usual motives for collaborating with Fascism. A

Marcello (Jean-Louis Trintignant) and Giulia (Stefania Sandrelli) in
The Conformist (1969)

civil servant, well grounded in the classics, he claims to seek stability
and security as he travels to Paris to assassinate his former professor,
Quadri. His real desire is to atone for his shooting, at the age of thirteen, a homosexual chauffeur. Bertolucci brings this psychological
drama to a head in Rome, with the announcement of Mussolini's resignation, so that the collapse of the regime counterpoints Marcello's
moral bankruptcy. Hypocrisy, cowardice, betrayal: these are the issues
that swarm within the elaborate web of a film that captivated
Bertolucci's peers and established him definitively as an *auteur* in his
own right. And what a web, spun to perfection by the intricate
arabesques of Storaro's cinematography, and by the luminous performances by Dominique Sanda and Stefania Sandrelli. The style of the
piece owed more of a debt to Ophüls, Sternberg and Welles than to
Godard; but Bertolucci could not resist at least one reference to his
inspirational ex-comrade.

Left margin: © Marianne Productions/Mars Film/Paramount Pictures

BERTOLUCCI: *In* The Conformist, *when he gets to Paris, Marcello goes to see his old professor of philosophy, Quadri. And first he calls him, and gives his number to the operator, and the number was Jean-Luc's at the time. Then he takes a cab and gives an address in rue St Jacques, where Jean-Luc was living then. So there is this kind of hidden message throughout the film!*

Lindsay Anderson had helped to draft the original manifesto for the Free Cinema movement, the declared aim being to make films 'which share an attitude: a belief in freedom, in the importance of the individual, and the significance of the everyday'. But his best film, *If . . .*, shot in 1968 and winner of the Palme d'Or at Cannes the following spring, was set in the privileged milieu of the British public school. Some of the traditions that come under fire in this film are commendable traditions; Anderson always felt that a satirist should give everyone his due.

If . . . (1969): Malcolm McDowell as Mick Travis huddles with director Lindsay Anderson

While *If . . .* may at first sight appear to be securely anchored in public-school waters, it becomes on reflection accessible to more and more interpretations. When, in the final shot, Mick fires at the camera with his back to the roof, he is hurling his defiance between the eyes of the audience, challenging each spectator to take sides in the confrontation between youth and age, between anarchy and discipline. (Anderson reputedly declared to a rapturous audience after an early screening of the film, 'The rest is up to you . . .') *If . . .* was conceived, however, neither as an assault on the public-school system nor as a journalistic report on the student unrest of the late sixties – but rather as a speculation on the nature of individualism and authority.

Some would argue that Cannes in 1969 was almost more significant than the previous year's notorious festival. The top prize for *If . . .* seemed to legitimize the spirit of revolt that had swept through Europe and much of the United States. The runner-up, Bo Widerberg's *Ådalen 31* (see below), pulled no punches either. The impact of *Easy Rider* in the competition was extraordinary, prefiguring the pattern of independent film-making in America over the coming decades. Costa-Gavras's *Z* delivered a stinging rebuke to the junta in Greece, while Glauber Rocha's *Antonio das Mortes* offered an exotic – and trenchant – image of Brazilian life and customs. And a group of radical directors, predominantly French and chaired by the *Cahiers* veteran Jacques Doniol-Valcroze, formed the Société des Réalisateurs de Films in order to show works outside the staid official section of the festival in Cannes. This sidebar programme, quickly dubbed the 'Directors' Fortnight', opened the way to a bevy of new *auteurs*.

In the later sixties, the Beatles endorsed for an immense public the trend towards psychedelic surrealism. Their 'pilgrimage' to Bangor in North Wales to meditate with the Maharishi rhymed with screen experiments such as Conrad Rooks' *Chappaqua* and Dennis Hopper's *Easy Rider*, as well as stage productions like *Hair!*. Asian musicians, Ravi Shankar in particular, exerted a powerful impact on certain bands – not least on George Harrison. Moreover, after the death from an overdose of their manager, Brian Epstein (at just thirty-two years of age), the Beatles felt less constrained about public pronouncements. John Lennon in particular would make plain his opposition to the Vietnam War, and, with Yoko Ono, would become one of the decade's most influential proponents of non-violence.

TOP Nicolas Roeg and Donald Cammell, co-directors of *Performance* (1970)

BOTTOM 'The wicked Anita': Ms Pallenberg in *Performance* (1970)

Anyone watching *Performance*, co-directed by Donald Cammell and Nicolas Roeg, would have assumed that all Britain was awash with drugs and debauchery. Cammell, a true child of the sixties, had spent much time in Paris, and had taken a walk-on part in Rohmer's *La collectionneuse*. Colin MacCabe has called *Performance* 'the finest British gangster film ever made'. Shot in 1968 but released only in 1970, the film pulsates with a sinister undertow of violence 'legitimized' in some way by its veneer of high living and rock music. The class war and the political tensions of the era take lethal shape in this brilliantly controlled movie. Infinitely more searching than any of its successors in the genre (*Get Carter*, *The Long Good Friday*, *Mona Lisa*), it indicates that crime and decadence are indissolubly married, as they were at the time of Jack the Ripper. As the malevolent and reclusive rock star Turner, Mick Jagger gives an excellent 'performance': if any one icon of the sixties belonged in this *fin de siècle* masterpiece, it had to be Jagger.

Another arresting film from Britain in 1970 was Jerzy Skolimowski's *Deep End*. The Pole had come to London a year earlier at the behest of United Artists, who gave him several million dollars to make *The Adventures of Gerard*, a misbegotten tribute to Conan Doyle's Colonel of the Hussars. But *Deep End* catches the mysterious awakening of adolescence, when fantasies are nourished by a frustration that only the experience of adult life can interpret. Young Mike (John Moulder Brown) acquires a job at a municipal baths in London, and there meets an attractive female colleague named Susan (Jane Asher), who swiftly teaches him the means of survival in this strange environment. One can almost smell the chlorine and sense the shabbiness of the changing rooms. Surrealism permeates the film – as Susan skirmishes with the cashier, a man's hand and a brush move into sight at the end of the corridor, painting the green walls an unexpected and faintly alarming red (a foretaste of the film's tragic finale). Then there is a startling moment when Mike dives into the water and clings to the cut-out replica of Susan he has found outside a Soho strip-club; or a hilarious search for Susan's missing diamond in an eternity of snow. Skolimowski's best film, *Deep End* dovetails the best of Eastern European humour with the obsessive realism of the British cinema in the sixties. Jane Asher, as the simmering object of desire, was also cast boldly against type: she had long been regarded as the demure English rose, involved for some years with Paul McCartney before his surprise marriage to Linda Eastman.

Someone who should be mentioned, but who fits no category, and indeed has ploughed a lonely furrow throughout his career, is **Ken Russell**. Recognized for his sensitive documentaries on music for the BBC, Russell would become one of the most controversial figures in the British film landscape. His adaptation of D. H. Lawrence's *Women in Love* contained an instantly notorious nude wrestling match between Alan Bates and Oliver Reed, and won Russell an Academy Award nomination in 1969 for Best Director. He cared little for trends, and his style can be likened to no other director's. Transparent, wilful and yet unnervingly watchable, his films thumb their nose at taboos and society alike.

Still, even if the ferment of British cultural life in the sixties had proved a lodestone for many directors from other countries, the local film industry seemed uncertain of its role or its future. By 1968, the American studios were investing some $40 million a year in so-called 'British' films. Yet the number of cinemas operating in Britain plunged dangerously by comparison with Germany, France, Spain, Japan and the US. In one of the worst years, 1967, attendances fell by more than 900,000 per week.

Dušan Makavejev, that fervent disciple of Godard, continued to produce celluloid collages typical of the period. In 1942, a professional strong man named Dragoljub Aleksić had intermingled documentary footage of his own gymnastic feats with stretches of wide-eyed melodrama, in a Serbian film entitled *Innocence Unprotected*. Makavejev resurrected this feature, tinting many of the most outrageous sequences by hand and adding further layers of meaning in the form of up-to-date interviews with Aleksić and his cameraman as well as a selection of wartime newsreels. The result is a 'peculiar cinematic time machine', says Makavejev, offering an indepth portrait of the war period (the rape of the heroine is juxtaposed with Hitler's 'rape' of Europe) and of Aleksić, who even twenty-five years later appears in real life to be just as vain and mock-courageous as he was in his original film.

> MAKAVEJEV: *When researching for* Innocence Unprotected, *I managed to get some facts about life during the war, which showed that it was not the big liberation fight as we had been taught. Most of the people had been sitting in restaurants having beer, not necessarily collaborating but going through black-market operations. There were a lot of things about our existence that I did not put in the film because I did not want to compromise, because I got lots of material*

about the guy in Innocence Unprotected, *and I could easily have destroyed him. He was a trickster, an operator. For example, to cement his links with the occupying power, he showed his film in a theatre that had been half-owned by a Jew (who had been sent to a concentration camp) and half by a Serbian. The Jew's part had gone to the Volksreich, and his property was probably being stolen, so I didn't like the idea of this guy choosing a theatre like that. I was detecting autobiography in his film – so it was like a kind of research. The original film was in black-and-white and mine was in colour.*

Innocence Unprotected *was shown in Berlin in June of 1968. During the riots in Paris of May 1968, I was editing the film.* Switchboard Operator *was playing in a Left Bank theatre in Paris during the demonstrations. I mixed the film at the beginning of June, and on 2 June there was the big uprising in Belgrade. So I took part in the student marches, and half of the day I would be filming these protests, and had most of it confiscated by the police. The film won the Special Jury Award and also the FIPRESCI Prize. Then, without me, it went on to Chicago and took the Golden Hugo for Best Film. Roger Ebert discovered me and wrote enthusiastically about the picture. The film travelled wonderfully, to Zürich, to all kinds of places. It became, to my surprise, even more of a trendsetter than the previous two films I'd made.*

In 1968, **Bo Widerberg** filmed not just one, but two indignant critiques of the political right – *The White Sport* (about demonstrators protesting at the Sweden–Rhodesia tennis match) and *Ådalen 31* (harking back to an acrimonious industrial dispute in northern Sweden that ended with men gunned down by the authorities). Widerberg at his adventurous best was the godson of both Truffaut and Godard, evincing the former's romantic warmth and the latter's technical brio and smouldering anger. Two years later, Widerberg travelled to the United States to make, on location, a stirring screen biography of Joe Hill, the immigrant singer who wandered from city to city during the early twentieth century. Hill wrote campaign lyrics, competed against the Salvation Army from any number of soap-boxes, endured punches, prison and finally suffered what in effect was legalized murder. 'He was a swell guy,' said Widerberg at his press conference at Cannes in 1971, and *Joe Hill* remains a poignant romance, charting a young man's eager, awed discovery of the good emotions life can stir, and his stalwart rebellion in the face of

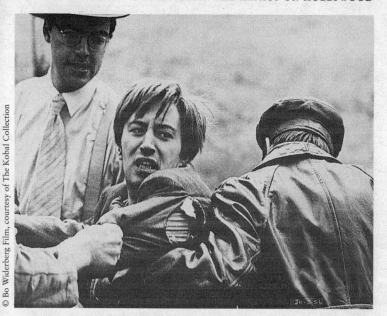

Joe Hill (1971): Thommy Berggren as the eponymous, ill-fated hero

treachery and guile. The film's achievement lies in its observation – the poetry of Joe's encounter with a young Italian woman (Anja Schmidt) on a fire-escape outside the opera house in New York, the carefree thrill of train-jumping with Blackie (Evert Anderson), and the Keatonesque humour of a restaurant sequence in Manhattan, with Joe (Thommy Berggren) declining to taste the wine before a baffled waiter.

Krzysztof Zanussi brought a dispassionate sophistication to 1969 with his first feature, *The Structure of Crystals*. If, for Astruc, the camera is merely a pen, for Zanussi it is a microscope, in the lens of which are reflected the curious forces that shape our lives. Two contrasting individuals meet and clash in *The Structure of Crystals*. Once college friends, they find themselves on opposing sides of the ideological fence when they meet again in the countryside in their thirties.

ZANUSSI: *When I wrote* The Structure of Crystals, *I recall that we had a clear feeling of disgust with the prevailing social reality. We had a dream of getting away from society, from careers, from the system, and finding a niche where you could have a single human relationship. This was a strongly felt reaction to the enormous wave of drabness that was passing through Poland. It had been easy to get the screenplay accepted because we were going to talk about village life and the inhabitants of a rural area. When my colleagues had seen the first cut of the picture, however, they urged me to hide it and pretend that it was unfinished, as they found it so depressing – one character obsessed by the need for recognition in life and the other resigned to a quiet, unprotesting life in the provinces. Then one colleague of mine advised me to cut the film down to the shortest possible length; maybe it will seem better to the bureaucrats. So we did just that, cutting it down from three hours to just eighty minutes, to the point where the lack of action was bearable.*

The following year, Zanussi attended the Bergamo Festival in Italy with the film, and found that *The Structure of Crystals* had been judged in advance by the Italian media. Some had taken the synopsis at its face value, and assumed that the director endorsed the quiet life of the man who lives in the countryside.

ZANUSSI: *There was a crowd on the street shouting 'Fascisti borghesi!' and 'Corrupt!' And I was furious and thought, For God's sake, you are the bourgeois! Who am I? I cannot even pay for my coffee, and these people are all arriving in luxury, in big cars. Ahead of time, these people said my film was wrong and should not be screened in the festival. I had no way of arranging a screening of it, and so it was not shown at all in Bergamo. I remember that when that festival was interrupted, I had problems in getting home, because I had a fixed-date return ticket, and so I had to camp a couple of nights near the railroad station!*

In Latin America, the revolution in cinema had percolated steadily from the late fifties onwards. Standing tall among his contemporaries was the imperious figure and personality of **Leopoldo Torre Nilsson**. His father, Leopoldo Torres Rios, had been Argentina's dominant director of the thirties and forties. His wife, Beatriz Guido, proved an expert screenwriter, creating with Torre Nilsson a sickly aristocratic world in which indecision, decadence and betrayal circled each other warily. Their breakthrough occurred in 1957, with *The House of the Angel*. A young girl's life is blighted by her mother's puritanical insistence on her growing up at once free of sin and in ignorance of the facts of life. Not surprisingly, she throws herself into the arms of the first handsome man – a political deputy – who pays attention to her. But he does not marry her, and the young woman is condemned to live alone with her ageing father in the 'house of the angel', locked in a claustrophobic limbo until her death. Torre Nilsson's symbolism and his endemic fear of evil revealed his keen admiration for Bergman's work of the fifties. But the subjective, furtive camera movements owe much to Welles and Hitchcock, and the undercurrent of perversion in childhood recalls Buñuel. Two features released in 1961, *The Hand in the Trap* and *Summer Skin*, confirmed Torre Nilsson's deft touch in revealing corruption and tedium among the upper classes in Argentina. Their controlled languor rhymed perfectly with Antonioni's work across the ocean, and indicated that the *Zeitgeist* was alive and well in Latin America too.

In neighbouring Brazil, **Nelson Pereira dos Santos** directed *Rio 40 Degrees* as early as 1955. Its authentic locations and its fidelity to ethnic traditions served as a harbinger of 'Cinema Nôvo', a Brazilian equivalent of the French New Wave that for some ten to fifteen years galvanized Latin American film-making. *Barren Lives* (1963) is a searing masterpiece, relentless in its depiction of migrant workers and their families struggling to survive the drought. There was a lighter side to Pereira dos Santos, however, manifest in *How Tasty Was My Little Frenchman* (1971), a tongue-in-cheek satire on the clash between native Indian culture and the blundering European adventurers of the sixteenth century.

Ruy Guerra, born in Mozambique, moved to Brazil in 1958 and became a portal figure in that country's Cinema Nôvo movement. Films like *Oz Fuzis* (1964) and *Sweet Hunters* (1969) presented country locales as they had not been shown before in Brazil, while capturing the underlying beat of Latin American life and music. Cinema Nôvo was driven by the need to combat poverty, and in France some critics dubbed their work 'Cinéma de la faim' – cinema of hunger.

Glauber Rocha, a disciple of Italian neo-realism, attracted the attention of the French magazine *Positif* in the early sixties. Bernardo Bertolucci sung his praises, and Walter Salles continues to do so today. Rocha's maiden feature, *Barravento*, resembled *La terra trema* in its devoted, yet also objectively structured, study of fisherfolk. At Cannes in 1964, his *Black God White Devil* took part in the official competition, alongside his compatriot dos Santos's *Barren Lives*. Carlos Diegues

TOP Glauber Rocha's *Black God White Devil* (1964)

BOTTOM Mauricio Do Valle as *Antonio das Mortes* (1969)

recalls the atmosphere at the Rocha press screening: 'As its strange images and barbaric sounds filled the cinema, the audience looked at each other, in turn amazed, confused, shocked and delighted by the absurd human geography, the savage dramaturgy, by characters and situations never before seen in cinema.' Half the audience walked out; the other half remained to give *Black God White Devil* a standing ovation. But Rocha's finest hour came in May 1969, when he won the Best Director award at Cannes for *Antonio das Mortes*. This story is constructed on several levels – political allegory, folkloric ballad, opera, western – and paid graphic tribute to Brazilian culture as well as defiantly rejecting the country's feudal economy and the exploitation of labour. Bernardo Bertolucci met Rocha in the sixties in Rome, and later told an interviewer, 'We immediately agreed on something: the relation between author and audience. We were not seeking for understanding. Our fight was like that between bull and torero. We did not want praise. Maybe corpses . . .'

The Bertolucci of 2003 laments the fact that so few young people today know the work of Glauber Rocha:

BERTOLUCCI: *We were a little group, you know – some Italians, some French, some Canadians (Michel Brault, Claude Jutra, Pierre Perrault) – and we all had the same kind of passion for cinema, and we loved so many aspects of the Nouvelle Vague.*

Glauber Rocha had an extraordinary capacity. When he was doing a movie, the movie was like the tension and the effort to find a way or an order out of the chaos – it was his imagination, and going really to the roots of what they were calling 'tropicalismo' at the time. It was a real movement. But he and others all had to leave Brazil, and he spent a long time in Italy, and he was in Paris, and Cuba. It's very sad to realize now, when you speak to young people, that nobody has heard his name.

But while his angry work symbolized Cinema Nôvo for most European observers, at home Rocha found himself in the firing line. The right-wing regime in Brazil banned *Antonio das Mortes* and Rocha fled to Cuba. Altogether, he spent seven years abroad, including lengthy spells in Italy and France, before returning to his native country to die in Rio de Janeiro at the age of just forty-three.

Reinaldo Arenas, the Cuban novelist, wrote in *Before Night Falls*: 'In spite of everything, youth in the sixties managed to conspire, not against

Nagisa Oshima (centre) directs *Diary of a Shinjuku Thief* (1968)

the regime but in favour of life.' Yet Cuban cinema under Castro, like Yugoslav cinema under Tito, seemed to enjoy more liberty and public support than it actually did. The Castro government established the ICAIC (Cuban Institute for the Art and Industry of Film), but for some years output was restricted to didactic documentaries – a field in which Santiago Alvarez proved an unrivalled master. In 1968, **Tomás Gutiérrez Alea** analysed on screen his disenchantment in the wake of Castro's revolution, in *Memories of Underdevelopment*. Both this and his earlier *Death of a Bureaucrat* (1962) have a sophisticated, allusive mood, a blend of Antonioni and Kafka, anxiety and satire.

The spirit of rebellion against social structures and political platitudes gathered momentum outside Europe and America as the decade wore on, and in Japan in 1968 the young Nagisa Oshima made *Diary of a Shinjuku Thief*. This febrile, disorganized and yet gripping snapshot of a modern Tokyo far removed from the hierarchical world of Kurosawa or the placid domesticity of Ozu's middle-class amplified what the West had been saying for some time. Individual films by New Wave directors like

© Sozosha Production, courtesy of The Kobal Collection

Scene from *Diary of a Shinjuku Thief* (1968)

Hiroshi Teshigahara and Susumu Hani had reached festivals during the early sixties, but Oshima, born in the same year as Truffaut, focused most imaginatively on the plight of young people out of tune with their elders in the aftermath of World War II. *The Catch* (1961), his first feature, underlined Japan's responsibility for the war and its intolerance towards foreigners. *Night and Fog in Japan* (1961) expressed Oshima's fury at the signing of the US–Japan security treaty. A film filled with stylized debate among opponents of the treaty, its title pays homage to Resnais' 1956 documentary. Oshima's suppressed rage was barely contained within the rigorous framework of traditional film-making, and in *Death by Hanging* he again pursues the theme of xenophobia, as a young Korean faces execution on very ambiguous grounds. The film also works in a Godardian way, analysing the very act of hanging itself, with the police obliged to re-enact the crime in an attempt to convince their victim of his guilt.

By the time he made *Diary of a Shinjuku Thief*, Oshima had become enamoured of what Godard and his ilk were doing in Europe, and he refused to kowtow to the tenets of a courteous Japanese cinema that upheld rigid values and evaded contemporary reality. Birdey Hilltop, the student who dominates the film, steals everything (including books!) for sexual satisfaction and hooks up with a girl who is willing to enter his world of erotic fantasy. This flight from an outmoded reality eventually opens the way – at least in theory – to a new and more valid way of life. As Claire Johnston wrote, 'Oshima sees the failure of the older generation as being essentially a failure of imagination.' When *Diary of a Shinjuku Thief* reached the West, audiences for the first time saw on screen the urban life of a new Japanese generation. Indeed, Oshima's direction was so advanced for its time that even today its influence can be located in film-makers like Takeshi Kitano, Kinji Fukasaku, and the Korean Kim Ki-Duk.

The United States had to run hard to catch the Europeans during the later sixties and early seventies. Indeed, the most engaging achievements of Hollywood and off-Hollywood in the post-*Godfather* era revealed the influence of Europe's great directors. Whether it was Coppola and Scorsese responding to *The Conformist*, Woody Allen genuflecting before Bergman, or Robert Altman echoing Godard, the European New Wave undoubtedly meant a good deal more to the 'Movie-Brat' generation than did the legendary 'journeymen' directors of Old Hollywood.

By the end of the sixties, Hollywood's traditional power base seemed to be crumbling. The feisty moguls of yesteryear were dying, or 'ankling', to use *Variety* parlance. Only Twentieth Century Fox and Columbia Pictures retained their independence. MGM even shuttered its studio for some years, auctioning off Clark Gable's raincoat and Judy Garland's red sequin shoes from *The Wizard of Oz*. Gulf and Western, a conglomerate dealing in everything from sugar to insulated wire, had absorbed Paramount; a garage giant, Kinney Services, had assumed control of Warner Bros.; and Lew Wasserman's MCA agency was running Universal. United Artists had become a mere division of Transamerica Inc., alongside other subsidiaries such as Budget Rent-a-Car and Transamerica Life Insurance. In short, Hollywood was going corporate.

The studios at first regarded the New Waves in France, Italy and Scandinavia with some caution. They loved the low-budget concept and loathed the small returns. They eventually dipped their toes into the fresh waters, assigning modest investments to the work of François Truffaut, Claude Lelouch and Ingmar Bergman, for example. This was usually achieved via the local offices of corporations such as United

Artists. For their part, MGM financed Antonioni's *Blow-Up* and then invited him to America to make *Zabriskie Point* at the end of the decade.

However, trouble lay in store. As Cassavetes noted, 'What's basically wrong with Hollywood is that you cannot really have teamwork. I couldn't make a good film without it. Once you set up an employer–employee relationship, you divide people.' It was teamwork that had shored up the most conspicuous individual talents of the fifties and sixties in Europe, whether it was Bergman and his troupe of players from the Swedish stage, or Fellini and his habitual costume designers and cinematographers.

Hollywood's attempts to capitalize on the laid-back, smoke-laden mood of the late sixties, in films like *The Strawberry Statement* and *Alice's Restaurant*, failed miserably. Even Columbia was baffled by the success of its own release, *Easy Rider*, Dennis Hopper and Peter Fonda's road movie that had come out of left field and enunciated many of the misgivings that Americans felt about their country's role in the world, and about the intolerance that marked the United States at home. 'A man went looking for America,' ran the film's tag-line, 'and couldn't find it anywhere . . .'

In 1969, United Artists thought they would have some fun by backing Gillo Pontecorvo's *Burn!* (also known as *Queimada*), which dealt with the British attempts to undermine – and destroy – the Portuguese presence in Latin America during the mid-nineteenth century. Marlon Brando was cast as the English mercenary and *agent provocateur*, Sir William Walker. But still the studio found itself at a loss – literally.

PONTECORVO: *Things were good for me in the States at that time, because* Kapò *had been nominated for an Oscar, and* The Battle of Algiers *had been a success and won three Academy Award nominations. Franco Solinas had worked together with me on the script of* Burn! *and we were convinced that the part needed someone with the face of Brando, who was then felt to be one of the greatest actors ever to work in cinema. But when I proposed this to our Hollywood co-production partners, they said, 'Why don't you take Steve McQueen?' He was then at the top of the box-office tree. Then Sidney Poitier was suggested for the role of the black man. I said I admired his work, but that I wanted a face that was altogether more wild.*

Anyway, time went by, we had to start shooting, and I still had not found the protagonist for Brando. We were scouting locations in

Colombia, looking for a forest to burn down. And suddenly I saw a peasant riding past on horseback; he was riding without a saddle. And I knew that was the face I needed. But when I called to him, he rode off at high speed. It was 40 degrees in the shade, and that evening I said to my colleagues, 'This is too good a chance to miss.' They thought I was mad, and said that it would be like looking for a needle in a haystack. But we did in fact find him, in a village with earthen huts, and I phoned United Artists. When they asked who the man was, I fibbed, I told them he was 'a local actor'. They asked if he spoke English. We said no, but that we could post-sync his lines.

Then I called Marlon, who was in Polynesia, and he was very generous, asking if this was really the face I had been looking for and if it was, then he would go along with it. The actor, Evaristo Márquez, turned out to be very gifted, and excellent on camera. For his first scenes, we had to tell him when to look up, when to move here and there and so on, but by the end we were giving him instructions as you would to a Method actor.

Ironically, Pontecorvo was probably posed more problems by Brando than by Márquez, as an already arduous shoot was punctuated by various disagreements between director and star. The picture that emerged was as remarkable as it was unclassifiable, but it promptly vanished from view.

Nevertheless, the more astute Hollywood executives glimpsed hopes for the future in unorthodox films like Mike Wadley's *Woodstock* documentary and Robert Altman's free-wheeling satire, *M*A*S*H*, which won the Palme d'Or at Cannes in 1970 and proved that a movie without stars could appeal to a wide public. George Roy Hill's hugely popular *Butch Cassidy and the Sundance Kid*, made the previous year, revelled in montage sequences reminiscent of *Jules et Jim*, and featured music (especially over the robbery scenes) that evoked *Les Parapluies de Cherbourg*.

JOHN BOORMAN: *Hollywood at that point was very unsure of itself. It hadn't yet learned how to deal with television and it was a very ageing place. I went out there in 1966 to do* Point Blank. *The great if finally declining studio, MGM, was still functioning in all departments, still had its lab, its costumes, its special effects, but there was this ageing population there, and a great sense of uncertainty. During the early and mid-sixties, all these American producers were camping out in London, trying to make pictures, because there was this feeling that somehow the younger European directors held the secret of how to attract an audience. There was a huge loss of confidence in the States, in the studios.*

There was a great sense of inferiority in the States at that time, and I suppose that's how I came to do Point Blank, *because they felt, we don't know how to do it any more, and maybe this weird kind of thriller will work. Resnais was a big influence on* Point Blank, *Alex Jacobs and I were very aware of Resnais when we did our script, and also of Pinter in terms of the very cryptic dialogue.*

Hollywood placed no value on its past, and it was the French in particular who had such admiration for the American movies of the forties and so forth. Disney was in total decline, hardly functioning, MGM was falling apart, there was a struggle going on for Paramount and Fox, and they were all just hoping . . . The English films made during the sixties were very influential on Hollywood and it wasn't until much later that they began to pick up steam over there.

I met John Cassavetes when I first went out to Hollywood. He was a great friend of Lee Marvin's, and he was very depressed about the difficulty of making his kind of picture. He was acting to earn money to make his films. There were very few new directors working in Hollywood at that time. The people I got to know were Sam Peckinpah, Cassavetes and Robert Altman. These guys knew what they wanted to do and were trying to battle the system.

There was something somewhat fraudulent about the whole thing, because what the studios did was to say, we don't know what to do, so we'll put ourselves in the hands of these directors, and there was a kind of faith, a belief . . . and we achieved great power, and out of that came films like Five Easy Pieces *and* Easy Rider. *What changed everything was the success of Spielberg's and Lucas's films, because the studios suddenly realized that the audience was composed of teenagers, and they went after that audience, and suddenly they knew what their function was. So gradually that ground was lost – that middle ground where we used to function disappeared. Looking back, I suppose we can say that we were lucky in that the studios didn't understand enough about their audience in the sixties and early seventies.*

Boorman in effect remodelled the gangster film with *Point Blank*, even more profoundly than Arthur Penn did with *Bonnie and Clyde* or Sam

Peckinpah with *The Getaway*. He retained the essential brutality of the genre, while devising a complex chronological structure worthy of *Hiroshima mon amour*. He also used the 'Scope format and the garish Metrocolor system to give *Point Blank* a brash and vulgar look absolutely suited to Lee Marvin's ruthless hoodlum and his bent for vengeance.

Boorman's own bent was for subjects that showed men at odds with themselves and their environment. *Hell in the Pacific* (1968) could have been made by Bresson, so rigorous and so austere was its language. Lee Marvin and Toshiro Mifune, veterans of a Pacific war that has long vanished over the horizon, strive to outwit one another on a remote, sunbleached atoll. Immaculate in its visual composition, *Hell in the Pacific* prefigures Boorman's ultimate masterpiece, *Deliverance*, made in 1972, that *annus mirabilis* of the Hollywood resurrection.

Sam Peckinpah found himself at odds with Columbia over the costly Civil War epic, *Major Dundee*. The film, sporadically brilliant, emerged in a truncated form and left its embittered director on the sidelines for four years. When his finest work, *The Wild Bunch*, appeared at the tail end of the sixties, its unforgiving violence and savage shootout aroused the wrath of many a censor. Set somewhat later – 1914 – than the traditional western, *The Wild Bunch* made Peckinpah's name a synonym for carnage, with William Holden and his gang fighting for survival in a hostile Mexico. Peckinpah admitted to a fondness for the new European cinema, and in particular for the naked bitterness of Carlos Saura's *La caza*, which he saw at the Berlin Festival in 1966. (Yet another example of how festivals provided the essential forum for an exchange of ideas among film-makers.)

Francis Ford Coppola would dominate the seventies as the most confident and imperious of the 'Movie Brats'. During the sixties, however, he came of age with his early feature films, *You're a Big Boy Now* (screened at Cannes in 1967) and *The Rain People*. He had served as principal aide to the prolific, cheerfully trashy producer Roger Corman, doctoring scripts, shooting second-unit material and even recording sound. In 1963, Corman accepted Coppola's pitch for a horror movie called *Dementia 13*. 'As I described it,' recalled Coppola, 'a man goes to a pond and takes off his clothes, picks up these dolls, ties them together, goes under the water, dives down . . . and Roger says, "Change the man to a woman, and you can do it." So I said, "Sure" . . .'

Shirley Knight's role in *The Rain People* bore the hallmark of Monica Vitti in Antonioni's *L'avventura*. Coppola brought a sympathetic, searching eye to bear on a woman fleeing her responsibilities and failing to adjust to new partnerships in an aimless odyssey across the Midwest of the United States. Coppola's disenchantment with Middle America chimes with that of *Easy Rider*, which was being shot around the same time, while his admiration for the New Wave explains his desire for filming on location. Even on the musical *Finian's Rainbow* (1968), he managed to escape from the studios in Burbank to shoot out and about for eight days, in Monterey, Carmel, Modesto and San Francisco.

While Agnès Varda clung cheerfully to her conservatory–studio in Paris, and Ingmar Bergman edited *Persona* in a converted hotel room in central Sweden, **John Korty** had set up a small studio in Marin County, California, far from the razzmatazz of Hollywood and influenced to some degree by Mogens Skot-Hansen's Laterna Studios in a leafy suburb of Copenhagen:

> KORTY: *Francis Coppola had been talking to George Lucas for ages about getting out of LA. George and I were speaking at an English teachers' conference up here in the Bay Area in the summer of 1969, and Francis was finishing up* The Rain People *in Arkansas. George got all excited when I talked about what I was doing in this tiny town, Stinson Beach. So he called Francis from a pay phone in the Hilton Hotel, and urged him to come out to see what I was doing.*
>
> *They arrived in two station wagons at my studio in Stinson Beach. I showed them our projection set-up, our editing rooms, our sound transfers . . . We were all very excited at meeting each other and Francis promised that they would be back the following week. So they drove to LA, they unpacked their station wagons, caught up on their sleep for a few days, and literally came back in a week. They began looking for a home for a new studio that would become Zoetrope: we searched on the coast of Marin, and we went up as far as Bodega Bay at one point. When I gently protested that this was getting pretty far from civilization, Francis said we could do it with helicopters, we could bring in a sound module, and a camera module! Then we started going over the hill the other way. We even looked at the wealthiest part of Ross, with its huge mansions. Of course, we ended up down and dirty, south of Mission on Folsom Street in San Francisco, exactly the opposite!*

Antonioni brought the sixties to a close with *Zabriskie Point*, his inimitable compositions of the Arizona Desert and Death Valley over-

Verna Bloom observes the National Guard massing for battle outside the 1968 Democratic convention in Haskell Wexler's *Medium Cool* (1969)

whelming the banal story of a radical Los Angeles student on the run from the authorities. The film – a financial catastrophe for an already ailing MGM – bemused audiences and critics alike, although the painting of an aircraft in the desert, and the climactic explosion of a house and its lavish contents, are memorable Antonioni scenes, clothed in an intriguing aura that masks the *naïveté* of the director's approach to a foreign social situation.

As young Americans increasingly reacted against the war in Vietnam, so violence on college campuses continued to spread. But the authorities were in no mood to compromise, and so the Democratic Convention in Chicago in 1968 became a virtual killing-ground. Cinematographer Haskell Wexler recorded enough damning footage to form the backbone of his *Medium Cool* (1969), which cast a jaundiced eye at the American media and its cynical disregard for human dignity, perhaps for life itself. Though a photo of Belmondo in *À bout de souffle* adorns the apartment

Left margin: © Paramount Pictures, courtesy of The Kobal Collection

of news cameraman Robert Forster, the cynicism that is everywhere else around him seems to confirm that the sixties dream has gone sour. As he is sucked into the turmoil enveloping the Democratic Convention, Forster's anti-hero winds up a victim of circumstance. Wexler, a superb cinematographer in his own right, closed his film with a tribute to Godard's *Le mépris*, as the camera is turned upon us, the audience. He handled his fictitious narrative with the force of a *cinéma-vérité* documentary. One saw the armoured cars drawn up in readiness by Mayor Daley's regime, and one realized that this was for real – a moment of which Pontecorvo would have been proud. Soon afterwards, the 'Chicago Seven' were put on trial for allegedly 'conspiring to incite a riot' at the Convention.

The Altamont Speedway killings in December 1969, recorded so compellingly in *Gimme Shelter*, sounded the death-knell of the sixties. The laid-back ideals that had percolated through the cafés and movie theatres of San Francisco's Haight-Ashbury neighbourhood, along with the rebellious sounds of Jerry Garcia and the Grateful Dead, seemed to have dispersed for ever. Richard Lester's *Petulia*, one of those films withdrawn from Cannes the previous year, filtered into theatres in the United States and Europe. In Lester's words, '*Petulia* was a deeply troubled and serious and disturbed film about the destruction of the Haight-Ashbury flower-power and the beginnings of Vietnam and the beginnings of real dishonesty.'

The most engaging, if not quite definitive, lament for the sixties came with Bob Rafelson's *Five Easy Pieces*, shot in and around a bleak Puget Sound during the autumn of 1969. Its primary producer, Bert Schneider, had been behind Rafelson's first film, *Head*, in 1968, and also served as executive producer on *Easy Rider*. Close friends with Jack Nicholson, Schneider embodied a fresh approach to film financing – not so grungy and tongue-in-cheek as Corman, but still offbeat and anti-Establishment. Bobby Dupea in *Five Easy Pieces* is a fallible nonconformist, a seemingly coarse-cut oil-rigger whose rejection of society is not simply to be admired. Discontented with the physical vulgarity of life in the South, and unable to immerse himself in the musical mediocrity of his upper-middle-class relatives in upstate Washington, he remains solitary and tormented. He is smart enough to dispute the rules of the menu with a stupid waitress at a roadside diner, but he breaks down in tears before his crippled father on the family island. Still, for all the moral ambivalence of his behaviour, Bobby Dupea is a likeable and intriguing

Bobby Dupea (Jack Nicholson) gets into a barking contest with a car-bound dog in Bob Rafelson's *Five Easy Pieces* (1970)

character, and Jack Nicholson plays him with a dreamy pensiveness that heralded his arrival as the key American star of the seventies. Few anticipated that, just two years later, the carefully plotted box-office triumph of *The Godfather* would herald a revolution in American film-making, and the start of a long period of hegemony and global popularity – even among the cognoscenti – for Hollywood product.

10 The Long Goodbye

'What have I been doing? Different things, different jobs, here and there. Nothing that interesting.'
  Bobby Dupea (Jack Nicholson) in *Five Easy Pieces*

Many of the masters whose work so illuminated the sixties continue to make films, if at increasingly sporadic intervals. Fashion has not been kind to Michelangelo Antonioni. In *Sight and Sound*'s 1962 poll for the Best Film of All Time, *L'avventura* came second. Forty years later, it had disappeared from the list, with only ten of 145 critics selecting it as a favourite. Visconti, and *La terra trema*, have suffered a similar eclipse. But Antonioni will survive as one of the fundamental reformers of the cinema, a director working in an altogether different register from his more popular compatriot, Fellini. He has never much cared that his films are an acquired taste, much like Chinese porcelain, Dos Passos, Webern, Kandinsky and the very dry martini.

Antonioni's legacy still vibrates in a *tour de force* such as Theo Angelopoulos's *Eternity and a Da*y, and during the seventies many directors sought to emulate his languorous mood, from Radivojević in Yugoslavia to Wenders in Germany. Paralysed and able to communicate only with a very few intimates, Antonioni has continued to conceive and partly direct films like *Beyond the Clouds* (1995) and *Just To Be Together* (2001). His greatest post-sixties work is undoubtedly *The Passenger* (1975), with Jack Nicholson and Maria Schneider drifting through southern Spain in that eternal, Antonionian quest for meaning.

Others, though, have passed away – Truffaut, Fellini, Pasolini, Demy, Malle, Anderson, Richardson, Reisz, Losey, Widerberg, Kubrick . . .

Although Truffaut would enjoy commercial and critical success throughout his career – particularly in the United States – he could not quite recapture what Browning called the 'first fine careless rapture'. *Baisers volés* and *Domicile conjugal* pursued the on-screen career of

Truffaut's *alter ego*, Antoine Doinel, while adaptations of American thrillers (*La mariée était en noir*, *La sirène du Mississippi*) underlined Truffaut's skill with actors, but lacked the innovative flair of his most pristine work. If one were to take just one of his later films to a desert island, it would have to be *La nuit américaine* (1973), in which Truffaut succeeds gloriously in capturing the frenetic joy and frustration of making a film with a team of actors and technicians.

Fellini's other films of the sixties merely threw the magic of *8½* into relief. However idiosyncratic, however stunning in terms of visual legerdemain, *Juliet of the Spirits*, *Histoires extraordinaires* and *Fellini-Satyricon* proved complaisant and over-wrought. Artifice became Fellini's trademark, albeit artifice of an enchanting, forgivable kind. In terms of popular success, only *Amarcord*, his affectionate evocation of his childhood in Rimini, would match *La dolce vita*. 'In *Amarcord*, I built the sea,' confessed Fellini. 'And nothing is truer than that sea on the screen. It is the sea I wanted, which the real sea would never have given me. How do you build the sea? That's a trade secret I would not want to reveal. A couple of sheets of plastic and a couple of good-natured operators, and you have it. I work for this, to be there, to cut and nail, paint and set up lights. The cinema is an illusion: an image that must emerge for what it is.'

A committed Marxist, whose work was none the less shot through with spiritual craving, Pasolini never quite achieved the art-house status of Fellini, Visconti, Antonioni or even his most avid disciple, Bertolucci. But his influence has survived, in as recent a film as Bellocchio's *My Mother's Smile* (2002) and in the moving episode of Nanni Moretti's *Dear Diary* when the director visits the seashore outside Rome where, in 1975, Pasolini met his ugly death.

Jacques Demy's talent, glittering fondant-sweet in the bright morning of the New Wave, melted away in subsequent years. For all his innovative use of camerawork, music and production design, he seemed to hark back to a vanished era, that of Jacques Prévert with his poignant farewells. But his remains a gossamer-light, fairy-tale world where a fleeting kiss is enough to suggest the most earth-shattering of passions.

Wajda, awarded an honorary Oscar in 2000, continues to make ambitious films. He first anticipated and then caught the spirit of Solidarity in his two masterpieces, *Man of Marble* (1977) and *Man of Iron* (1981). And few films about the French Revolution have understood the rashness and perfidy of those hectic months as well as *Danton* (1982). Aged seventy-five, Wajda still surges into the room with the energy and purpose of a senator in Republican Rome (and he did indeed serve a term in the Polish Senate from 1989 onwards). His remains a distinctive language, rich in gesture and romantic metaphor.

Zanussi's heyday proved to be the seventies, with a stream of intelligent, compelling studies of life in Poland: *Illumination*, *Camouflage*, *The Spiral*, *The Constant Factor*. His scientific approach to cinema endows his films with a singular geometry, while his gift for discourse sets him apart from his contemporaries. Physician-like, he regulates the temperature of his work so that it never appears either overheated or excessively cold. A polymath, endowed with an Ustinovian facility for languages, Zanussi still heads the TOR production unit in Warsaw, and continues to direct interesting features himself every other year.

Equally bright, Volker Schlöndorff has addressed political and social themes in many countries, sometimes falling flat on his face (*Voyager*, *Palmetto*), and sometimes grabbing the issue by the throat (*Circle of Deceit*, about the chaotic fighting in Lebanon). His masterpiece will long remain his fiendishly accurate adaptation of Grass's novel, *The Tin Drum*, which in 1979 shared the Palme d'Or at Cannes with *Apocalypse Now*.

Jerzy Skolimowski, almost as gifted a painter as he is a director, contributed one further, splendidly idiosyncratic, film to the British cinema, *The Shout* (1978), probing beneath the coded life of the English middle class with a ferocity that excelled even Pinter and Losey, while using sound to an imaginative degree. (Four years earlier, Ray Dolby had changed the landscape of sound design when *Callan*, the first film with an optical mono soundtrack encoded with A-type noise reduction, was screened at Cannes.)

For his part, Bertolucci has enjoyed a roller-coaster ride, gaining notoriety for *Last Tango in Paris*, winning Academy Awards for his epic, *The Last Emperor* (1987), suffering the derision of critics with flops like *La luna*, *Little Buddha* and *Stealing Beauty*, restoring faith in himself with the low-budget *Besieged*, and most recently returning to the events of the sixties with *The Dreamers*, based on Gilbert Adair's novel about the riots in Paris in early 1968.

Television would claim the talent of Ermanno Olmi for many a long day, until 1978, when *The Tree of Wooden Clogs* won the Palme d'Or at Cannes. Although his fresco of medieval history, *The Profession of Arms*, was awarded many national prizes in 2001, its soporific verbosity contradicted the zest and visual eloquence of Olmi's youth.

Francesco Rosi has remained true to his early ideals, even if, in what seems likely to be his final film, *The Truce* (1995), a certain tinge of sentimentality seeps into the landscape. Time cannot detract, however, from that sublime analysis of family relationships, *Three Brothers* (1980), or from the relentless investigative power of *Il caso Mattei* (which won at Cannes) and *Cadaveri eccellenti*, about the corruption at the heart of the Italian judicial system.

Ken Loach, of course, has sustained a neo-realist approach for three decades, from *Kes* to *Sweet Sixteen*, with his tribute to the international brigade in the Spanish Civil War (*Land and Freedom*) perhaps the finest example of neo-realism outside Italy.

John Schlesinger (*Midnight Cowboy*), Karel Reisz (*Who'll Stop the Rain?*), John Boorman (*Deliverance*) and Roman Polanski (*Chinatown*) all responded to the siren call of the West Coast, although Reisz made most impact in America with *The French Lieutenant's Woman* in 1981. Boorman has never quite settled down in Hollywood, and some of his most engaging work has been achieved elsewhere (*The General*, *Hope and Glory*, *The Tailor of Panama*). When Polanski returned at last to his native country, he resurrected World War II with such devoted passion in *The Pianist* that the film beguiled the jury at Cannes, winning the Palme d'Or in 2002, and three major Academy Awards in the spring of 2003. Miloš Forman made his permanent home in New York, harvesting kudos for his sharp-eyed comedy, *Taking Off*, and then numerous Academy Awards for *One Flew Over the Cuckoo's Nest* and *Amadeus*. His friend Ivan Passer also went to the US, but has kept a lower profile. His cult thriller *Cutter's Way* (1981) fixed a malevolent gaze on the sleepy town of Santa Barbara and tapped into the guilt and resentment felt by many Americans in the aftermath of Vietnam. Jan Němec made the engaging, fastidious *Martyrs of Love* in 1968 and, long after compatriots like Forman and Passer, managed to settle for a while in the United States. But something in the air of the sixties had inspired him, and when life and politics changed, the urgency slipped away from his work.

Dušan Makavejev zigzagged through the seventies and eighties. His dazzling collage, *WR: Mysteries of the Organism* (1971), paid tribute to Wilhelm Reich, inventor and sexologist extraordinaire, and *Sweet Movie*, made three years later, touched on nearly every taboo in sight, including coprophilia. Makavejev made his most joyous romp, *Montenegro*, for a Swedish production company, with Susan Anspach finding erotic fulfilment among a group of Serbian gipsies.

Wim Verstappen, who once tracked the 'Provos' on the streets of Amsterdam for *Joszef Katús*, became a banker. (And why not, when Jerry Rubin, of the 'Chicago Seven', achieved success on Wall Street in the eighties?) Fons Rademakers directed a masterly analysis of the Dutch colonial experience in *Max Havelaar* (1976), and ten years later won the Academy Award for Best Foreign Film with *The Assault*, set during World War II.

Some have continued to plough their familiar furrow: Chabrol, with his unsettling, often brilliantly controlled psychological thrillers; Rivette, with his sporadic observations on Parisian intellectual life, most recently celebrated in *Va savoir* (2001); Costa-Gavras, still incensed by the duplicity of those in power (even in his latest, *Amen*, released in 2002), and a potent influence on directors like Oliver Stone and John Sayles; and Rohmer, still writing exquisite dialogue for men and women a third of his age. Yet paradoxically, *Ma nuit chez Maud*, which in 1969 won universal acclaim (even two Oscar nominations), can now be seen as one of the more tiresome exercises in Rohmer's career. Shot for the most part indoors, with its camera rarely on the move, its protracted arguments between Jean-Louis Trintignant, Françoise Fabian and Antoine Vitez about Pascal's wager and the nature of emotional commitment are just too theatrical. The acting, as always in Rohmer, is excellent, but the film gasps for air at several points, the action stifled by an intellectual élitism that now looks curiously dated and light years removed from films like *Easy Rider* and *Five Easy Pieces* which owed so much to Rohmer's earliest work.

At least ten to fifteen years would elapse before the world could appreciate Alain Resnais' personality in three dimensions, with his mischievous humour, his affection for *outré* authors like H. P. Lovecraft, Alan Ayckbourn and Marvel Comics' Stan Lee, and his gift for sophisticated musical comedy. *On connaît la chanson* (1997) is a miraculous riff on so many aspects of musical comedy, not to mention the dubbing that is such an integral element in French film-going. Still strolling around at eighty in sneakers and a windcheater, Resnais has slipped the bonds of the average career, excelling in a wide variety of genres and never taking himself too seriously. His latest project is a 'comedy with music' entitled *Pas sur la bouche*, featuring his favourite actors and actresses.

Others have deviated into fresh fields – Saura with his musical dramas like *Blood Wedding*, *Carmen*, *Flamenco* and *Tango*, or Varda with her documentary investigations of life in the margins of France. Indeed,

Varda still seems the youngest of all the surviving New Wave film-makers. Her passion and commitment are evident in her documentary, *Les glaneurs et la glaneuse* (2001), and *Vagabond*, made in 1986, reveals the sombre mid-winter nether-world of Provence.

Bergman has outlived his old friend, Fellini. Together, they constituted a mutual admiration society. 'Bergman's way of telling a story,' said Fellini, 'the richness of his temperament and above all his way of expressing himself exactly as I feel a showman ought to – that is, as a mixture of magician and conjurer, prophet and clown, travelling salesman and preacher – makes him exactly what a showman ought to be.' Bergman felt similarly about Fellini, spending three weeks with him during the late sixties, preparing a portmanteau film that would have comprised episodes from Kurosawa, Fellini and Bergman himself. Kurosawa had fallen ill with pneumonia, and while waiting for him to arrive in Rome, Bergman watched Fellini at work in Cinecittà on the final scenes of *Satyricon*. 'I loved Fellini's personality,' he said recently. 'I went to see him at home with Giulietta Masina, on the coast, and had a memorable Easter dinner with them. We had a lot of affection for each other. And of course I still watch his films. I adore *La strada*, and above all *Amarcord*.'

Bergman admits that he enjoyed the scene in *Les 400 coups* where the kids steal the still of Harriet Andersson in *Summer with Monika* from the front of a cinema. 'I liked Truffaut very much, and admired his work. His way of addressing his audience, of telling a story, was fascinating and appealing.' Godard, though, left him very cold. 'I've never been capable of communicating with any of his films, and I've never understood them either. I find his films affected, intellectual, imbued with themselves and, from a cinematic point of view, without interest and frankly deadly dull.' For Bergman, Chabrol remains the most intriguing of the New Wave directors – 'a marvellous story-teller in a particular field; I've always had a weakness for his thrillers.' Bergman made his magnum opus, *Fanny and Alexander*, in 1982 and then announced his retirement from the cinema. That did not prevent his writing and directing for television, nor his staging plays and operas in Stockholm, nor his writing screenplays about his parents for others, like Bille August and Liv Ullmann, to direct. In 2003, he completed *Saraband*, a 'sequel' to *Scenes from a Marriage*.

For Bergman, as for Welles, the cinema was a medium created by magicians like Méliès. 'I think it's quite tragic that electronics have taken over now,' he told me in 1982. 'Of course, it must be so if we think about it. Film was invented in 1895, and we still work with it in exactly the same way. Something else has to happen, and I think that's to be welcomed, but I don't want to be involved in it. I like to work with a screen and projectors, with the sound of the projectors and the shadows. To me, that has enormous fascination . . .'

Godard, the most acclaimed director of the sixties, and still contentious, still cantankerous, has worked more prolifically in film and television than anyone of his generation. He even dipped his toe into the American pool in the late seventies, when Francis Coppola and Tom Luddy advanced him money for a picture about Bugsy Siegel – which was never made – at Zoetrope Studios, and when he helped Coppola modestly on *One from the Heart*. By the turn of the seventies, however, the joys of life seemed to be drying up for Godard. Even in his films of the very late sixties he was swinging away into a jungle of self-referential drivel. But during that earlier, spellbinding burst of energy, he, more than any single director, embodied the title of this book – *Revolution!*. Detached, derisive, infinitely inventive, he changed for ever the way in which films were shot and edited. To quote a story by Borges that Godard himself adored: 'There once was a man who wanted to create a world: so he began by creating houses, provinces, valleys, rivers, tools, fish, lovers, etc., and at the end of his life, he noticed that this patiently elaborated labyrinth was nothing other than his own portrait.' To paraphrase the late Richard Roud, that portrait is indeed Godard's.

Orson Welles regarded Godard as 'the definitive influence' of the sixties; 'and his gifts as a director are enormous. I just can't take him very seriously as a *thinker* – and that's where we seem to differ, because *he* does.' The influence of Godard can be found today in a legion of directors, from Scorsese to Tarantino and Kaurismäki. His insolent, innovative spirit hovers at the shoulder of Lars von Trier and his Dogme 95 doctrine, with its insistence on naturalism and its abhorrence of special effects. The once-despised neo-realism has made a comeback, too, thanks to lighter cameras and digital methods. Films as diverse as Michael Winterbottom's *In This World*, Danis Tanović's *No Man's Land* and Samira Makhmalbaf's *Blackboards* attest to the need to ally fiction and non-fiction that stood at the very core of Visconti's *La terra trema* – or, for that matter, Varda's *La Pointe Courte*.

Finally, I asked my interviewees to assess the period from the perspective of the present day.

VOLKER SCHLÖNDORFF: *At that juncture we really had a young audience that liked our films. We had the feeling that films were as much the expression of what was going on in the* Zeitgeist *as was music. Of course, you can't beat the Beatles or the Stones, but next best to music was the cinema. Films were the medium of the generation of the sixties . . .*

We were anti-consumerism in our film-making: the strong undercurrent of the student revolt was partly Vietnam, but an equal part was anti-consumerism. And the first thing Andreas Baader did before he created the Baader-Meinhof Gang was to set fire to department stores – it did little damage as such, but people could not believe it was happening, because society at large – the parents' generation – were total consumers. They didn't want to hear about politics ever again, because they felt they had been betrayed by Hitler. I think that throughout Europe, the fifties were a consumerist time, coming in the wake of the hardship of the post-war years. So it was logical that in our films we would take characters who were not successful, who did not want to succeed within the economic miracle, and who generally were anti-consumerism.

We shunned the studio reality of the forties and the fifties, which had pretended to show life and reality – but did neither. And it took almost ten years before any of the New Wave directors themselves had to go into the studio and reverse it somehow. Even if we were treating a piece of fiction, we still wanted to approach it in some kind of documentary way. And anything that was stagy, like delivering a punchline with a certain reading so that it would get a laugh – that was forbidden, because it was the old way, with the timing and the looking for laughs. As was the habit of creating a certain vibrato in the voice to express emotion – NO WAY! Because in real life, people didn't do that! So you needed a different kind of actor, actors who had not been trained in stage routine, going for the artificial pause, going for the punchline.

In the screenplay, we wanted to avoid any melodramatic construction, and any attempt to press real-life relationships and occurrences into the traditional three-act canon of melodrama.

So it was an aesthetic revolution in the name of truthfulness, of authenticity – not to turn life upside-down but rather to put life back on its feet.

MILOŠ FORMAN: *The sixties were absolutely vital – we got a taste, a taste of what we could do when we were allowed to make what we wanted to make, freely.*

You are always under pressure in the film business. In the Communist countries, you were not under commercial pressure, but you were under strong ideological pressure. In the United States, you are not under ideological pressure at all, but you are under commercial pressure. To be honest, I prefer commercial pressure, because then I am at the mercy of the taste of an audience. Under ideological pressure, I am at the mercy of one or two idiots. Besides, it's a mistake to regard Hollywood as one entity. Hollywood doesn't exist – hundreds of Hollywoods exist, and behind every door you'll find a different Hollywood. If you are lucky, and find the right door at the right moment, you can do interesting things in America.

FRANCESCO ROSI: *The sixties were a period of major cultural revolution, which brought together a generation and different countries, throughout Europe and even the United States. It was very profound. You've only got to look at a film by Godard or Fellini or Antonioni to see that it was really revolutionary. The problem is to live one's own period with a passion for self-expression, for making films that say something, however modest or even humble. That's why I want the audience for my films to be active, not passive.*

In the hands of publicity and consumerism, the world is changing so fast – whether in the domain of technology, publicity, music, television – that we can no longer control the way it's evolving. In this culture of change, young people have no knowledge of the past – there's an enormous lack of 'memory'. Even in Italian schools and colleges, they are often unaware of Rossellini. Television may be the most rapid medium of communication, but the cinema remains the most profound.

GILLO PONTECORVO: *I think that before the New Wave films began exploding all over Europe, there was, in the minds of those cinéastes, an awareness that the world could not remain as it then was. For the past fifteen, twenty years, the intellectuals have abdicated their primary responsibility of being vigilant towards reality – but at least in Italy there are one or two signs that the intellectuals are now changing their tune . . .*

KRZYSZTOF ZANUSSI: *We had a far bigger margin of freedom back then. And what did we do with that freedom? I think that first and foremost we were trying to discover the historical condition – men versus history. And it was always implicit polemics, with Marx and with Hegel, Man as a tragic victim of History. As Marx's teaching dictated that History is always right, our colleagues were often shouting that History is often wrong. This was a very strong message, very close to the spirit of Greek tragedy, with no good way out.*

My generation – Kieślowski, myself and others – with its focus on a cinema of 'moral anxiety', was trying to discover the role of the individual versus society – there is no such thing as society, only individuals, and that History is not on our account. This was a reaction against a long period of Marxist collectivism. We were insisting on that because most post-modernists were trying to put good and evil together, saying that there's no distinction. We were screaming that there is a very clear distinction between good and evil, between truth and life, and that no class struggle can obscure this distinction. Don't tell us that torture is good, if it's for a good purpose! Violence is evil.

JERZY KAWALEROWICZ: *The themes are different today than they were in the sixties. Now commercial considerations are more important. This, allied to the arrival of satellite television, has changed the situation for Polish cinema. I have never made a film for television; for me, the TV screen cannot accommodate a big film! The size of the screen plays an important role in my cinema. I always liked to give audiences something that would touch their emotions, and a big screen – not necessarily a specific 'Scope process – helped to do just that.*

There's no doubt in my mind that the sixties marked the greatest period of Polish cinematography. Today, television dominates to such a degree that there are few important screenwriters around. In the sixties, as in the time of Balzac, there was a surge in writing about historical subjects, and screenwriters who could bring them to life.

PHIL KAUFMAN: *When film books came out in the sixties, people read them with a real curiosity. Now they do so with a calculation: how can I transform my knowledge into dollars? But I want to insist upon the right to be naïve – even if I made* The Right Stuff *about this unknown guy, Chuck Yeager, who had gone up into space for practically no money at all, and then when the movie comes out, he's doing TV commercials and becoming a multi-millionaire!*

I believe that young and old were interested in serious things in the sixties. An excitement was in the air. I don't think it's just my adrenal flow, the flush of my youth, my libidinous adolescence. Was this childhood's end? I mean, it's a tragedy that Italian cinema's not vital right now . . . I just wish that young film-makers were making more truly experimental movies and not just calling cards for Hollywood. Films in the sixties had this irreverent vitality, but they spoke to everybody, you didn't have to be particularly a hipster to understand what was going on.

Our business is, as film-makers, to create dreams, get us through the darkness of every day. In the sixties, we would look forward for weeks and weeks to the next Fellini or the next Bergman movie with bated breath.

JOHN BOORMAN: *There was a mixture of influences, really. In terms of Britain, there's one thing that's never really acknowledged, and that's that the explosion of music that occurred in the early sixties was to do with the Education Act of 1947, where you had these secondary-modern schools which taught music and drama and so forth which hadn't done so before. Prior to that, it was either the grammar school or the technical school. If you look at the timing, by 1960 these people were coming out of those schools having learned to play a musical instrument. The Beatles were heavily influenced by Dylan, who was a crucial influence, and rock 'n' roll – all came from America. But it was the French cinema that really influenced us, or certainly Richard Lester.*

À bout de souffle was really the picture that made us all interested in the New Wave and what was happening in France at that time. The Japanese cinema was also very powerful then, too. The Academy Cinema and the Cameo-Poly were the places in London where I first encountered those kinds of films.

WALTER MURCH: *The filming technique behind even something so personal as Bergman's The Seventh Seal, unless you really know cinema, is a little opaque as to what's going on and how they achieved some of those effects. Prior to being a film student, I had no inkling. I looked at À bout de souffle and instantly I knew how that was made, in the sense that I just had to be given a few clues. They placed a camera in a wheelchair, and suddenly I saw that it was done very simply, using natural light and real locations and simple things like wheelchairs and hand-held cameras. Our family had a little 8mm camera, so I saw this as a slightly larger version of that.*

Godard's work was both inspirational in terms of the freedom of its technique but also in that the very technique allowed you to see how you could do that – it made it possible. As opposed to a more traditional Hollywood film, or even a more controlled film-maker like Kurosawa (and Fellini to a certain extent), who achieved marvellous individual effects, but where the freedom and lightness of technique was not quite so evident as it was in Godard.

JÖRN DONNER: *I still have a longing for that period, because so many things were happening, not just the Nouvelle Vague. What I liked especially in the Eastern European cinema – especially in the Czech films – was a sort of anarchist humour. I don't remember any American films from that period! And of course the Italian film was nothing new to me, because in 1953 already I had gone to Rome and interviewed and seen and met most of those film-makers who would become famous, Visconti, Antonioni and so on.*

RICHARD LESTER: *The sixties will always be the period of my life. I've always said that when I die, the* Evening Standard *will say, 'Beatles Director in Death Drama'. I can't change that. It was an absolutely extraordinary period for me. One felt immensely alive, and we all got through a huge body of work. I look at my diaries from that time, from the late fifties onwards, and the amount of things that I did in a week was probably what I'd do in a year now. Everything came together for something that turned out to be extraordinary, and that I think will remain so. Of course it is too soon to judge it. It's like if you look at the seventeenth century compared to Georgian England – the transition periods become really wonderful when you poke around in them.*

AGNÈS VARDA: *I have the feeling that this film revolution broke out in France. I think that it was Godard and Truffaut and others in France who influenced Miloš Forman and other European directors. Of course the Polish cinema, the Czech cinema, had their way of working, as did Coppola and Scorsese a few years later. Even Lelouch had a way of embracing the cinema. Then in Britain you had Lindsay Anderson and the documentarists, then* If . . .

For me, the Nouvelle Vague was composed of cinéastes under the age of thirty, who made films for less than thirty million francs at the time. Because there was a constant flow of young people, not yet fully developed, who loved cinema intensely and who were auteurs. Many of these talents have survived and continued – Godard, Chabrol . . . Lelouch, Rozier, Rohmer and Rivette started a little later. You could say that the older members of the Nouvelle Vague have kept rather fresh, with a lot of creative energy still. I don't think that they've laid down their arms . . .

BERNARDO BERTOLUCCI: *What was important for me in the sixties was that a 'political film' was not necessarily a film with a political subject. Instead, such a film could treat politics in the essence of cinema, which means style – the way you produce a film, the way you break the conventions and clichés of narrative structure. Sometimes, and we were very fundamentalist in that, we rejected movies that were politically aimed at the audience that was going to see them, and in a way they were enriched politically – but for us they weren't, because they were told and filmed in the same old-fashioned way. So to be <u>really</u> politically correct then, a movie had to be revolutionary not only in its content but especially in its form.*

The cinema was feeding this need for hope in the sixties. About three years ago, I saw Before the Revolution *for the first time in some thirty-five years. I was so surprised at how sure we were at that time. We were sure because our hopes were so powerful, so strong. Young people could dream of an incredible future in the sixties. Is there room for that kind of hope today?*

Doubtless, 1956 to 1970 comprised a fifteen-year freewheeling lifetime, replete with icons and calamities that burned their way into the collective psyche – Algeria, the Hungarian Uprising, the Vietnam War, the Kennedy assassinations, the death of Marilyn Monroe, the Cuban missile crisis, the Beatles, the Stones, the invasion of Czechoslovakia, the miniskirt, tanks in the streets of Athens, the murder of Martin Luther King, May '68 . . .

The movie actor, too, became an icon personified: from Jeanne Moreau and Monica Vitti to Liv Ullmann and Max von Sydow, from Jean-Paul Belmondo to Marcello Mastroianni.

Will Hutton would write in the London *Observer* in 2001:

The sixties provoked a romantic revolt against deference, authority and unthinking social conformity that opened the way to a very English approach to individuality captured in the idea of social individualism. We wanted the freedom to explore our inner selves – 'Strawberry Fields Forever' or 'Lucy in the Sky with Diamonds' – while expressing the solidarities of 'All You Need is Love'.

Herbert Marcuse had excoriated industrial materialism, saying that it handicapped the individual in society, and that freedom for the aesthetic imagination was indispensable. There may be two distinct ways of remembering the sixties, in fact. For many, the decade throbbed with a new-found liberty – in fashion, in music, in art, even, to some extent, in politics. For others, it was a time of levity, when speculation was skin-deep and each new weekend offered both a demonstration and the chance to pass the pipe and listen to Frank Zappa and the Mothers of Invention. If a common factor can be discerned in this tumultuous period as it hastens back into history, it is the need to shock – technically, aesthetically and socially,

And so it is that cinematic images of desolation have outlasted the frivolities of Carnaby Street or Haight-Ashbury: Cybulski dying in agony amid the refuse in *Ashes and Diamonds*, Léaud on the beach at the end of *Les 400 coups*, Nicholson mumbling an apologia to his father on a hillside in *Five Easy Pieces*. Their troubling relevance still sends, to quote Lindsay Anderson, 'both a threat and a reproach' to later decades.

Notes

INTRODUCTION

'Economic expansion began', Arthur Marwick, *The Sixties* (Oxford and New York, Oxford University Press, 1998)

'Tennessee Williams told Elaine Dundy', Elaine Dundy, *Life Itself!*, (London, Virago Press, 2001)

'If there is still any doubt', Tony Palmer, *Observer* (London, November 1968), quoted on LP sleeve for *Yellow Submarine*

'All we knew was that we were having fun,' Andrea R. Vaucher, 'New Wave Girl Karina Hasn't Lost It', *Variety* (Los Angeles, 3–9 December, 2001)

'Michelangelo Antonioni's *L'avventura*', Penelope Houston, 'Cannes 1960', *Sight and Sound* (London, Summer 1960)

'The absolutely contemporary, sixties film', Penelope Houston, *Sight and Sound* (London, Winter 1961–2)

'I liked Truffaut very much', interview with Ingmar Bergman, by Jan Aghed, *Positif* (Paris, July–August 2002)

'If I watch my old films', Peter Cowie, *Max von Sydow* (Stockholm, Swedish Film Institute, 1989)

'As Mark LeFanu . . .', Mark Le Fanu, 'Art House Lives', *Prospect* (London, November 2000)

1 ONCE UPON A TIME IN THE FIFTIES

'The only useful way', Peter Cowie, *Antonioni–Bergman–Resnais* (London, The Tantivy Press; New York, A.S. Barnes & Co., 1963)

'Eroticism is the disease of our age', quoted in *Antonioni–Bergman–Resnais*, op. cit.

'Some film-makers decide to tell a story', cited in Peter Cowie (ed.), *Fifty Major Film-Makers* (London, The Tantivy Press; New York, A.S. Barnes & Co., 1975)

'*Summer with Monika* is the most original film', cited in Tom Milne (ed.), *Godard on Godard* (London, Secker and Warburg, 1968)

'Wild Strawberries proves Ingmar', op.cit.

'Polish film-makers', Boleslaw Michalek, 'The Polish Drama', *Sight and Sound* (London, Autumn 1960)

'As far as I know', Ado Kyrou, *Positif* (Paris, February 1957)

'For us it was a film of tremendous importance', cited in Boleslaw Michalek, *The Cinema of Andrzej Wajda* (London, The Tantivy Press, 1973)

'I wanted to show a society', cited in Peter Cowie (ed.), *Fifty Major Film-Makers* (London, The Tantivy Press; New York, A.S. Barnes & Co., 1975)

2 CINÉPHILES TO CINÉASTES: FRANCE IN TRANSITION

'All of us at *Cahiers*', Tom Milne (ed.), *Godard on Godard* (London, Secker and Warburg, 1972)

'Nobody can enter the Olympus', Antoine de Baecque and Serge Toubiana, *François Truffaut* (Paris, Editions Gallimard, 1996)

'Only speaks of what he knows well', ibid.

'With *Voyage en Italie*', ibid.

'I was trying to portray a new generation', Philip French (ed.), *Malle on Malle* (London, Faber and Faber, 1993)

'This autumn, in the studio', Henry Chapier, *Louis Malle* (Paris, Editions Seghers, 1964)

'When I made *Ascenseur pour l'échafaud*', ibid.

'The moment I first touched the camera', *Truffaut par Truffaut* (Paris, Chêne, 1985)

'The sincerity of a film', Peter Cowie, *Eighty Years of Cinema*, (New Jersey, A. S. Barnes & Co., 1977)

'A hymn to love', *Truffaut par Truffaut*, op. cit.

'I've always wanted, basically', *Godard on Godard*, op. cit.

"Perhaps as important a film as *Citizen Kane*', *Positif*, no. 31 (Paris, November 1959)

'His idea was to film the screenplay', interview with Richard Roud in *Sight and Sound* (London, Winter 1960–1)

'It was a good time to be alive', Foreword to *François Truffaut, Letters*, translated by Gilbert Adair (London, Faber and Faber, 1989)

3 THE REALIST'S EYE

'When I started, I thought it would take me only a few months', Ray Carney (ed.), *Cassavetes on Cassavetes* (London, Faber and Faber, 2001)

'Dreamed up some characters', ibid.

'The real difference between *Shadows*', ibid.

'First we improvise', ibid.

'Though on *Shadows* I had to scrap', John Russell Taylor, 'Cassavetes in London', *Sight and Sound* (London, Autumn 1960)

'It was an essential training for me', Preface to Freddy Buache, *Le Cinéma Français des Années 60* (Renens, Switzerland, Les 5 Continents, 1987)

'If I watch my old films', *Max von Sydow, from The Seventh Seal to Pelle the Conqueror* (Stockholm, Swedish Film Institute, 1989)

'Assertiveness, his impetuosity', cited in Boleslaw Michalek, *The Cinema of Andrzej Wajda* (London, The Tantivy Press, 1973)

'We didn't even have enough money', Ray Carney (ed.), *Cassavetes on Cassavetes* (London, Faber and Faber, 2001)

4 THE BIG NEW WAVE

'Everyone thought the New Wave was so natural', Andrea R. Vaucher, 'New Wave Girl Karina Hasn't Lost It', *Variety* (Los Angeles, 3–9 December, 2001)

'I've always wanted, basically, to do research', Tom Milne (ed.), *Godard on Godard* (London, Secker and Warburg, 1972)

'Whereas the Odyssey of Ulysses', ibid.

'Sensitivity, intuition, good taste', cited in Peter Cowie (ed.), *Fifty-Major Film-Makers* (London, The Tantivy Press; New York, A.S. Barnes & Co., 1975)

'My very soul revolts', Louis Marcorelles, 'In the Picture', *Sight and Sound* (London, British Film Institute, Winter 1959–60)

'Little by little, the cinema has been recognized', Raymond Borde,

Nouvelle Vague (Lyon, Premier Plan/SERDOC, 1960)

'In both these films', cited in Peter Cowie, *Antonioni–Bergman–Resnais* (London, The Tantivy Press; New York, A.S. Barnes & Co., 1963)

'It implies a high degree of involvement', from Richard Roud, 'The Left Bank', *Sight and Sound* (London, Winter 1962–3)

'The Dome was not only a rendezvous', ibid.

'There is another factor that obliged me from the start', Rohmer, Preface to *Six Moral Tales* (London, Lorrimer Publishing, 1980)

'They refuse to commit themselves', Robert Benayoun, 'The King Is Dead', *Positif*, no. 46, cited in Peter Graham (ed.), *The New Wave* (London, Secker and Warburg, 1968)

'I prefer blue to black', cited in Peter Cowie (ed.), *Fifty Major Film-Makers* (London, The Tantivy Press: New York, A.S. Barnes & Co., 1975)

'The term "political film"', author's interview with Francesco Rosi (see separate listing)

'If Antonioni was the anatomist', Naomi Greene, *Pier Paolo Pasolini, Cinema as Heresy* (Princeton, NJ, Princeton University Press, 1990)

'For the boy [in *Il posto*]', Charles Thomas Samuels, *Encountering Directors* (New York, G. P. Putnam's Sons, 1972)

'We started off in the middle of the night', Anna Keel and Christian Strich (eds), *Fellini on Fellini* (London, Eyre Methuen, 1976)

'Michelangelo Antonioni's *L'avventura* was shown', *Sight and Sound* (London, British Film Institute, Summer 1960)

'I think it is much more cinematic', cited in *Antonioni–Bergman–Resnais*, op. cit.

'Man deceives himself when he hasn't courage enough', ibid.

'I think it is the normal ratio', Peter Graham (ed.), *The New Wave* (London, Secker and Warburg, 1968)

'In fact, satire was as much of a force', Elaine Dundy, *Life Itself!*, op. cit.

'As Marx's teaching dictated', author's interview with Krzysztof Zanussi (see separate listing)

'I remember seeing Pasolini's *Accattone*', author's interview with Phil Kaufman (see separate listing)

'I identified with black people,' interview with Shirley Clarke by DeeDee Halleck (New York, 1985, see http://208.55.137.252/shirleyclarkeinterview.html)

'That's what I was looking to do', ibid.

'When we made *The Manchurian Candidate*', Gerald Pratley, *The Films of Frankenheimer* (London, Cygnus Arts; Bethlehem, Lehigh University Press, 1998)

'I wanted to do a picture', ibid.

'In *Through a Glass Darkly* the predominant thing', Vilgot Sjöman, *L136, Diary with Ingmar Bergman* (Anna Arbor, Karoma Publishers, 1978)

5 BURYING 'PAPA'S CINEMA'

'There is no New Wave', Guy Braucourt, *Claude Chabrol* (Paris, Editions Seghers, 1971)

'The Swedish Institute expresses in this way', quoted in Peter Cowie (ed.), *Swedish Cinema* (London, The Tantivy Press/A. Zwemmer; New York, A. S. Barnes & Co., 1966)

'Easily the bravest and most original film', *International Film Guide 1966* (London, The Tantivy Press; New York, A.S. Barnes & Co., 1965)

'There's a good deal of blood,' *Godard on Godard*, op. cit.

'Your film is as stupid as Jean Renoir', *Varda par Agnès* (Paris, Les Editions de *Cahiers du cinéma*, 1994)

'What interested me about *La peau douce*', quoted in *Truffaut par Truffaut* (Paris, Editions La Chêne, 1985)

'Those who live before the revolution', quoted in Mira Liehm, *Passion and Defiance, Film in Italy from 1942 to the Present* (Berkeley, University of California Press, 1984)

'What interests me passionately,' quoted in *Fifty Major Film-Makers*, op. cit.

6 TOWARDS A FRESH AESTHETIC

'We were very interested in what cinema is', interview in the *Observer* (London, 21 October 2001).

'All the most important and immediate conflicts in life', quoted in *Fifty Major Film-Makers*, op. cit.

'We pursue our professions,' ibid.

'The death of Cybulski was a real story', from author's interview with Andrzej Wajda (see separate listing)

'I think I'll be crying', quoted in *Fifty Major Film-Makers*, op. cit.

'I work very fast', ibid.

'Normally we'd have needed three days', from author's phone interview with Hercules Bellville (28 January 2003)

'All these people who amuse themselves', ibid.

'There were five of us in the crew', Gunnar Bergdahl, *Interlude in Smygehuk: Jan Troell on His Films* (Göteborg, Göteborg Film Festival/Swedish Film Institute, 2001)

'Cassavetes stayed until the last disdainful Parisian', *Cassavetes on Cassavetes*, op. cit.

'Of all the scripts I have turned down', *François Truffaut, Letters,* op. cit.

'Young people felt excluded from a society', quoted in *Fifty Major Film-Makers*, op. cit.

7 COMMITMENT COMES IN FROM THE COLD

'Instead of trying to reconcile the myth', quoted in *Fifty Major Film-Makers*, op. cit.

'These people are offered real love', ibid.

'The film is shot with a plaintive simplicity', *Projections* 4½ (London, Faber and Faber, 1995)

'The situation here is different', interview in *International Film Guide 1968* (London, The Tantivy Press; New York, A. S. Barnes & Co., 1967)

'The *cinéma des auteurs* is not merely a question', ibid.

'In his innovative use of high-contrast film stock', Rob Stone, *Spanish Cinema* (London, Longman/Pearson Education, 2002)

'Strong, intelligent personalities grouped together', Jean-Michel Frodon, *L'Age Moderne du Cinéma Français, de la Nouvelle Vague à nos jours* (Paris, Flammarion, 1995)

'The Free Speech movement [in Berkeley] began', *San Francisco Chronicle,* 13 April 2001

'Is that under the pretence of reforming', Richard Roud, *Jean-Luc Godard* (London, Thames and Hudson, 1968)

8 1968 AND ALL THAT . . .

'Actor Jean-Pierre Léaud', Gilbert Adair, *The Holy Innocents* (London, Heinemann, 1988)

'All directors, producers, distributors', *Le Monde,* Paris, 10 May 2001

'It is inconceivable that people should be seeing films down here', Jacques Sternberg, 'Révolution culturelle au Festival de Cannes', cited in Danièle Heymann and Jean-Pierre Dufreigne, *Le Roman de Cannes, 50 années de Festival* (Paris, TF1 Editions, 1996)

'I'm talking to you about solidarity', Jean-Michel Frodon, *L'Age Moderne du Cinéma Français, de la Nouvelle Vague à nos jours* (Paris, Flammarion, 1995)

'This film is being shown against the will', Penelope Houston, 'Revolutionary '68 events triggered coup de cinema', *Variety*, 24–30 March 1997 (Cannes 50 Years supplement)

'The saddest figures in this boisterous political carnival', ibid.

'Is this a revolution?', ibid.

9 AFTERMATH: THE IMPACT ON HOLLYWOOD

'Looking back, I suppose we can say', from author's interview with John Boorman (see separate listing)

'Cinema Nôvo was driven by the need', Leif Furhammar and Folke Isaksson, *Politics and Film* (London, Studio Vista, 1971)

'As its strange images and barbaric sounds', *Projections* 4½, op. cit.

'We immediately agreed on something,' quoted at http://www.italian-network.it/cinema/cinema41/cinema_e.htm

'In spite of everything, youth in the sixties', Reinaldo Arenas, *Before Night Falls* (New York, Viking Penguin, 1993)

'Oshima sees the failure', Claire Johnston, 'Nagisa Oshima', *Fifty Major Film-Makers*, op. cit.

'What's basically wrong with Hollywood', *Cassavetes on Cassavetes*, op. cit.

'As I described it,' Peter Cowie, *Coppola* (London, André Deutsch, 1989; Faber and Faber revised edition, 1998)

'*Petulia* was a deeply-troubled', from author's interview with Richard Lester (see separate listing)

10 THE LONG GOODBYE

'In *Amarcord,* I built the sea', *Fellini on Fellini*, op. cit.

'There once was a man', Introduction to *Godard on Godard*, op. cit.

'And his gifts as a director are enormous', Orson Welles and Peter Bogdanovich, *This Is Orson Welles* (New York, HarperCollins, 1992)

'When you've been a critic, and start making films', from interview on Criterion Collection DVD of *Contempt* (New York, 2002)

'Bergman's way of telling a story', *Fellini on Fellini,* op. cit.

'I loved Fellini's personality,' Jan Aghed, interview with Ingmar Bergman, *Positif* (Paris, July–August 2002)

'I liked Truffaut very much', ibid.

'I think it's quite tragic that electronics have taken over now', interview with Peter Cowie at National Film Theatre, London, September 1982

'The sixties provoked a romantic revolt', Will Hutton, 'Why the Death of a Sixties Idol Is So Affecting', *Observer,* London, 2 December 2001

'Both a threat and a reproach', from Lindsay Anderson's speech at National Film Theatre, London, November 1987

Interviews

The main interviews for this book were conducted as follows:

Bernardo Bertolucci, by phone (London), 3 February 2003
John Boorman, by phone (Eire), 20 November 2001
Jörn Donner, Stockholm, 26 March 2001
Miloš Forman, by phone (New York), 16 March 2002
Phil Kaufman, San Francisco, 14 March 2001
Jerzy Kawalerowicz, Warsaw, 10 July 2002
John Korty, Point Reyes Station, California, 8 April 2001
Walter Lassally, by phone (Crete), 7 March 2002
Richard Lester, Twickenham Studios, 22 April 2002
Dušan Makavejev, Paris, 23/24 April 2001
Walter Murch, London, 20 December 2000
Gillo Pontecorvo, Rome, 11 December 2001
Fons Rademakers, Rome, 11 December 2001
Karel Reisz, London, 9 May 2002
Alain Resnais, Paris, 11 April 2002
Francesco Rosi, Rome, 10 December 2001
Volker Schlöndorff, Berlin, 12 February 2002
Vilgot Sjöman, Stockholm, 26 March 2001
Bertrand Tavernier, Paris, 23 April 2001
Agnès Varda, Paris, 13 November 2001
Andrzej Wajda, Warsaw, 9 July 2002
Krzysztof Zanussi, Warsaw, 10 July 2002

Filmographies of Directors Interviewed

BERNARDO BERTOLUCCI

Born 1940, Parma (Italy). At first a promising poet, he accepted an offer in 1961 to assist Pasolini on *Accattone*. Won Academy Award in 1988 for his direction of *The Last Emperor*. Features: *La commare secca/The Grim Reaper* 1962; *Prima della rivoluzione/Before the Revolution* 1964; *Partner* 1968; *La strategia del ragno/The Spider's Stratagem, Il conformista/The Conformist* 1970; *Ultimo tango a Parigi/Last Tango in Paris* 1972; *Novecento/1900* 1976; *La luna* 1979; *La tragedia di un uomo ridiculo/The Tragedy of a Ridiculous Man* 1981; *The Last Emperor* 1987; *The Sheltering Sky* 1990; *Little Buddha* 1994; *Stealing Beauty* 1996; *Besieged* 1998; *The Dreamers* 2003.

JOHN BOORMAN

Born 1933, Shepperton (UK). Began career in British television, and in 1962 became head of BBC documentary unit in Bristol. Features: *Catch Us if You Can/Having a Wild Weekend* 1965; *Point Blank* 1967; *Hell in the Pacific* 1968; *Leo the Last* 1970; *Deliverance* 1972; *Zardoz* 1974; *Exorcist II: The Heretic* 1977; *Excalibur* 1981; *The Emerald Forest* 1985: *Hope and Glory* 1987; *Where the Heart Is* 1990; *Beyond Rangoon* 1995; *The General* 1998; *The Tailor of Panama* 2001; *Country of my Skull* 2003.

JÖRN DONNER

Born 1933, Helsinki (Finland). Published books before he was twenty, and began writing film criticism for various magazines and papers in Finland. Made short films, and published a trenchant study of Ingmar Bergman's work, before embarking on a career as a director, producer and prize-winning novelist. Continues to direct and produce for television. Features: *A Sunday in September* 1963; *To Love* 1964; *Adventure Starts Here* 1965; *Rooftree* 1967; *Black on White* 1968; *Sixty-nine* 1969; *Portraits of Women, Anna* 1970; *Fuck Off! – Images of Finland* 1971; *Tenderness* 1972; *Men Can't Be Raped* 1978; *Dirty Story* 1984.

MILOŠ FORMAN

Born 1932, Cáslav (Czechoslovakia). Graduate of the Prague FAMU college, he began writing for the cinema during the mid-fifties. Features: *Audition/Competition, If It Weren't for Music* 1963; *Black Peter/Peter and Pavla* 1964; *Loves of a Blonde/A Blonde in Love* 1965; *The Firemen's Ball* 1967; *Taking Off* 1971; *One Flew over the Cuckoo's Nest* 1975; *Hair* 1979; *Ragtime* 1981; *Amadeus* 1984; *Valmont* 1989; *The People vs Larry Flynt* 1996; *Man on the Moon* 1999.

PHILIP KAUFMAN

Born 1936, Chicago. Studied at University of Chicago and Harvard Law School. Then turned all his attention to cinema, teaching himself the technique and financing of films as he went along. Features: *Goldstein* (co. Benjamin Manaster) 1964; *Fearless Frank/Frank's Greatest Adventure* 1967; *The Great Northfield Minnesota Raid* 1972; *White Dawn* 1974; *Invasion of the Body Snatchers* 1978; *The Wanderers* 1979; *The Right Stuff* 1983; *The Unbearable Lightness of Being* 1987; *Henry and June* 1990; *Rising Sun* 1993; *The Blackout Murders* 2003.

JERZY KAWALEROWICZ

Born 1922, Gwozdziec (Poland, now Ukraine). Graduated from the Kraków Film Institute, and made his directorial début in 1950. Five years later, appointed head of the influential KADR Studio Unit. Features: *The Village Mill* (co. Kazimierz Sumerski) 1950; *A Night of Remembrance, Under the Phrygian Star* 1954; *The Shadow* 1956; *The Real End of the Great War* 1957; *Night Train* 1959; *Mother Joan of the Angels* 1961; *Pharaoh* 1965; *The Game* 1969; *Maddalena* 1971; *Death of a President*

1978; *Chance Meeting on the Atlantic* 1979; *Austeria* 1982; *Hostage of Europe* 1989; *Bronstein's Children* 1990; *Why?* 1996; *Quo Vadis* 2001.

JOHN KORTY

Born 1936, Lafayette (Indiana). Started shooting amateur films at sixteen and showed early talent for animation. Specialist in low-budget documentaries and, during the sixties, noted for his offbeat comedies of social observation. Won Oscar in 1977 for his feature-length documentary, *Who Are the De Bolts? . . . And Where Did They Get 19 Kids?* Founded his own studio in northern California. Features: *The Crazy Quilt* 1966; *Funnyman* 1967; *Riverrun* 1970; *Silence* 1974; *Alex and the Gypsy* 1976; *Oliver's Story* 1978; *Twice Upon a Time* 1983.

WALTER LASSALLY

Born 1926, Berlin. Came to the UK as a refugee during World War II, and started his career in 1945, as a clapper-boy. Known for his collaboration with directors such as Lindsay Anderson, Tony Richardson, James Ivory and above all Michael Cacoyannis in Greece. Won Academy Award for his cinematography on *Zorba the Greek*. Main features: *A Girl in Black* 1956; *Every Day Except Christmas* (docu), *A Matter of Dignity* 1957; *Beat Girl/Wild for Kicks* 1960; *Electra, A Taste of Honey* 1961; *The Loneliness of the Long Distance Runner* 1962; *Tom Jones* 1963; *Zorba the Greek* 1964; *The Day the Fish Came Out* 1967; *Oedipus the King, Joanna* 1968; *Savages* 1972; *Heat and Dust* 1983; *The Bostonians* 1984; *The Ballad of the Sad Café* 1991.

RICHARD LESTER

Born 1932, Philadelphia. Settled in the UK in 1956, directed several segments of *The Goon Show* for British television and earned an Academy Award nomination for his short, *The Running Jumping & Standing Still Film*. Features: *It's Trad Dad* 1962; *The Mouse on the Moon* 1963; *A Hard Day's Night* 1964; *The Knack . . . And How To Get It, Help!* 1965; *A Funny Thing Happened on the Way to the Forum* 1966; *How I Won the War* 1967; *Petulia* 1968; *The Bed Sitting Room* 1969; *The Three Musketeers, Juggernaut* 1974; *The Four Musketeers, Royal Flash* 1975; *Robin and Marian, The Ritz* 1976; *Butch and Sundance: The Early*

Days, Cuba 1979; *Superman II* 1980; *Superman III* 1983; *Finders Keepers* 1984; *The Return of the Musketeers* 1990; *Get Back* 1991.

DUŠAN MAKAVEJEV

Born 1932, Belgrade (Yugoslavia). Degree in psychology from Belgrade University, then enrolled in film school. Made documentaries for Zagreb Studios. Has made his features in various countries, from Australia to Sweden as well as in his native Yugoslavia. Features: *Man Is Not a Bird* 1966; *Love Dossier/Switchboard Operator* 1967; *Innocence Unprotected* 1968; *WR: Mysteries of the Organism* 1971; *Sweet Movie* 1974; *Montenegro* 1981; *The Coca-Cola Kid* 1985; *Manifesto* 1988; *Gorilla Bathes at Noon* 1993; *Hole in the Soul* 1994.

WALTER MURCH

Born 1943, New York. Studied film technique at University of Southern California, and made early friends with Francis Ford Coppola and George Lucas. Joined Coppola as one of the early stalwarts of Zoetrope Studios in San Francisco. Became one of the foremost sound designers and editors of his time, winning Academy Awards for his innovative work on *Apocalypse Now*, and *The English Patient*. Also directed *Return to Oz* in 1985. Main features: (sound) *The Rain People* 1969; *Gimme Shelter* 1970; *THX 1138* 1971; *American Graffiti* 1973; *The Conversation, The Godfather Part II* 1974; *Apocalypse Now* 1979; *The English Patient* 1996. (editing) *Julia* 1977; *The Unbearable Lightness of Being* 1987; *Ghost, The Godfather Part III* 1990; *House of Cards, Romeo Is Bleeding* 1993; *I Love Trouble* 1994; *First Knight* 1995; *The English Patient* 1996; *The Talented Mr. Ripley* 1999; *K-19: The Widowmaker* 2002.

GILLO PONTECORVO

Born 1919, Pisa (Italy). Took degree in chemistry before becoming a journalist. 1941: joined Italian Communist Party, and became a leader of the Italian resistance during World War II. In 1945 he became assistant to Monicelli, Yves Allégret and other directors, and began specializing in documentaries. Won Golden Lion at Venice for *The Battle of Algiers*. Features: *La grande strada azzurra/The Long Blue Road* 1957; *Kapò*

1960; La battaglia di Algeri/The Battle of Algiers 1966; Queimada/ Burn! 1969; Ogro/The Tunnel 1979.

FONS RADEMAKERS

Born 1920, Roosendael, Netherlands. Stage actor, then assistant to Jean Renoir, Vittorio De Sica and Charles Crichton. Won Academy Award for Best Foreign-Language Film for *The Assault*. Features: *Village on the River/Doctor in the Village* 1958; *The Joyous Eve* 1960; *The Knife* 1961; *The Spitting Image* 1963; *The Dance of the Heron* 1966; *Mira* 1971; *Because of the Cats* 1973; *Max Havelaar* 1976; *Mysteries* 1978; *My Friend/The Judge's Friend* 1979; *The Assault* 1986; *Diary of an Old Man* 1987; *The Rose Garden* 1989.

KAREL REISZ

Born 1926, Ostrava (Czechoslovakia). Died London 2002. Flew for Czech squadron of RAF during World War II, then studied at Cambridge University. Took up teaching and contributed to influential film magazine, *Sequence*. 1953: publishes *The Technique of Film Editing*, a standard textbook. Shorts: *Momma Don't Allow* (co. Tony Richardson) 1955; *We Are the Lambeth Boys* 1959. Features: *Saturday Night and Sunday Morning* 1960; *Night Must Fall* 1964; *Morgan: A Suitable Case for Treatment/Morgan!* 1966; *Isadora/The Loves of Isadora* 1968; *The Gambler* 1974; *The Dog Soldiers/Who'll Stop the Rain?* 1978; *The French Lieutenant's Woman* 1981; *Sweet Dreams* 1985; *Everybody Wins* 1990.

ALAIN RESNAIS

Born 1922, Vannes (Brittany, France). Attended IDHEC film college in Paris, and took up film editing. In 1948 he directed short on *Van Gogh*, which won an Oscar the following year. During the fifties, Resnais became the leading European documentarist of his time, with classics like *Night and Fog* and *Toute la mémoire du monde*. Features: *Hiroshima mon amour* 1959; *Last Year at Marienbad/L'année dernière à Marienbad* 1961; *Muriel ou le temps d'un retour* 1963; *The War Is Over/La Guerre est finie* 1966; *Je t'aime je t'aime* 1968; *Stavisky . . .* 1974; *Providence* 1977; *My American Uncle /Mon oncle d'Amérique* 1980; *Life Is a Bed of Roses/La vie est un roman* 1983; *Love unto Death/L'Amour à mort* 1984; *Mélo*

1986; *I Want to Go Home/Je veux rentrer à la maison* 1989; *Smoking/No Smoking* 1993; *Same Old Song/On connaît la chanson* 1997.

FRANCESCO ROSI

Born 1922, Naples (Italy). Entered the Italian film industry as assistant to Visconti on *La terra trema*, then worked with Emmer, Antonioni and Monicelli, honing his talent as a screenwriter. Won Special Jury Prize at Venice for his directorial début, *La sfida*. Has won numerous top prizes at Cannes and Venice. Features: *La sfida* 1958; *I magliari* 1959; *Salvatore Giuliano* 1962; *Le Mani sulla città/Hands over the City* 1963; *Il momento della verità/The Moment of Truth* 1965; *C'era una volta* 1967; *Uomini contro* 1970; *Il caso Mattei/The Mattei Affair* 1972; *Lucky Luciano* 1973; *Il contesto* 1975; *Cadaveri eccellenti/Illustrious Corpses* 1976; *Cristo si è fermato a Eboli/Christ Stopped at Eboli* 1979; *Tre fratelli/Three Brothers* 1981; *Carmen* 1984; *Cronica d'una morte anunciata/Chronicle of a Death Foretold* 1987; *Dimenticare Palermo/To Forget Palermo* 1990; *La tregua/The Truce* 1997.

VOLKER SCHLÖNDORFF

Born 1939, Wiesbaden (Germany). Moved with his parents to Paris in 1956, passed out second in France in Philosophy exams, and studied film-making at IDHEC. Assistant to Louis Malle, Alain Resnais and Jean-Pierre Melville. Shared Palme d'Or at Cannes for *The Tin Drum*, which went on to win an Oscar. First head of resurrected Babelsberg Studios in the nineties. Features: *Young Törless* 1966; *A Degree of Murder* 1967; *Michael Kohlhaas/Man on Horseback* 1969; *The Sudden Wealth of the Poor People of Krombach*, *The Morals of Ruth Halbfass* 1971; *A Free Woman/Summer Lightning* 1972; *The Lost Honour of Katharina Blum* (co Margarethe von Trotta) 1975; *Coup de grace* 1976; *The Tin Drum* 1979; *Circle of Deceit* 1981; *Un amour de Swann/Swann in Love* 1984; *The Handmaid's Tale* 1990; *Voyager* 1991; *The Ogre* 1996; *Palmetto* 1998; *The Legends of Rita* 2000.

VILGOT SJÖMAN

Born 1924, Stockholm (Sweden). Began working at age fifteen, but wrote plays in spare time, eventually parlaying an early novel into a screenplay,

Defiance (1952). Wrote book about Bergman's making of *Winter Light*. *I Am Curious – Yellow* smashed box-office records in Europe and the United States. Features: *The Mistress* 1962; *491*, *The Dress* 1964; *My Sister My Love* 1966; *I Am Curious – Yellow* 1967; *I Am Curious – Blue* 1968; *You're Lying!* 1969; *Blushing Charlie* 1970; *The Karlsson Brothers* 1972; *Troll* 1973; *A Handful of Love* 1974; *The Garage* 1975; *Taboo* 1977; *Linus* 1979; *I Am Blushing* 1981; *Malacca* 1986; *The Pitfall* 1989.

BERTRAND TAVERNIER

Born 1941, Lyons (France). Studied law but early devotee of cinema. Co-founded the Nickel-Odéon film society, wrote articles for *Cahiers du cinéma* and became successful film publicist. Directed shorts from 1963 onwards. Features: *The Clockmaker /L'Horloger de Saint-Paul* 1974; *Let Joy Reign Supreme/Que la fête commence* 1975; *The Judge and the Assassin /Le Juge et l'assassin* 1976; *Spoiled Children /Des enfants gâtés* 1977; *Death Watch/La Mort en direct*, *A Week's Vacation/Une Semaine de vacances* 1980; *Clean Slate/Coup de Torchon* 1981; *A Sunday in the Country/Un dimanche à la campagne* 1984; *Round Midnight* 1986; *Beatrice/La Passion Béatrice* 1988; *Life and Nothing But/La Vie et rien d'autre* 1990; *Daddy Nostalgie* 1991; *The Undeclared War/La Guerre sans nom* (docu), *L627* 1992; *D'Artagnan's Daughter/La Fille de D'Artagnan* 1994; *The Bait/L'Appât* 1995; *Captain Conan/Capitaine Conan* 1996; *It All Starts Today/Ça commence aujourd'hui* 1999; *Safe Conduct/Laissez-passer* 2002.

AGNÈS VARDA

Born 1928, Brussels. Brought up in France, Varda studied at the Sorbonne, at first training as a museum curator and then turning to photography. She soon became the official photographer to the prestigious Théâtre National Populaire in Paris. Made numerous shorts. Married to Jacques Demy. Features: *La Pointe Courte* 1954; *Cléo de 5 à 7/Cleo from 5 to 7* 1961; *Le Bonheur* 1964; *Les Créatures* 1965; *Lions Love* 1969; *Daguerréotypes* (docu) 1975; *L'Une chante l'autre pas/One Sings the Other Doesn't* 1976; *Murs murs* (docu) 1980; *Documenteur* (docu) 1981; *Sans toit ni loi/Vagabond* 1985; *Jan B. par Agnès V.* (docu) 1987; *Kung-Fu Master* 1987; *Jacquot de Nantes* 1990; *L'Univers de Jacques Demy* (docu) 1995; *Les Glaneurs et la glaneuse* 2000.

ANDRZEJ WAJDA

Born 1926, Suwalki (Poland). Son of a cavalry officer, he studied painting at the Kraków Academy of Fine Arts. In 1950 he joined the Łódź Film School, and two years later served as assistant on Aleksander Ford's *Five Boys from Barska Street*. Appointed a senator in 1989, and received lifetime achievement Academy Award in Hollywood in 2000. Features: *A Generation* 1954; *Kanal* 1957; *Ashes and Diamonds* 1958; *Lotna* 1959; *Innocent Sorcerers* 1960; *Samson* 1961; *Siberian Lady Macbeth* 1962; *Ashes* 1965; *The Gates to Paradise* 1966; *Everything for Sale* 1967; *Hunting Flies* 1969; *The Birchwood* 1970; Landscape *After the Battle* 1971; *The Wedding* 1972; *The Promised Land* 1974; *The Shadow Line* 1976; *Man of Marble* 1977; *Without Anaesthetic, The Young Ladies of Wilko* 1979; *The Orchestra Conductor* 1980; *Man of Iron* 1981; *Danton* 1982; *A Love in Germany* 1983; *A Chronicle of Amorous Incidents* 1986; *The Possessed* 1987; *Dr Korczak* 1990; *The Crowned-Eagle Ring* 1993; *Nastasya* 1994; *Holy Week* 1995; *Miss Nobody* 1996; *Pan Tadeusz* 1999; *The Revenge* 2002.

KRZYSZTOF ZANUSSI

Born 1939, Warsaw (Poland). Took a physics degree at the University of Warsaw, started making amateur movies and then enrolled at the Łódź Film School. Won awards for his short to medium-length films, *Death of a Provincial* and *Face to Face*. For past quarter-century has headed the TOR Studio Unit in Warsaw, producing the films of, among others, Krzysztof Kieślowski. Prolific director of television movies and documentaries. Features: *The Structure of Crystals* 1969; *Family Life, Behind the Wall* 1971; *Illumination* 1973; *The Catamount Killing* 1974; *Quarterly Balance* 1975; *Camouflage* 1977; *Ways in the Night* 1979; *The Constant Factor, Contract, From a Far Country: Pope John Paul II* (docu) 1980; *The Temptation, Imperative* 1982; *Bluebeard, The Year of the Quiet Sun* 1984; *The Power of Evil* 1985; *Life for a Life* 1991; *The Silent Touch* 1992; *At Full Gallop* 1996; *Our God's Brother* 1997; *Life as a Fatal Sexually Transmitted Disease* 2000; *The Supplement* 2002.

Index

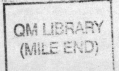